OLD FRENCH
A CONCISE HANDBOOK

OLD FRENCH

A CONCISE HANDBOOK

E. EINHORN

M.A., Ph.D.
Department of Romance Studies
University of Cape Town

 **CAMBRIDGE**
UNIVERSITY PRESS

Published by the Press Syndicate of the University of Cambridge
The Pitt Building, Trumpington Street, Cambridge, CB2 1RP
40 West 20th Street, New York, NY 10011-4211 USA
10 Stamford Road, Oakleigh, Melbourne 3166, Australia

Library of Congress catalogue card number: 73-90648

ISBN 0 521 20343 0 hard covers
ISBN 0 521 09838 0 hardback

First published 1974
Reprinted 1979 1980 1985 1987 1990 1994

Printed in Great Britain at
Athenæum Press Ltd, Newcastle upon Tyne

Contents

Contents

APPENDICES

Tables

Preface

This book treats the Old French of northern France and England as a language in its own right. A knowledge of Latin is not essential, and this work can even be used by medieval scholars who may not be versed in French.

Exercises with a key have been added to the first chapters for illustration and practice; word-lists are given for convenience, but further words will be found in the glossary.

Old French phrases used as examples have been selected where possible for their clarity and general interest. Variant forms have at times been normalised, especially in earlier chapters; translations where added are fairly literal. Three Old French passages have been included for further study.

The norms and rules suggested here have been carefully checked against original texts. All the same they can only provide a rough guide, since Old French was a living, fluctuating language, and the written word could vary according to the year, the region, or the whim of the scribe.

I gratefully acknowledge my debt to the scholars whose works are recorded in the bibliography, and to many others. In particular I would like to thank Professor D. J. A. Ross and Dr C. A. Robson for their interest and valuable advice.

It is hoped that this work will encourage many students to enjoy Old French literature, which is rich and varied, a vivid reflection of the life and thought of the medieval world.

E.E.

Symbols and abbreviations

For abbreviations referring to works quoted, e.g. (Rol.2550), see p. 178.

>	becomes, became.
<	from, comes from, came from.
+	plus, used with, followed by.
=	equals, is, was.
≠	by analogy with.
ʌ	word or syllable omitted.
§	paragraph.
[ ]	square brackets indicate phonetic transcriptions, with sounds pronounced according to tables in §6 and §9 and examples below.
[k]	as in *keen*.
[g]	as in *go*.
[s]	as in *so*.
[z]	as in *zone*.
[š]	as in *show*.
[ž]	as in *azure*.
[ts]	as in *its*.
[dz]	as in *beds*.
[tš]	as in *church*.
[dž]	as in *judge*.
[t]	as in *thin*.
[ḍ]	as in *then*.
[ł]	a velarised *l* as in *milk*.
[l′]	a palatal *l* as in Italian *figlio*.
[n′]	a palatal *n* as in French *agneau*.
[w]	as in *word*.
[ẅ]	as in *whip*.
[y]	as in *yet*.
[é]	as in French *né*.
[é:]	probably longer than in French *né*.
[è]	as in *ten*.
[ó]	higher than in French *vos*.
[ó:]	higher and longer than in French *vos*.
[ò]	as in *port*.
[ü]	as in French *tu*.

[ŏ]	as in French *peu*.
[ə]	a weak *e*, the first vowel in *about*.
ſ	[ts], becoming [s] in the 13th c.
~	a tilde, placed over a nasalised vowel.
··	a diaeresis, indicating a juxtaposed vowel (§14).
˘ ¯	symbols for short or long Latin or Germanic vowels, e.g. ĕ, ē.
′	placed after a consonant indicates a palatal pronunciation, e.g. *l′*.
-	separates syllables, e.g. *por-ter*, or stem and flexion, e.g. *port-er*.
'	the following syllable or diphthongal element is stressed, e.g. *sone'rai*.
''	the following syllable is semi-stressed, e.g. *''sone'rai*.
/	separates paired forms or alternatives, etc.; indicates a new line of verse in quotations.
|	marks a caesura.
L., Lat.	Latin.
VL	Vulgar Latin.
G., Germ.	Germanic.
OFr	Old French.
ModFr	Modern French.
Ch.	Chapter.
App.	Appendix.
Cl.	Class.
M, (M), masc.	masculine.
F, (F), fem.	feminine.
Neut.	neuter.
N, Nom.	nominative case.
O, Obl.	oblique case.
NS	nominative singular.
OS	oblique singular.
NP	nominative plural.
OP	oblique plural.
PI, Pres.Ind.	present indicative.
PS, Pres.Subj.	present subjunctive.
Impf.(Ind.)	imperfect indicative.
I've, Iv.	imperative.
P, Perf.	perfect tense.
IS, Impf.Subj.	imperfect subjunctive.
Pres.Part.	present participle.
PP, Past Part.	past participle.

C, Cond. conditional.
F, Fut. future.
Inf. infinitive.
R, Rs rule, rules (see §§38 or 73).
S stressed.
U unstressed.
St/ strong (perfect).
Wk/ weak (perfect).
St/s strong (perfect) of the s-type.
Wk/a weak (perfect) of the a-type.
SA syllabic alternation.
VA vocalic alternation (apophony).
adj. adjective.
adv. adverb.
art. article.
cf. compare.
conj. conjunction.
def. definite.
dem. demonstrative.
dir. direct.
esp. especially.
i.f. inflected form.
indir. indirect.
interr. interrogative.
irr. irregular.
lit. literally.
nf. feminine noun.
nm. masculine noun.
pers. person.
pl. plural.
pron. pronoun.
refl. reflexive.
rel. relative.
sing. singular.
syll(s). syllable(s).
v., vb verb.
var. variant (of).

Letters in round brackets:

(*b*), (*d*), (*t*)
 (used in App.E): consonants found in the infinitive which are not part of the stem (§75).

(*e*), (*i*), (*s*)
 forms are found with or without *e, i, s*.

(*h*) *h* not pronounced, frequently omitted in spelling.

(*n*) *n* disappears in pronunciation and spelling in the 12th c.

ş can disappear or be doubled (§69.2).

ţ, đ these consonants disappear in the early 12th c.

ie/e stem vowel *ie* when stressed, otherwise *e*.

1, 2, 3 in verbs: 1st, 2nd and 3rd person singular.
4, 5, 6 in verbs: 1st, 2nd and 3rd person plural.
Stress differentiation (Chapter 7 and Table 12):
tu   stressed or unstressed.
toi   stressed.
te   unstressed.

Note: the symbols [š], [ž], [tš], [dž], *ț*, *d̦*, *l'* and *n'* were chosen to fit in with
standard works on OFr, such as those by M. K. Pope and A. Ewert
(see bibliography).

Technical terms

The following are practical definitions, to elucidate points in the text. They are not necessarily comprehensive.

analogy: by analogy with = under the influence of.

articulation point: the point at which the air passage is constricted in the production of a sound. In [i] and [n′] the articulation point is palatal, i.e. the tongue is raised towards or up to the hard palate.

depalatalised: in which the articulation point (q.v.) has shifted away from the hard palate, often resulting in a new phoneme; thus [l′], [n′] can be depalatalised to [l], [n]. Depalatalisation can be accompanied by the palatalisation (q.v.) of a neighbouring sound (§39.13) or by the development of a new palatal sound, e.g. [i].

elision, elided: see §19.

enclisis, enclitic: see §20.

expletive: serving to fill out the phrase or metrical line, but adding little or nothing to the meaning.

flexion, inflexion: a suffix or ending added to the stem of a word to indicate tense, person, number, case, etc.

generalise: bring into general use.

glide or intrusive sounds: transitional sounds produced before or after a sound, or during the passage from one sound to another; these can develop into independent sounds (§8.6).

graphy: spelling; variant spelling.

hiatus: vowels in hiatus = juxtaposed vowels belonging to separate syllables, as in *païs, a ele*.

inflected: with a flexion.

initial vowel: a vowel found in the first syllable of a word.

nasal, nasalised: produced while lowering the soft palate, thus allowing the main stream of air to pass through the nose. The degree of lowering can result in partial or complete nasalisation.

palatal consonants or vowels: those with a palatal articulation point (q.v.), e.g. [l'], [n'], [ü].

palatalised: in which the articulation point (q.v.) has shifted towards the hard palate under the influence of a neighbouring palatal sound (q.v.). This can result in a new phoneme, thus [n] can be palatalised to [n'], or [s] to [ts].

palatalised stems in OFr: stems in which the final consonant had been palatalised (q.v.) between the fourth and ninth centuries. A final [l'] and [n'] remained palatalised, while other consonants were subsequently depalatalised (q.v.), often giving rise to a preceding palatal glide which became [i]; thus [r'], [s'] became [ir], [is].

phoneme: a distinctive sound in a language. Phonemes may be pronounced differently in different words, e.g. [k] in 'king', 'cool'.

phonology: a study of the sounds of a language, which can include their historical development.

pleonastic: redundant; e.g. a pronoun echoing the noun to which it refers.

stem: the distinctive part of a word, which is often inflected. The stem can be partially modified by the addition or omission of flexions (§8).

syllabic alternation: see §16.

syllables, open or closed: see §10.

tonic syllable or vowel: a syllable or vowel carrying the main stress (see §4).

unvoiced: no longer produced with the vibration of the vocal cords; thus *b* is unvoiced to *p*.

vocalic alternation: see §16.

voiced consonants: consonants produced with the vibration of the vocal cords, e.g. *b*, *d*, *g*.

voiceless consonants: those pronounced without the vibration of the vocal cords, e.g. *p*, *t*, *k*.

vowels, free or blocked: see §10.

vowels, low or high: vowels formed with the tongue low or relatively high, e.g. *a*, *i*.

weak *e*: an unstressed *e*, pronounced [ə]. See §§11.4–7, 19.

Introduction: sounds and spelling

1. The origin of Old French

Old French, like its descendant Modern French, is a Romance language, derived mainly from Vulgar Latin, the colloquial Latin introduced into Gaul from the second century B.C. onwards as a result of the Roman conquest and occupation.

After the Germanic invasions of the fifth century A.D. the Vulgar Latin spoken in Gaul, which had already undergone certain modifications, began to change more rapidly and developed into a new language, splitting at the same time into numerous dialects. Gradually two main dialect groups emerged with basic differences: the *Langue d'Oc* in the south and the *Langue d'Oïl* in the north, so called because of the words *oc* and *oïl* used for 'yes'.

By the twelfth century, which saw the emergence of Old French literature, the *Langue d'Oïl* itself included many regional dialects, such as Picard in the north-east, Anglo-Norman in England, and Francien, taken as standard Old French in this work, in the royal domain of the Ile de France. It is the special form of Francien spoken in Paris which, from the twelfth century onwards, supplanted the other dialects for political reasons and developed into Modern French.

Six periods can be roughly distinguished in the transition from Latin to Modern French:

> Vulgar Latin: from the second century B.C., when Latin was first spoken in Gaul, to the late fifth century.
> Gallo-Roman: from the end of the fifth century to the middle of the ninth.
> Early Old French: from the middle of the ninth century to the end of the eleventh.
> Later Old French: from the end of the eleventh century to the beginning of the fourteenth.
> Middle French: from the early fourteenth to the early seventeenth century.
> Modern French: from the early seventeenth century onwards.

2. Vocabulary

Old French of the twelfth century contained, usually in modified form, a few dozen words from the original Celtic spoken by the Gauls (e.g. *vassal, charue*), a few hundred Germanic words, introduced during and after the Germanic invasions (e.g. *guerre, heaume, harpe, blanc, fief*) and a few hundred Low Latin words, drawn from the medieval Latin of the clerks to supplement the vocabulary in religious, scholastic and political fields, etc. (e.g. *humilité, argument, justice*), many of these words having originally come from the Greek (*eglise, allegorie, filosofie*, etc.).

These loan-words, however, formed well below 10 per cent of the vocabulary, and Old French remained basically a descendant of colloquial Latin.

3. Syllabic division

In the flow of an Old French phrase, each syllable began, where possible, with a sounded consonant:

Il i avoit un home = I-li-a-voi-tu-n(h)o-me.

The linking of a final consonant to a following syllable beginning with a vowel is termed 'liaison', and is found only within a breath group.

Two consonants were divided:

terre, cest ami, saint Urbain = ter-re, ces-ta-mi, sain-tur-bain

and three consonants were split between the last two:

cest pere, saint Marc = cest-pe-re, saint-marc

except that there was no division in the case of:

1. the digraphs *ch* or *ss*: *ri-che, va-ssal,*
2. consonant groups for [l'] or [n'] (see §7.1): *fi-lle, di-gne,*
3. a consonant (other than *l, r*) followed by *l* or *r*:

an-gle, com-pren-dre, en-sem-ble.

For the elision of final vowels, see §19.

4. Word stress

Monosyllabic words could usually carry a stress, unless the vowel was a weak *e* (see §11.7); thus ꞌ*serf*, ꞌ*lion* (stressed), but *se, ne* (unstressed).

Polysyllabic words were stressed on the last syllable:

ba-ꞌron, ci-ꞌté, ge-ne-ꞌral,

or on the second last, if the final vowel was a weak *e* (see §11.6):

ꞌ*si-re*, ꞌ*Char-les*, *pa-ꞌro-le.*

This stressed syllable is termed the tonic syllable.

Initial syllables and prefixes were probably semi-stressed:

ǁ*chan-*ǀ*ter,* ǁ*chan-te-*ǀ*rai,* ǁ*en-*ǁ*chan-te-*ǀ*rai.*

This secondary stress, however, tended to disappear within a breath group (see §17).

Adverbs composed of an adjective plus *-ment* had a double stress:

ǀ*fort-*ǀ*ment,* ǀ*ten-dre-*ǀ*ment.*

5. Old French phonemes

The exact pronunciation of sounds in OFr is often uncertain, and dates and areas of sound changes cannot always be determined with precision. Specialised works on phonology are listed in the Bibliography, but for practical purposes the following indications should prove adequate. The later twelfth-century pronunciation of Francien has been taken as a standard, and notes on thirteenth-century changes have been added.

6. Consonants

1. In the second half of the twelfth century OFr probably contained twenty-one consonant phonemes (see Symbols, p. xi):

> Plosive: *p, b, t, d, k, g.*
> Affricative: *ts, dz, tš, dž.*
> Nasal: *m, n, n'.*
> Lateral: *l, l'.*
> Rolled: *r.*
> Fricative: *f, v, s, z, h.*

The articulation point of [t], [d] and [n] was dental, not alveolar, while [r] was an alveolar [r], slightly more rolled than in 'rose'; [n'] and [l'] were palatal consonants, while [s], [z] and the affricatives were possibly slightly palatalised.

2. The following eleventh-century phonemes had disappeared from the sound system:

> Fricative: *t, d.*
> Lateral: *ł.*

3. During the thirteenth century three semi-consonants, [y], [w], [ẅ], were added to the sound system, but the four affricatives, [ts], [dz], [tš], [dž], lost their plosive element, becoming the corresponding fricatives [s], [z], [š], [ž].

7. Consonant notation

1. Later twelfth-century Old French used eighteen consonants and at least ten digraphs to represent twenty-one consonant phonemes:

> *p, b, t, d, k, m, n, l, r, f, v* normally stood for one phoneme only, corresponding roughly to the English equivalent. (For the digraphs *gn, ng, ll*, and for the rare use of *l* for [l'], see below.)

c = [ts] before *e, i: cel, merci*,

> [k] before *a, o, u*, before consonants, or when final:

> > *car, acort, cuer, croc.*

> Where *c* (+ *a, o, u*) = [ts], it is usually represented nowadays by *ç: ça, ço, reçu.*

g = [dž] before *e, i: gent, engin*,

> [g] before *a, o, u*, or before consonants:

> > *gai, gole, agu, grant.*

gu = [g], used before *e, i: guerre, guise.*

ch = [tš]: *chat, manche.*

j = [dž]: *je, jambe.*

> *j* replaced *g* pronounced [dž] before *a, o, u*; thus in the verb *jugier*: PI.5 *jugez*, but PI.4 *jujons.*

h = silent and usually omitted in words of Latin origin: (*h*)*onor*, but sounded in those of Germanic origin: *harpe.*

gn between vowels, *ng* when final = [n']: *digne, poing.*

ill between vowels, *il* when final, or *ll, l* respectively after *i* = [l']: *vie-ille, vie-il, fi-lle, fi-l.*

qu (sometimes *q*) = [k]: *qui, quanque, qe* (=*que*).

s = [s] in initial and final positions, after a consonant or before [p], [t], [k]: *sac, bons, ainsi, est*,

> [z] between vowels: *usage, aise.*

> Note: *s* had usually disappeared before consonants other than [p], [t], [k], but was still found in the spelling; thus *s* was silent in *isle, asne*, but sounded in *espee, escu.*

ss = [s]: *vassal, assez.*

z = [ts] when final: *avez*,

> [dz] before a vowel: *onze.*

> Note: *z* replaced the groups *t + s, d + s, st + s*, all pronounced [ts], resulting from flexional *s* (see § 38.2).

2. The following consonants were found in the eleventh century:

l (+ consonant) = [ł]. By the early twelfth century it had either vocalised to [u] or had disappeared after *i* or *u*:

> *halt > haut, nuls > nus.*

ţ, ḑ: In certain positions *t* and *d* were pronounced 'th' as in 'thin' and 'then' respectively, recorded here as *ţ* and *ḑ*, in which case they had disappeared in pronunciation and usually in spelling by the early twelfth century:

> *merciţ > merci, riḑre > rire.*

3. During the thirteenth century:

(a) Affricatives lost their plosive element and changed to the corresponding fricatives, as follows:

	Phonemes	
Notation	12th c.	13th c.
c ($+e, i$)	[ts]	[s]
ch	[tš]	[š]
g ($+e, i$)	[dž]	[ž]
j	[dž]	[ž]
z (before vowels)	[dz]	[z]
z (final)	[ts]	[s] at times spelt *s*.

(b) The first elements of the diphthongs spelt *ie, ieu, oi, ui* became the semi-consonants [y], [w], [ẅ] (see §12.3).

(c) The *s* previously retained before [p], [t], [k] disappeared, but was still recorded graphically. It was pronounced, however, in a few later borrowings or words influenced by Latin, e.g. *ester, espoir, juste*, in which the *s* is still sounded today.

(d) Final [n'] was possibly depalatalised to [n], although still spelt -*ng*. This change may however have taken place earlier.

(e) In colloquial speech final consonants gradually disappeared before a following consonant and were sometimes omitted by scribes; *s* was the first to disappear, and was followed by [p], [t], [k] after a consonant. Final consonants were retained before a pause, however, or in liaison before a vowel, in which case *s* and *f* were soon voiced to [z] and [v] respectively.

8. Consonant modifications

Changes in the phonetic circumstances of consonants could lead to phonetic or spelling changes, and often to both. The more important are listed below and the forms chiefly affected have been added in brackets and referenced.

1. The final stem consonant could be effaced or modified owing to the addition of:

(a) flexional -*s*: *serf+s > sers, cest+s > cez*. (Nouns, adjectives, participles and verbs: §§38, 73.)

(b) flexional *-t*: *dorm + t* > *dort*. (Verbs: §73.)
(c) the suffix *-ment*: *fort + ment* > *forment*. (Adverbs: §142.)

2. Voiced consonants were unvoiced when final, e.g. *servir / serf.* (Verbs: §72.)

3. Final unvoiced consonants were sometimes voiced before a weak *e*, e.g. *vif / vive*. (Past participles and Class I adjectives: §48.)

4. A final *m* could become *n*, thus *nom* or *non*. (Nouns.)

5. Forms ending in *-g*, [dž] or *-ch*, [tš], or in consonants (other than *r,l*) + *r, l*, needed a supporting vowel, thus *tremble*, not *trembl*. (Verbs: §71.)

6. Glide or intrusive consonants developed between *l, m, n, s*, etc., and a following *-r*, leading to the groups *ldr, mbr, ndr, sdr*, etc.; e.g. *tenir*, but *tendrai*. (Class III verbs: §75.)

9. Vowels

Vowels in use in the second half of the twelfth century were probably the following:

1. Twelve monophthongs, probably falling into the articulation pattern shown below, symmetrical except for [ó], [ó:], which were fairly high, possibly even [u], [u:].

	Front	Central	Back
High	i	ü	u
			ó ó:
High-mid	é é:	ö	
Low-mid	è	ə	ò
Low	a		

[é:] was probably a long [é], or even the diphthong [éé].
[ó:] was a long [ó], possibly even the diphthong [óó] or [óu].
[ə] was an unrounded central *e*, like the first vowel in 'about'. It was never stressed, and is often called 'weak *e*'.

These monophthongs, short except for [é:] and [ó:], were probably slightly longer when stressed in open syllables.

2. Six diphthongs: four falling diphthongs, ['ei], ['oi], ['ui], ['au], with the stress on the first element, and two rising diphthongs, [i'é], [i'ö], with the stress on the second element.

3. One triphthong, [é'au], with the stress on the central element.

4. Two nasal monophthongs, [ã] and [õ]; the latter was a fairly high vowel, possibly even [ũ].

5. Two nasal diphthongs: one rising, [i'ẽ], with the second element nasalised, and one falling, ['ẽ̄], with both elements nasalised.

10. Vowel notation

The phonemic value of later twelfth-century graphies is given below. Note that the term 'vowel' covers diphthongs as well as monophthongs. For vowels followed by *m*, *n*, *n'*, see §13.

A syllable ending in a vowel is termed an open syllable, and the vowel is described as free. A syllable ending in a consonant is termed closed, and the vowel is described as blocked.

For the identification of tonic syllables, see §4.

11. Monophthongs

1. *a*, *i*, *u* = [a], [i], [ü] respectively in all positions:

av'ra, i'ci, va'lu, pu'nir.

Exceptions: For *i* used to indicate [l'], see §7.1. For the graphy *i*, *u* for *j* and *v*, see §21.12.

i in hiatus, as in *avi'ons*, became [y] in the later thirteenth century.

2. Tonic *e* or *é* = [é:] (if < VL or Germ. a). This vowel is found:

(a) in the stressed Class 1a verb endings *-er*, *-'erent*, *-é* (<-*ét*) and *-'ee* (<-*'ede*): *so'ner, so'nerent, por'té, por'tee* (stems *son-*, *port-*).
(b) in the stressed verb ending *-ez*: *de'vez, de'vrez* (v. *devoir*).
(c) in stressed syllables ending in a single consonant, including *z* (=*ts*), e.g. *'mer, 'nef, 'tel, 'quel, mor'tel, a'ssez, ci'tez*.
(d) in stressed open syllables, e.g. before *-re*, or in the common ending *-'té* (<-*'tét*): *'pe-re, 'me-re, 'pré, bon-'té* (<*bon-'tét*).

Note: [é:] is somtimes accented by editors to avoid confusion; thus *'parleṭ* > *'parle*, 'he speaks', but *par'léṭ* > *par'lé*, 'spoken'.

3. Tonic *e* = [è] (if < VL or Germ. ĭ, ē, ĕ), e.g. *'cest, 'ele, 'letre, 'herbe, chas'tel, con'seil, 'ceing, 'bele'ment, a'pres*.

4. *e* in initial syllables or prefixes =
[è] if blocked or followed by [l']:

ser-'vir, es-'poir, me-'illor,

[ə] if free: *ve-'nir, de-'voir, re-le'ver,*
[é] before [tš], [dž] or *s*+consonant (except where *s* is retained in the thirteenth century: §7.3c):

pe'chier, le'gier, es'cu, despe'chier.

Note: *e* in the prefix *des* (+vowel) = [ə], or [é] by analogy with *des* (+ consonant).

5. Non-initial, pre-tonic *e* = [ə]:

   ape¹lons, chante¹rai, pri¹vee¹ment.

6. Final unstressed *e* = [ə].
Note: a final *e* was unstressed (unless nowadays spelt *é*):

(a) in an open syllable: ¹*vi-ve*, *a-¹mi-e*, *por-¹te-e*,
(b) if followed by flexional *-s*: ¹*ro-ses*, ¹*par-les*, ¹*on-ques*,
(c) in verbal inflexions consisting of, or ending in *-e*, *-ent*:

   ¹*parle*, ¹*chantent*, *porte¹roie*, *a¹voient.*

In other cases a final syllable with *-e* was usually stressed (see (2) and (3) above).
Note: Where *-es* was stressed, e.g. in spelling variations or because of dropped consonants, it is usually marked *-és* by editors.

7. *e* in open monosyllables (unless nowadays spelt *é*) = [ə], e.g. *me, ne, que.*
   Exception: *e*, 'and', often spelt *et* = [é].

8. Tonic *o* =
[ó:] (>[ö] during the thirteenth century, spelt *eu*) if from a free vowel:

   ¹*flor* (< ¹flō-re), *ne¹vo* (<ne-¹pō-te), ¹*gole* (< ¹gŭ-la),

[ó] (>[u] during the thirteenth century, spelt *ou*) if from a blocked vowel other than ŏ:

   ¹*tor* (< ¹tŭr-re), ¹*tot* (< ¹tōt-tu), ¹*cort* (< ¹cōr-te),

[ò] if from blocked ŏ, or from *au*:

   ¹*mort* (< ¹mŏr-te), ¹*cor* (< ¹cŏr-nu), ¹*porte* (< ¹pŏr-tat),
   ¹*fol* (< ¹fŏl-le), ¹*chose* (< ¹causa), ¹*ot* (< ¹audit).

9. *o* in initial syllables or prefixes =
[ó] (>[u] during the thirteenth century, spelt *ou*):

   tor¹ment, *do¹lor*, *o¹ïr*, *porpar¹ler*,

but sometimes [ò], by analogy with stressed stems in [ò]:

   mor¹tel (≠ ¹*mort*), *fo¹lie* (≠ ¹*fol*),
   por¹ter (≠ ¹*porte*).

Note: A Modern French spelling of *eu*, *ou* or *o* usually reflects a later twelfth-century pronunciation of [ó:], [ó] or [ò] respectively.

12. Diphthongs and triphthongs

1. The following graphies represent diphthongs or triphthongs in the later twelfth century:

ai = ['ei] in an open syllable: *rai-son, vrai-e, se-rai.*
oi = ['oi], often from early twelfth-century *ei* = ['ei]:
   toi (< *tei*), *devoir* (< *deveir*), *choisir.*
ui = ['üi]: *lui, nuit, puisse.*
au = ['au]: *autre, haut, maudire.*
   The rare initial *au* (< VL au) = [ò], e.g. *augure.*
ie, ié = [i'é]: *chief, niés.*

This diphthong is found in the stressed verb endings *-ier, -iez, -'ierent,*
-ié and *-'iee*: *ai'dier, non'ciez,* etc.
Note: The diphthong *ie* is nowadays often spelt *ié* when final or when
followed by *-s* to avoid confusion with *-ie* or *-ies* containing a weak *e* (cf.
notes to §11.2, 6); thus *pi-e,* but *pié; vi-es,* but *viés.*
ieu = [i'ö]: *Dieu, vieuz.*
eau = [é'au]: *beaus, chasteaus, heaume.*

The triphthong *iau*, a common dialectal variant for *eau,* = [i'au], e.g.
biaus, for *beaus.*

2. The following diphthongs and triphthongs, pronounced ['ai], ['ou],
['ue], ['éu] and ['ueu] respectively in the early twelfth century and still
represented in the spelling, had been simplified by the later twelfth
century as follows:

ai = [è] in a closed syllable: *mais-tre, fait.*
ou = [u]: *coup, douce, foudre.*
ue, eu, ueu = [ö]: *buef, eus, dueus.*
   [ö] was occasionally spelt *oe, oeu*: *oef, oeuvre.*

3. In the thirteenth century *ie* and *ieu* soon became [yé] and [yö], while *oi*
and *ui* were gradually pronounced [wè] and [ẅi], except that *oi* in hiatus
before a stressed vowel or [y] remained ['oi], e.g. *loi'al, otroi'ier.*

13. Nasal vowels

From the tenth to the fourteenth century vowels were progressively
nasalised before *m, n, n',* starting with the lowest, [a], and ending with the
highest, [ü]. The following nasal was still pronounced.
   All the vowels were affected in all positions, but vowels in open initial
syllables or prefixes were only lightly nasalised. Weak *e*, however, was
probably nasalised only in the ending *-ent.*

1. In the later twelfth century the following vowels had already been
fully nasalised before *m, n, n'*:

a, e = [ã]: *en, agnel, amender* [ãn, ãⁱnˈèl, ãmãnˈdéːr].
o = [õ]: *ome, soner, Borgogne* [ˈõmə, sõⁱnéːr, bórⁱgõnˈə].
ie = [iⁱẽ]: *crieme, rien, tieng* [ˈkriẽmə, ˈriẽn, ˈtiẽn'].
ai, ei = [ˈẽɪ]: *aime, plein, seignor* [ˈẽɪmə, ˈplẽɪn, sẽɪⁱnˈóːr].

2. In the thirteenth century [i] and [ö], the latter spelt *ue, eu*, etc., were soon nasalised to [ĩ] and [õ]; [iⁱẽ] became [yẽ] and [ˈoi] was later nasalised to [wẽ].

14. Juxtaposed vowels

Vowel groups other than those representing diphthongs and triphthongs stand for juxtaposed vowels, e.g. *gaain* (*ga-ain*), often arising from flexions, as in *menee* (*me-ne-e*), *pooient* (*po-oi-ent*).

Where confusion is possible editors often place a diaeresis over *i, u* or *e*, in that order of preference, to distinguish vowels belonging to different syllables, e.g. *envïeus, seür, soëf*.

15. The group -ii-

The group -*ii*- in juxtaposed diphthongs, pronounced [-ii-], then [-iy-], was soon spelt -*i*-; thus *paiien* > *paien, proïier* > *proier, otroiiez* > *otroiez*, pronounced [peiⁱyẽn], [proiⁱyér], [otroiⁱyéts] in the early thirteenth century (§ 12.3).

The monophthong *i* is found in hiatus before *ie* in the verb endings -*iiens*, -*iiez*, and in a few loan-words, e.g. *anciien*. Here *iie* was pronounced [iⁱié] or [iⁱyẽ], then [iⁱyé] or [iⁱyẽ], and was soon spelt *ie*, nowadays usually noted as *ïe*; thus *aviiens* > *avïens, aviiez* > *avïez*, pronounced [aviⁱyẽns], [aviⁱyéts] in the early thirteenth century.

In the later thirteenth century *i* in hiatus became [y] (§ 11.1) and merged with the following [y]; thus *ancien*: [ãntsiⁱyẽn] > [ãnⁱsyẽn] and *avïez*: [aviⁱyéts] > [avⁱyés].

16. Vocalic and syllabic alternation

Stressed and unstressed (or semi-stressed) vowels had often developed differently in the past. Words from a common stem but with a different stem stress thus often displayed regular vowel changes, termed vocalic alternation or apophony, which can be expressed as follows:

VA *ie/e* = stem vowel *ie* when stressed, otherwise *e*.

This change in the stem vowel is found in:

1. Verbs: ˈ*tient*, teˈ*nons*, VA *ie/e*; ˈ*doit*, deˈ*vons*, VA *oi/e*; ˈ*dis*, deˈ*sis*, VA *i/e* (see §§65, 76 and Appendix D).

2. Class III nouns: ¹*ber*, *ba*¹*ron*, VA e̲/a; ¹*suer*, *se*¹*ror*, VA u̲e̲/e (see Appendix A.2).

3. Related words: ¹*per*, *pa*¹*reil*, VA e̲/a; ¹*buef*, *bo*¹*vier*, VA u̲e̲/o; *es*¹*poir*, *espe*¹*rer*, VA oi̲/e.

In a few words change of stress led to the loss of the unstressed vowel, and this resulted in syllabic alternation (see §77): *pa*¹*role*, *par*ᴧ¹*lons*, SA o̲/-.

Common types of vocalic alternation, together with their phonemic equivalents, are listed in Appendix D. For vocalic alternation dependent on group stress see §18.

17. Group stress

In a phrase, seen as a single concept or breath group, word stress diminishes and the main stress usually falls on the last tonic syllable. The tendency was for this position to be used for important words, mainly nouns and verbs.

The initial syllables of a rhythmic group were often emphasised; thus *tu* stands out in *Tu le verras!* but not in *Que as tu fait?* Within a breath group the stress on individual words depended on the syntax, and could be influenced by reason or emotion; more often, however, logical or emotional considerations, combined with rapid speech, could lead to a loss of individual stress for the benefit of the group; thus *Ferez a*¹*vant, baron!* (---¹--) (Or.824).

The rhythmic pattern of OFr phrases led to important changes such as double forms of words, and to elision or enclisis, where unstressed syllables contracted to form part of the following or previous words respectively. These are discussed below.

18. Doublets

Not only syllables (§16) but words can vary, depending on whether they are stressed in the phrase. This affected:

1. Pronouns, with stressed forms like *moi, toi, soi*, alternating with the unstressed forms *me, te, se*, etc. (VA oi̲/e) (see §§86–8);
　　　　e.g. *por* ¹*moi*, but *il me* ¹*dit*.

2. Possessives, where stressed forms like *mien, moie, nostres* alternate with unstressed *mon, ma, noz*, etc. (see §§54, 55);
　　　　e.g. *le* ¹*mien*, but *mon* ¹*oncle*.

3. A few other words, like *ço, iert, non, buen* (stressed), *ce, ert, ne, bon* (unstressed) (see Tables 4.2, 8 and §§144.4, 146);
　　　　e.g. ¹*Moi*, ¹*non!* but ¹*Rien ne me* ¹*vaut*.

19. Elision

Elision occurred where the final unstressed vowel of a word was dropped before a word beginning with a vowel; thus a weak *e* in polysyllabic words was elided within a breath group before a following vowel:

bele amie (be-la-'mi-e), une injure (u-nin-'ju-re).

For adverbial doublets due to elision, e.g. *ore / or*, see §144.5.
Elision was compulsory for the following monosyllables:
the articles *le*, *la* (§37.1),
the pronouns *me*, *te*, *se*, *le*, *la* before a verb (§85),
the possessives *ma*, *ta*, *sa* (§54),
the particles *ne* (§146) and *re* (§193),
and the preposition *de* (§165).
Elision was optional for the following monosyllables:
the singular article *li* (§37.1),
the pronouns *me*, *te*, *se*, *le*, *la* after a verb (§85),
the pronouns *je* (§85) and *ce* (§59),
the weak pronoun *li* before *en* (§85),
the adverb *si* (§150),
the conjunctions *si*, *se*, *ne* (§160),
que, and compounds of *que* (§§98, 160).
The elision of the vowel in monosyllables (or compounds of *que*) was usually reflected in the spelling.

20. Enclisis

Enclisis occurred when an unstressed vowel in a monosyllable was dropped before a following consonant, leaving the word linked to a previous word ending in a vowel. This affected the articles or pronouns *le* and *les*, which were reduced to *-l* and *-s* respectively after many common monosyllables such as *a*, *de*, *je*, *ne*, *qui*, etc. (§§37.2, 91);
thus: *a le roi > al roi, je les avrai > jes avrai.*
Enclitic forms of the unstressed pronouns *me*, *te*, *se* and *en* are occasionally found, e.g. *ne me > nem*.
For a list of enclitic forms see Appendix B.

21. Spelling variants

The standard twelfth-century spelling used here has been deduced mainly from early thirteenth-century transcripts, since there are few earlier manuscripts extant. In practice, however, there was considerable variation in spelling. This was partly due to dialectal, conservative and analogical influences, and partly due to hesitation in the graphy of certain

sounds, especially those in the process of changing. Thus *oeil*, [öl'], was also written *oil*, *oill*, *oel*, *oeul*, *ueil*, *hueil*, etc.

Among the more common spelling variants are the following:

1. The symbol *x* was at times used for *us*, thus *fox*, *Diex* for *fous*, *Dieus*, and gradually, through confusion, for *s* or *z* after *u*, thus *lieus* or *lieux*.

2. Variants for [n'] include combinations of *n*, *g*, *i*, such as *ngn*, *ign*, *in*, *ni*, also *g*.

3. Variants for [l'] include combinations of *l*, *g*, *i*, such as *ilg*, *lg*, *lli*, *illi*.

4. After [ł] became *u*, *l* could replace or reinforce *u* before a consonant, thus *mout*, *molt* or *moult*.

5. Consonants dropped before flexions were sometimes restored in the spelling, e.g. *chefs*, *vils*, *colps* for *ches*, *vis*, *cous*.

6. Under the influence of Latin, effaced consonants were occasionally reintroduced, thus *set* or *sept*, *pié* or *pied*.

7. An extra nasal sometimes indicates the nasalisation of the previous vowel: *aime* or *aimme*, *seignor* or *seingnor*.

8. *n* could replace *m* before *p*, *b*, *f*, *v* or *m*: e.g. *combat* or *conbat*.

9. Since *a* or *e* (+nasal) = [ã], words with *e* could be spelt with *a*, thus *ansanble*, see (8) above, for *ensemble*.

10. Since *ai* or *ei* (+nasal) = [ẽi], words with *ai* are found with *ei*, e.g. *seint* for *saint*.

11. Where *ai* = [ei] or [è], the graphies *ei* or *e* were also used, thus *raison*, *fait*, or *reison*, *fet*.

12. *u* and *i* were normally used in manuscripts for [v] and [dž] > [ž] respectively. They are replaced in edited texts by *v* and *j*.

13. A silent *h* was sometimes used, as in *huit*, to show that the following *u* was a vowel, not [v].

14. Since [ö] could be spelt *eu*, *ue*, *oe* (§§11.8, 12.2) these graphies were at times confused, thus *peut* or *poet* for *puet*.

15. When [ts], spelt *c*, *z*, became [s] in the thirteenth century there was at times confusion in the use of the graphies *c*, *z*, *s*; thus *ci*, *seinte*, *sez* for *si*, *ceinte*, *ses*.

16. Note that *o* could become *eu* or *ou* in the thirteenth century (§11.8, 9), thus *flor* > *fleur* and *tor* > *tour*.

Note: For variants which reflect a dialectal pronunciation or a regional scribal tradition, see Chapter 16.

I
Articles and nouns

22. General

There are three genders in Old French: masculine, feminine and neuter. The gender can reflect the natural gender:

>*le pere* (M), the father   *la mere* (F), the mother

Usually, however, the distinction appears arbitrary:

>*le mur* (M), the wall   *la rose* (F), the rose

The neuter is only used for adjectives, pronouns and participles.
   There are two numbers: singular and plural:

>*la rose* (sing.),   *les roses* (plural)

and two cases: nominative and oblique:

>*Charles* (nom.)   *Charlon* (obl.)   Charles
>*Aymes* (nom.)   *Aymon* (obl.)   Aymes

Articles and nouns are subject to regular systems of inflexions, indicating gender, number and case. These are tabulated in the form of declensions (see Table 1).

23. Articles

There are two articles in Old French (see Table 1):

>the definite article: *le* (M), *la* (F), the
>the indefinite article: *un* (M), *une* (F), a

The article agrees in gender, number and case with the noun to which it refers.

Table 1. *Articles and nouns*

1. Articles

	Definite		Indefinite	
	Masc.	Fem.	Masc.	Fem.
Nom.Sing.	*li*	*la*	*uns*	*une*
Obl.Sing.	*le*	*la*	*un*	*une*
Nom.Plur.	*li*	*les*	*un*	*unes*
Obl.Plur.	*les*	*les*	*uns*	*unes*

2. Masculine nouns

	Class I	Class II	Class III
NS	(*li*) *murs*	(*li*) *pere***	(*li*) *ber*
OS	(*le*) *mur*	(*le*) *pere*	(*le*) *baron*
NP	(*li*) *mur*	(*li*) *pere*	(*li*) *baron*
OP	(*les*) *murs*	(*les*) *peres*	(*les*) *barons*

3. Feminine nouns

	Class I	Class II	Class III
NS	(*la*) *rose*	(*la*) *loi(s)*	(*la*) *none*
OS	(*la*) *rose*	(*la*) *loi*	(*la*) *nonain*
NP	(*les*) *roses*	(*les*) *lois*	(*les*) *nonains*
OP	(*les*) *roses*	(*les*) *lois*	(*les*) *nonains*

* Class II (M) nouns at times add -*s* in the NS ≠ Class I (M).

24. Masculine nouns

These fall into three declension classes (see Table 1):

Class I: Most masculine nouns belong to this class, including infinitives used as nouns.

Class II: This includes a few masculine nouns ending in -*re*.†

Class III: This class, in which the NS differs markedly from the other cases, includes:

1. a fair number of nouns referring to persons,†

2. several hundred nouns composed by adding -(*i*)*ere* and -*eor* to the stem of a verb to form the NS and OS respectively; thus: *trovere*, *troveor*, 'lyric poet', from the verb *trover* (to find, to invent). The flexion -*iere* is used in the case of Class 1b verbs. These nouns are all the names of agents.†

† See Appendix A for nouns in this group.

25. Feminine nouns

These fall into three declension classes (see Table 1):

Class I: Most feminine nouns belong to this class, namely all those ending in a weak *e* (§§9.1, 11.6a), e.g. *la letre, la rose.*

Class II: This includes nearly all feminine nouns which do not end in a weak *e.** Here an *-s* often appears in the NS for etymological reasons, or ≠ Class I masculine nouns; thus NS: *la loi* or *la lois.*

Note: Feminine nouns in *-(i)é* belong to this class, e.g. *cité* (<*citét*).

Class III: This class, in which the NS differs markedly from the other cases, includes a few nouns referring to persons or animals, and some names of rivers.*

The NS and OS are usually formed by adding *-e, -ain* respectively to the stem.

  * See Appendix A for nouns in this group.

26. Indeclinable nouns

Nouns ending in *-s* or *-z* in the oblique case are indeclinable; thus: *le cors, la voiz* (OS), *les cors, les voiz* (OP). See examples in Appendix A.

27. Basic value of the oblique form

Nouns are usually listed in the oblique case (singular). All masculine nouns then add *-s* in the OP, while the feminine nouns take *-s* throughout the plural. The NS can easily be deduced from the OS, except in the case of a few Class III nouns, where the NS form should be noted in addition.

28. The nominative case is used:

1. for the subject:
    Charles est vieuz.   Charles is old.
2. for the person or thing addressed: *Aymes!*
3. for words qualifying or in apposition to nouns in the nominative case:
    Charles, li rois.   Charles, the king.

29. The oblique case is used:

1. for the direct object:
    La mere voit Aymon.   The mother sees Aymes.

2. after prepositions:

> *Por Charlon.*   For Charles.

3. fairly frequently to express possession or relationship, referring to persons in the singular:

> *La mere Aymon.*   The mother of Aymes.
> *L'eglise Nostre Dame.*   The church of Our Lady.

4. occasionally for the indirect object, usually referring to persons in the singular:

> *Porte Aymon la letre!*   Carry the letter to Aymes!

5. occasionally for nouns that reflect concepts rather than realities, to stress their hypothetical nature (e.g. in comparisons):

> *Plus fiers que lion.* (cf. Rol.1111)
> More arrogant than a lion.

6. for words qualifying or in apposition to nouns in the oblique case:

> *Por Aymon, le baron.*   For Aymes, the baron.

7. for adverbial phrases of time, manner, place, etc.:

> *Charles chevauche grant oirre.*
> Charles rides (at a) high speed.

> *Charles chevauche le grant chemin.*
> Charles rides (along) the highway.

30. The definite article

The definite article is used to distinguish or to give a slight demonstrative stress to a noun:

> *le chevalier*, the knight, that knight, the knight in question.

The definite article is thus frequently omitted, especially before nouns used in a general or partitive sense, before abstract nouns, names of individuals, countries or people:

> *Franceis fierent.*   The French strike.

It is also omitted after prepositions in many common expressions, thus *en maison*, 'at home', but *en la maison*, 'in the said house'.

Being essentially a demonstrative, it is occasionally used as a demonstrative pronoun:

> *L'ame son pere et la sa mere.*   (cf. Yv.663–4)
> The soul of his father and that of his mother.

In the thirteenth century the definite article appears more often, but with weakened demonstrative value.

For contracted forms of the article, see §37.

31. The indefinite article

1. The indefinite article is used in the singular to introduce and particularise a noun not previously mentioned:

> *Un Sarrazin.*   A (certain) Saracen.

2. The indefinite article is usually omitted:

(a) if the noun is not particularised (e.g. before abstract nouns, in many comparisons, or in negative, interrogative or conditional phrases):

> *Fresche com rose.*   Fresh as a rose. (Cl.330)

(b) if the noun is already distinguished by a word like *tel* (such), *autre* (another), etc.:

> *Tel chevalier.*   Such a knight.

(c) it is as a rule omitted in the plural:

> *Un chevalier voit et pelerins.*   He sees a knight and pilgrims.

3. The indefinite article is used in the plural, however:

(a) to indicate a pair, a group or a class of objects of the same kind:

> *Uns solers.*   A pair of shoes.
> *Unes noveles.*   Tidings.

(b) for plurals which have no singular:

> *Unes cisoires.*   A (pair of) scissors.

(c) for the plural form of nouns with a different meaning in the singular.

> *Unes armes noires.*   A suit of black armour.
> but: *Une arme.*   A weapon.

32. The partitive

To express part of an indefinite collective whole, the article is omitted:

> *Roses avrez.*   You will have (some) roses.
> *Pain ne mangerai.*   I will not eat (any) bread.

At times the noun is preceded by the partitive preposition *de* (of):

> *De viande avrez.*   You will have (some) food.

If a specific collective whole is implied, *de* is followed by a defining word like an adjective or the definite article:

De mes roses avrez. You will have some of my roses.

De la vïande mangerai. I will eat some of the (that) food.

From the fourteenth century onwards, with the weakening demonstrative value of the article, *de la vïande* came to mean merely 'some food', or, with restricted meaning, 'some meat'.

33. Declensions in the thirteenth century

Certain analogical modifications first appear in the twelfth century, but become more frequent in the thirteenth; thus:

1. Class II (M) nouns increasingly add *-s* in the NS ≠ Class I.

2. Class III (M) nouns are at times treated as Class I (M) nouns: either *-s* is added in the NS, e.g. *sires*, or the oblique form is used for the NS as well, with or without an added *-s*, e.g. *seignor(s)*.

3. Class I (M) proper nouns more and more often omit flexional *-s* in the NS, e.g. *Tristran* for *Tristrans*.

4. Class III (M) proper nouns can add or drop a final *-s* in the NS ≠ Class I (M) proper nouns, and double forms are found, e.g. NS *Gui(s)*, *Pierre(s)*.

34. Breakdown of the declension system

The case system was probably not rigorously observed in colloquial OFr, and this gradually influenced the written language. In the twelfth century already there were signs of a breakdown of the declension system, particularly in Anglo-Norman texts, the usual error being that the more common OS form was used for the NS as well, and this tendency was increased in the thirteenth century.

35. Word order

Word order was flexible in OFr, since the form of a noun often indicated its case, clarified at times by the form of the verb; thus:

> *Or fierent chevalier paiens.*
> Now the knights strike the infidels.

Word order is dealt with in more detail in Chapter 15, but it is helpful to realise from the outset that the verb often precedes the subject, as above. In practice whenever a sentence, as frequently happens, starts with the direct or indirect object, a predicative adjective or noun, or an adverb or adverbial phrase, the position of subject and verb is inverted; thus:

> *Hauz sont les murs.* (Or.193)
> High are the walls.

Tant ont François chevauchié. (Ch.N.1070)
For so long have the French ridden.

Erec m'apelent li Breton. (Er. 652)
The Bretons call me Erec.

36. Spelling

The later twelfth-century spelling of the Francien dialect, the forerunner of ModFr, is taken here as a standard and used in word-lists, tables and exercises, and usually also in examples quoted from texts. Early twelfth-century forms with *ṭ*, *ḍ* are added to explain consonant modifications. For common variations in spelling, such as the graphy *x* for *us* (e.g. *Diex* for *Dieus*) see §21.

VOCABULARY

Class I (M)

chevalier, knight
lion, lion
mur, wall
roi, king
paien, infidel
pelerin, pilgrim

Class II (M)

frere, brother
livre, book
maistre, master
pere, father

Class III (M)

NS *ber*, OS *baron*, baron, lord, husband
NS *cuens*, OS *conte*, count
NS *traïtre*, OS *traïtor*, traitor
NS *prestre*, OS *provoire*, priest
NS *sire*, OS *seignor*, lord
NS *trovere*, OS *troveor*, lyric poet
NS *Charles*, OS *Charlon*, Charles
NS *Aymes*, OS *Aymon*, Aymes

Class I (F)

fille, girl, daughter
letre, letter
mere, mother
novele, news
parole, word
reïne, queen
rose, rose

Class II (F)

clamor, clamour
flor, flower
loi, law
maison, house

Class III (F)

NS *none*, OS *nonain*, nun
NS *suer*, OS *seror*, sister
NS *Berte*, OS *Bertain*, Bertha
NS *Eve*, OS *Evain*, Eve

Indeclinable nouns

païs (M), country
palais (M), palace
voiz, (F), voice

Articles

le (M), *la* (F), the
un (M), *une* (F), a

Verbs

The pronoun subject is often omitted in Old French; thus *voit* can mean 'he, she or it sees', according to the context.

fiert, he, she, it strikes
fierent, they strike
fier! strike! (sing.)
ferez! strike! (plural)
ot, he, she, it hears

oient, they hear
porte! carry! (sing.)
voit, he, she, it sees
voient, they see
voi! see! (sing.)
veez! see! (plural)

Other

or (adv.), now (see §35)

TEST YOURSELF

(a) Decline in full:

> *le roi, le frere, un traïtor, une novele, la clamor, Evain.*

(b) Give the nominative plural of:

> *le maistre, la parole, la seror, le lion, le baron, le païs, la flor.*

(c) Give the nominative singular of:

> *la mere, un pelerin, Charlon, le pere, une loi, Bertain, un troveor.*

(d) Give the oblique plural of:

> *la maison, un livre, le seignor, la nonain, une letre, le paien.*

(e) Put into the plural:

> 1. *Li prestre ot la voiz.*
> 2. *Li frere fiert le traïtor.*
> 3. *Or voit la suer le maistre.*
> 4. *'Pelerins! fier le lion!'*
> 5. *Or ot li cuens le troveor.*
> 6. *'Sire! voi le baron!'*

(f) Translate:

> 1. *'Chevalier! veez la reïne!'*
> 2. *Or fierent li paien.*
> 3. *La fille le conte ot la clamor.*
> 4. *Or oient chevaliers.*
> 5. *Les nonains voient Charlon le roi.*
> 6. *'Porte le seignor la novele!'*
> 7. *Or voit li pelerins la maison le provoire.*

Use the key to check your answers.

2

Contracted and modified forms

37. Contracted forms of the definite article

1. *Le* and *la* become *l'* before a vowel:

l'ami (M), *l'amie* (F), the friend.

Li is sometimes abbreviated to *l'* ≠ *le*, but in the singular only:

NS: *li amis* or *l'amis*, but NP: *li ami*.

2. *Le* and *les* combine with the prepositions *a*, *de*, *en* (to, of, in, etc.) as follows:

a le > al	a les > as	to the, etc.
de le > del	de les > des	of the, etc.
en le > el	en les > es	in the, etc.

Towards the end of the twelfth century the final -*l* in these contracted forms was vocalised before words beginning with a consonant. First *al > au*, then *del > deu, dou, du* and *el > eu, ou, u*. In the thirteenth century *as > aus* ≠ *au*.

38. Modifications due to flexional -*s*

The only inflexion found in the declension of nouns is -*s*. This -*s*, however, could affect or be affected by preceding sounds, leading to regular changes in pronunciation and spelling.

These changes apply not only to nouns, but to adjectives, participles and verbs as well, and follow phonetic rules which are summarised below. The examples added show the OFr forms without and with flexional -*s*.

For the meaning of words see the vocabularies on pp. 24 and 32 or the glossary.

1. *p, f, c* and *b, v* disappear before -*s*:

drap, dras   serf, sers   blanc, blans

2. *t, ţ, st* and *d, ḍ* combine with -*s* to form *ts*, written *z*:

mont, monz   escu (<*escuţ*), *escuz   ost, oz*

(For *ţ, ḍ*, see §§7.2, 39.3.)

3. After a vowel *m + s* becomes *ns*: *nom, nons*.

4. *rm + s* becomes *rs*: *ferm, fers*.

5. *rn + s* becomes *rz*: *jor(n), jorz*. (See §39.5, 6.)

6. *n' + s* becomes *nz*: *poing, poinz*.
    (For *n'*, see §39.7, 13.)

7. *el + s* usually becomes *eaus*: *bel, beaus* (but see §39.9).

8. *l + s* becomes *us* after vowels other than *e* or *i*:

    cheval, chevaus   ciel, cieus   duel, dueus

    and the *u* merges with a preceding *u*:

    nul, nus   Raoul, Raous   seul, seus

9. *l + s* becomes *s* after *i*: *vil, vis*.

10. *l' + s* becomes *lz*, then *uz*, after vowels other than *i*:

    trava-il, travauz   conse-il, conseuz   vie-il, vieuz

    and the *u* merges with a preceding *u*: *genou-il, genouz*.

    (For *l'*, see §39.10, 13.)

11. *l' + s* becomes *lz*, then *z*, after *i*: *fil', fiz*.

39. Supplementary notes

1. If *p, f, c* are dropped after *e* or *ie* these vowels are usually spelt *é, ié* nowadays to avoid confusion with weak *e*; e.g. *nef, nés*.

2. Final *c* was always pronounced [k] (§7.1). Its voiced form [g] is not included in Rule 1, since the final *g* in verb stems was pronounced [dž], while in nouns and adjectives it had become unvoiced to [k], spelt *c* (§8.2). The graphy *g* occasionally found is conservative; thus *borg = borc*, NS *bors* (town).

The voiced consonants *b, v* (R.1) and *d, d̦* (R.2) are normally found only in verb stems (§72, 73).

3. Although *ț d̦* (R.2) disappeared well before 1150 (§7.2) the inflected forms normally retained *z* until *z > s* in the thirteenth century (§7.3a).

4. Sometimes a double change is found; thus *champ + s > chans* (R.1, R.3).

5. The final *n* in the group *rn* (R.5), recorded here as *(n)*, disappeared during the twelfth century. For the inflected form in *z* see §39.3.

6. Rule 5 could include: *nn + s > nz*, to explain the inflected form *anz* of *an* (< VL annu), where the final *n* had already disappeared.

7. *n'* is a palatal *n* (see p. xi), usually written *ng* when final and *gn* between vowels (see also §21.2).

8. *l*, *l'* before a consonant (Rs 7–11) were vocalised or disappeared well before 1150, but were sometimes still recorded through conservatism.

9. *el*+*s* (R.7) usually became *eaus*, but occasionally *eus* (if *e* < Lat. ĭ, ē̆), e.g. *chevel*, *cheveus*, or *ieus* (if *e* < Lat. a), e.g. *tel*, *tieus*; *quel*, *quieus*.

The rare forms in *-ieus* were soon supplemented by analogical formations (e.g. *tels*, *quels*) which usually escaped the vocalisation of *l*, although vocalised forms like *teus*, *queus*, exist.

10. *l'* is a palatal *l* (see p. xi), usually written *il* when final (*vie-il*) or *ill* between vowels (*conse-ill-ier*). See also §21.3. The *i* is omitted, however, after a stem ending in *i* (*peri-l*). In these rare cases *l'* is recorded as such in the word-lists, e.g. *fil'*.

11. The group *ueu* (Rs 8, 10) sometimes became *ieu*; thus *ueil*+*s* > *ueuz* or *ieuz* (eye, eyes).

12. Rules 7–11 show that *l* and *l'* normally became *u* before *-s*, but disappeared after an *i* or *u* sound.

13. Rules 6, 10 and 11 show that *n'* and *l'* were depalatalised to *n*, *l* under the influence of a final *-s*, which was itself palatalised to *z* in the process. (See Technical Terms, p. xv.)

14. For consonants recorded in scripts although no longer pronounced, as in *serfs* for *sers* and *nuls* for *nus*, see §21.5 and §39.8.

VOCABULARY

Class I (M)

ami, friend, lover
amirail, emir
an, year (§39.6)
chastel, castle
cheval, horse
chief, head
ciel, sky, heaven
col, neck
conseil, opinion
cor(n), horn
coup, blow
drap, cloth
duc, duke
duel, grief

escu (< *escuṭ*), shield
fil', son
gant, glove
genouil, knee
jor(n), day
mont, hill
nom, *non*, name
ost, army (also Cl.II.F)
peril', peril
pié (< *piéṭ*), foot
poing, fist, hand
saint, saint
sanc, blood
serf, serf
travail, toil
vaslet, youth

vassal, vassal, knight
Bernart, Bernard
Raoul, Raoul

Class I (F)

amie, friend, sweetheart
dame, lady

Class II (F)

cité (< *citéṭ*), city
cort, court
ṇef, ship

Indeclinable nouns

braz (M), arm
cors (M), body

Verbs

est, he, she, it is
sont, they are

a, he, she, it has
ont, they have
trenche, he, she, it cuts (off)
trenchent, they cut (off)
For *estre* (to be) and *avoir* (to have) see Tables 7, 8.

Prepositions

a, to, belonging to (a person), etc.
de, of, from, belonging to (an animal or object), etc.
en, in, into
sor, on, onto
a was still *aḍ* before a vowel in the early 12th c.
de > *d'* before a word beginning with a vowel.

Other

si, and, so, as, etc.

TEST YOURSELF

(Later 12th c. forms to be used)

(a) Give the nominative singular of the Class I (M) nouns above, applying the relevant phonetic rules.

(b) Put into the plural:

1. *Li chasteaus est sor le mont.*
2. *'Voi l'escu al vaslet!'*
3. *En la nef ot li fiz le corn de l'ost.*
4. *Li chevaus est a l'amirail.*
5. *Or ot li trovere le nom del serf.*
6. *Si trenche al paien le pié, le poing, le chief.*

(c) Translate:

1. *'Veez les sainz es citez!'*
2. *Li dus ot les conseuz des oz.*
3. *Or fiert li amis les vassaus.*
4. *Le cors voit as piez le conte.*
5. *Bernarz a el poing uns ganz.*
6. *'Raous, voi les nés as amirauz!'*

3
Adjectives and participles

40. General

There are four declension classes for adjectives and participles used as adjectives (see Table 2). The flexions should be compared with those for nouns (Table 1).

The uninflected neuter is used in the singular only, to qualify neuter pronouns, phrases or clauses:

> *Ce est bel.*   This is fine.   (Yv.507)

> *Il est escrit en la geste francor.*   (Rol.1443)
> It is written in the chronicle of the Franks.

The stressed *-e* in past participles in *-ez*, *-éṭ* > *é* and -ˡe̦de > ˡee was pronounced [éː], while the corresponding stressed diphthong *-ie* = [ié]. An accent is nowadays placed on *-(i)é* and *-(i)éṭ* to avoid confusion with forms ending in a weak *e* (see §11.2a and note; §12.1). Later final *-z* became *-s* (§39.3), e.g. *chantez* > *chantés*, and this stressed ending *-(i)és* is accented nowadays as well.

The Class I adjective *tot* (all) has an irregular masculine NP *tuit*. Since this adjective is frequently used, it has been added in Table 2.

Examples of adjectives belonging to Classes II, III and IV are listed in Appendix A.

See the vocabulary on p. 32 for the meaning of OFr words in this chapter.

41. Class I

Most adjectives and all past participles belong to this class. The inflexions are those of Class 1 (M) or (F) nouns.

The feminine form adds a weak *e* (*bon* / *bone*, *chanté* / *chantee*) except in a few cases where the masculine already ends in a weak *e*, as in *malade* (see also §49 below). The modified (F) form *chante̦de* is explained in §48.

Almost all past participles originally ended in *-ṭ* (e.g. *chantéṭ*, *gariṭ*, *venuṭ*, *eüṭ*); this led to feminine forms in *-de* > *e* and to inflected forms in

Table 2. *Adjectives and participles*

1. **Class I** (Adjectives and past participles)

	(a) Basic declension			(b) PP in *ţ* (early 12th c.)		
	Masc.	Fem.	Neut.	Masc.	Fem.	Neut.
NS	*bons*	*bone*	*bon*	*chantez*	*chanteḑe*	*chantéţ*
OS	*bon*	*bone*	*bon*	*chantéţ*	*chanteḑe*	*chantéţ*
NP	*bon*	*bones*		*chantéţ*	*chanteḑes*	
OP	*bons*	*bones*		*chantez*	*chanteḑes*	

	(c) PP in *ţ* (later 12th c.)			2. **Class II** (Adjectives)		
	Masc.	Fem.	Neut.	Masc.	Fem.	Neut.
NS	*chantez*	*chantee*	*chanté*	*tendre**	*tendre*	*tendre*
OS	*chanté*	*chantee*	*chanté*	*tendre*	*tendre*	*tendre*
NP	*chanté*	*chantees*		*tendre*	*tendres*	
OP	*chantez*	*chantees*		*tendres*	*tendres*	

3. **Class III** (Adjectives and present participles)

	(a) Adjectives			(b) Present participles		
	Masc.	Fem.	Neut.	Masc.	Fem.	Neut.
NS	*tels*	*tel†*	*tel*	*chantanz*	*chantant†*	*chantant*
OS	*tel*	*tel*	*tel*	*chantant*	*chantant*	*chantant*
NP	*tel*	*tels*		*chantant*	*chantanz*	
OP	*tels*	*tels*		*chantanz*	*chantanz*	

4. **Class IV** (Comparatives)   5. **Tot** (Irregular)

	Masc.	Fem.	Neut.	Masc.	Fem.	Neut.
NS	*mieudre*	*mieudre*	*mieuz*	*toz*	*tote*	*tot*
OS	*meillor*	*meillor*	*mieuz*	*tot*	*tote*	*tot*
NP	*meillor*	*meillors*		*tuit*	*totes*	
OP	*meillors*	*meillors*		*toz*	*totes*	

* Class II (M) adjectives at times add *-s* in the NS ≠ Class I (M).
† Class III adjectives and present participles sometimes add *-s* in the NS (F).

-z in the masculine (§38.2) which were retained until *z* > *s* in the thirteenth century.

The early and later twelfth-century declensions of past participles in *-ţ* are given in Table 2 to show these consonant changes.

The remaining past participles end in *-t* or *-s*, e.g. *covert, escrit, ocis*, and add *-e* in the feminine. Those in *-s* are indeclinable in the masculine, while those in *-t* have inflected forms in *-z*.

42. Class II

This includes a few adjectives ending in -*re* (see App.A). There is no gender distinction in the oblique case.

Whereas feminine adjectives follow the pattern of Class I, masculine adjectives, like Class II (M) nouns, are uninflected in the NS, although they gradually adopt an analogical -*s*, especially during the thirteenth century.

43. Class III

A fair number of adjectives and all present participles fall into this group, in which the feminine lacks a distinctive -*e*. An -*s* is sometimes found in the NS (F), but less often than in the corresponding Class II (F) nouns (§25).

All common Class III adjectives (see App.A) end in -*l*, -*t* or -*f* which are modified by flexional -*s* (§38). *Tel*, 'such', however also uses unmodified forms (§39.9), and these are given in Table 2 to show the flexions more clearly.

By the end of the twelfth century several feminine adjectives had affixed an -*e*, thus moving into Class I. This process continued in the thirteenth century, till most Class III adjectives had been assimilated into Class I.

Feminine present participles from the twelfth century onwards occasionally added an -*e*, but this never became general.

Since all present participles end in -*t*, they have inflected forms in -*z* (§38.2).

Quite a few present participles are mainly used as adjectives, thus *corant*, 'swift', from *corre*, 'to run' (see §185.2).

44. Class IV

This covers all synthetic comparatives, of which there are very few (see App.A). Here the NS ends in -*re*, the OS in -*or*, and the neuter in -*s* or -*z*. The NS thus differs markedly from the OS, as in Class III (M) and (F) nouns.

Where there was no longer a distinctive neuter, the -*or* form was used; thus *graignor*, (M) OS and neuter.

A few other words also fall into this group, such as *felon* (NS *fel*), 'treacherous', 'cruel', and Class III (M) nouns used as adjectives.

45. Basic value of the oblique form

Adjectives and participles are usually listed in the masculine oblique case, from which the feminine form, only differing in Class 1, can be deduced. All masculines then add -*s* in the OP, while feminines take -*s* throughout the plural.

The NS can easily be inferred from the OS, except for the few Class IV adjectives, where the NS and the neuter form should be noted in addition. Elsewhere the neuter form is that of the masculine OS.

46. Indeclinable adjectives

The following are indeclinable:

1. Adjectives ending in -*s* or -*z*, mainly found among Class 1 masculines. (All Class 1 (F) adjectives end in -*e* and are declined.)

2. The adjective *meïsme* (§90.5), which however sometimes adds -*s* ≠ the adverb *meïsmes*.

3. A few adjectives in -*or*, meaning 'of the', referring to the plural; e.g.

francor	of the Franks, French
paienor	of the infidels, infidel
ancïenor	of the ancients, ancient
crestïenor	of the Christians, Christian

47. Concord

Adjectives, and participles used as adjectives (§§185, 186) agree in gender, number and case with the word they qualify, but follow their own declension class; thus:

> *Ma douce* (Cl.I.F) *amor* (Cl.II.F), *la meillor* (Cl.IV.F) *et la plus loial!* (Cl.III.F) (cf. Ver. 885–7)
> My sweet love, the best and the most loyal!

If an adjective or participle qualifies more than one noun, it usually agrees with the nearest one:

> *Pais* (M) *e teres* (F) *tantes* (F). (Rol.2333)
> So many (*tantes*) lands and countries.

48. Feminine stem changes

Class 1 (F) adjectives and past participles end in a weak *e*. This led in certain cases to a further differentiation of (M) and (F) forms, e.g. the

final consonant could be unvoiced in the masculine (*f*, *t*, *ţ*, etc.) but voiced before -*e* in the feminine (*v*, *d*, *ḑ*, etc.).

The main variations in the OS are given below, with comments on the phonetic conditions under which they usually arose.

(M)	(F)	Example	Comments
-*f*	-*ve*	*vif*, *vive*	always applicable
-*t*	-*de*	*froit* (< L. frigidu), *froide*	usually only if -*t* < d, so not applicable to participles
-*ţ*	-*de*	*chenuţ*, *chenuḑe*	always applicable (e.g. early past participles in -*ţ*)
-*c*	-*ge*	*larc* (< L. largu), *large*	if -*c* < g
-*c*	-*che*	*blanc* (< G. blank), *blanche*	if -*c* < k after a consonant
-*is*	-*sche*	*freis* (< G.frisk), *fresche*	if -*is* < sk

Sometimes the stem change is one of spelling only:

-*s*	-*sse*	*las* (< L.lassu), *lasse*	[s], from -s after a consonant, remains unvoiced between vowels, spelt *ss*
-*z*	-*ce*	*tierz*, *tierce*	-*z* = [ts], -*ce* = [tsə]
-*c*	-*que*	*grec*, *greque*	-*c* = [k], -*que* = [kə]
-*il*	-*ille*	*vermeil*, *vermeille*	[l'] is usually -*il* if final, -*ill* between vowels

Occasionally a phonetic change is not reflected in the spelling:

-*s*	-*se*	*ocis* (< L. occisu), *ocise*	[s], from -s after a vowel, is voiced to [z] between vowels, spelt *s* (§7.1) (e.g. past participles in -*s*)

49. Remodelled masculine adjectives

Modifications due to flexional -*s* increased the difference between the genders:

e.g. *vis* / *vive*,   *beau* / *bele*,   *fers* / *ferme*,

the NS masculine and feminine forms of *vif*, *bel*, *ferm*.

Many masculine adjectives were therefore subsequently remodelled on the feminine, hence later masculine OS forms like *ferme*, *large*, *chauve*, instead of *ferm*, *larc*, *chauf*.

50. Comparatives

Comparatives are usually formed analytically by the addition of the adverbs *plus* or *moins*, e.g. *plus puissant*, *moins fort*, 'more powerful', 'less strong'.

There are a few synthetic comparatives like *meillor*, 'better', all belonging to Class IV. These are listed in Appendix A.

The comparative is followed by *de* (before nouns, pronouns or numerals) or by *que* (often *que ne* before a verb), both meaning 'than':

> *Meillor vassal de lui.*   (Rol.3532)
> A better knight than he.

> *Plus froide que marbres.*   (Yv.381)
> Colder than marble.

> *Plus fresche que n'est rose.*   (Ad.228)
> Fresher than a rose.

When equivalents are compared, the comparatives are linked by *com* (also *come*, etc.), meaning 'as':

> *Blanche com flor.*   White as a flower.   (cf. Rol.3521)

51. Relative superlatives

Superlatives used in comparisons are formed analytically by adding the definite article to the comparative:

> *Le meillor e le plus bel.*   (Ad.644)
> The best and the most beautiful.

Since the superlative at times omits the article, e.g. after a possessive adjective, the sense must be inferred from the context:

> *Vostre meillor palefroi.*   Your best palfrey.   (Er.2579)

52. Absolute superlatives

These, very common, are usually formed analytically by the addition of adverbs such as *molt, assez, tres, trop*, all meaning 'very':

> *Une dame molt bele.*   (Er.2803)
> A very beautiful lady.

Note: Elsewhere *assez* and *trop* can have their modern meaning.

Par is often used as an intensive particle, separated by *estre* or *avoir* from the adjective it modifies. It is usually preceded and reinforced by *molt, tant, trop*, or *com*:

> *Tant par est bele.*   (Er.535)
> She is so very beautiful.

There are a few synthetic superlatives. They usually end in *-i(s)me*, like *grandisme*, *fortisme* (very large, very strong, etc.), and belong to Class I.

> *Cherismes amis!*   Dearest friend!
> *La saintime Virge.*   The most holy Virgin.

Some, like *pesme* (very bad, etc.) and *proisme* (very close), are used as emphatic positives, and can be modified:

> *Molt par est pesmes.*   (cf. Rol.2550)
> (The lion) is extremely fierce.

VOCABULARY

Adjectives
Class I

bel, fine, beautiful
blanc, white
bon, good
chaitif, wretched
chauf, bald
chenu (< *chenut*), hoary
douz, sweet
dur, hard
enferm, ill
ferm, strong
franc (< G.frank), noble,
  Frankish, French
freis, fresh
froit, cold
grec, Greek
irié (< *iriét*), angry
larc, wide
las, weary, unhappy
lonc (< L.longu), long
malade, ill
nul, some, any
prest, ready
saint, holy
seul, alone, only
tart (< L.tardu), slow
tierz, third
tot, all
vermeil, scarlet
vieil, old
vif, alive

Class II

autre, other
povre, poor
tendre, tender

Class III

brief, short
corant, rapid
fol, foolish
fort, strong
gentil (R.9), noble
grant, large
loial, loyal
mortel (*el* + *s* > *ieus*), mortal
novel, new
puissant, powerful
roial, royal
tel (§ 39.9), such
vaillant, valiant
vil, vile

Class IV

NS (M/F), OS (M/F), NS/OS
  (Neut.)
graindre, *graignor*, —, greater
mieudre, *meillor*, *mieuz*, better
pire, *peior*, *pis*, worse

Past participles (Class I)

chanté (< *chantét*), sung
covert, covered
escrit, written

eü (< *eüt*), had
gari (< *garit*), saved, etc.
ocis, slain
trové (< *trovét*), found
venu (< *venut*), come

Present participles
(Class III)

chantant, singing
trenchant, cutting, (adj.) sharp

Other

com, come, etc., as, like
e, et, and
moins, less
molt, mout, etc., very
plus, more
e was still *et* in the early 12th c., pronounced *et* (or *ed* before a vowel). The graphy *et* often found later is conservative.

TEST YOURSELF
(Later 12th c. forms to be used)

(a) Give the masculine NS of the above adjectives and participles, applying the relevant phonetic rules (§§ 38, 39).

(b) Give the feminine OS form of the Class 1 adjectives and of the participles listed above. Include early 12th c. forms where these differ.

(c) Give the regular feminine NS of the following:

   brief, autre, fort, graignor, povre, peior.

(d) Give the nominative singular of:

   1. *Une bone seror.*
   2. *Nul peior peril.*
   3. *Grant sont li ost.*
   4. *Un serf loial e fort.*
   5. *Le vieil duc povre et enferm.*
   6. *Li baron sont mort et ocis.*

(e) Put into the singular:

   1. *'Ferez, franc chevalier!'*
   2. *Or oient li provoire les briés conseuz des nonains.*
   3. *Molt par sont puissant li seignor.*
   4. *Li pelerin chaitif voient les paiens iriez.*

4
Possessives and demonstratives

53. Possessive pronouns and adjectives

Declensions are given in Table 3. Possessives are often declined like Class
I or Class II adjectives. Stressed and unstressed plural possessives are
identical, except that *nostres, vostres*, when unstressed, are contracted to
noz, voz.

Vostre is often used instead of *ton*, although the possessor is singular
(cf. §90.3):

> *Ostez vostre lion, beaus sire!* (Yv.5676)
> Remove your lion, fair lord!

Lor is indeclinable.

54. Unstressed forms

These are normally only used as adjectives, agreeing in gender, number
and case with the noun they qualify:

> *Son frere voit, sa mere et ses serors.*
> He sees his brother, his mother and his sisters.

Ma, ta, sa are elided to *m', t', s'* before a vowel:

> *M'amie, t'espee.* My friend, your sword.

55. Stressed forms

These, less common, are used:

1. as pronouns, agreeing with the noun they replace, often accompanied
by the definite article:

> *La dame est moie et je sui suens.* (Er.4800)
> The lady is mine and I am hers.

> *De vostre mort et de la moie.* (Yv.3745)
> About your death and about mine.

Table 3. *Possessive pronouns and adjectives*

1. Unstressed forms (adjectives)

	1st person sing. my		2nd person sing. your		3rd person sing. his, her, its	
	Masc.	Fem.	Masc.	Fem.	Masc.	Fem.
NS	*mes*	*ma*	*tes*	*ta*	*ses*	*sa*
OS	*mon*	*ma*	*ton*	*ta*	*son*	*sa*
NP	*mi*	*mes*	*ti*	*tes*	*si*	*ses*
OP	*mes*	*mes*	*tes*	*tes*	*ses*	*ses*

	1st person plural our		2nd person plural your		3rd person plural their	
	Masc.	Fem.	Masc.	Fem.	Masc./Fem.	
NS	*nostre*	*nostre*	*vostre*	*vostre*	*lor*	
OS	*nostre*	*nostre*	*vostre*	*vostre*	*lor*	
NP	*nostre*	*noz*	*vostre*	*voz*	*lor*	
OP	*noz*	*noz*	*voz*	*voz*	*lor*	

2. Stressed forms (pronouns and adjectives)

	1st person sing. mine, my		2nd person sing. yours, your		3rd person sing. his, her(s), its.	
	Masc.	Fem.	Masc.	Fem.	Masc.	Fem.
NS	*miens*	*moie*	*tuens*	*toe*	*suens*	*soe*
OS	*mien*	*moie*	*tuen*	*toe*	*suen*	*soe*
NP	*mien*	*moies*	*tuen*	*toes*	*suen*	*soes*
OP	*miens*	*moies*	*tuens*	*toes*	*suens*	*soes*

	1st person plural ours, our		2nd person plural yours, your		3rd person plural theirs, their	
	Masc.	Fem.	Masc.	Fem.	Masc./Fem.	
NS	*nostre*	*nostre*	*vostre*	*vostre*	*lor*	
OS	*nostre*	*nostre*	*vostre*	*vostre*	*lor*	
NP	*nostre*	*nostres*	*vostre*	*vostres*	*lor*	
OP	*nostres*	*nostres*	*vostres*	*vostres*	*lor*	

2. as stressed adjectives, occasionally on their own, but usually preceded by a qualifying word, like an article or a demonstrative adjective:

Mien escïent. To my knowledge. (Ch.N.63)
La soe amie. His sweetheart. (Er.296)

Un mien enemi mortel. (Yv.4912)
A mortal enemy of mine.

56. Alternative forms

1. The early twelfth-century form of *moie* was *meie*. The form in *ei* was retained, however, in many dialects, including Anglo-Norman (§212.2).

2. *Noz, voz* were sometimes used for *nostres, vostres*, especially in the west and north-west.

3. *Mis, tis, sis* often replaced NS *mes, tes, ses* ≠ the NP in western and north-western dialects.

4. For forms used in the Picard dialect (*me, men, nos, no*, etc.) see §213.5.

5. During the twelfth century additional stressed (F) forms *toie, soie* came into use ≠ *moie*, followed by (M) *tien, sien* ≠ *mien*.

6. During the thirteenth century:

(a) *mon, ton, son* began to replace *m', t', s'* before vowels.

(b) *mienne, tienne, sienne* were added as stressed feminine possessives ≠ *mien*, etc.

(c) *toe*, [tó:ə], > *teue*, [töə] (§11.8); similarly *soe* > *seue*, while *lor*, pronounced [ló:r], became [lör], spelt *leur*. The spelling *toe, soe, lor*, however, was often retained.

57. Demonstrative pronouns and adjectives

Declensions are given in Table 4. Note the correspondence in vowels and flexions between the definite article and the demonstratives *cest* (this) and *cel* (that): *li, le, li, les* / *cist, cest, cist, cez* (< *cests*) etc. These demonstratives have additional OS forms, ending in *-ui* (M) or *-i* (F). The initial (*i*) is often omitted.

   (*I*)*ceus* and (*i*)*cez* soon replace the early twelfth-century forms (*i*)*cels* and (*i*)*cestes*; in later OFr the (M) OS form *cest* can become *cet* or *ce* when unstressed.

58. Masculine and feminine demonstratives

1. These can be used either as pronouns (stressed) or as adjectives (unstressed):

> *Une vertuz que tuit cil et toutes celes ont.* (Gr.213)
> A quality which all those (men) and all those (women) have.
>
> *Cist moines est morz.* This monk is dead. (F.9.449)

2. Although masculine and feminine demonstratives are both pronouns and adjectives, yet there is a gradually increasing tendency to use the *cel* group as pronouns and the *cest* group as adjectives (see examples above).

Table 4. *Demonstrative pronouns and adjectives*

1. Masculine and feminine forms (pronouns and adjectives)

| | (*i*)*cel*, that one, that | | (*i*)*cest*, this one, this | |
	Masc.	Fem.	Masc.	Fem.
NS	(*i*)*cil*	(*i*)*cele*	(*i*)*cist*	(*i*)*ceste*
OS	(*i*)*cel*	(*i*)*cele*	(*i*)*cest*	(*i*)*ceste*
OS*	(*i*)*celui*	(*i*)*celi*	(*i*)*cestui*	(*i*)*cesti*
NP	(*i*)*cil*	(*i*)*celes*	(*i*)*cist*	(*i*)*cestes* > (*i*)*cez*
OP	(*i*)*cels* > (*i*)*ceus*	(*i*)*celes*	(*i*)*cez*	(*i*)*cestes* > (*i*)*cez*

* Additional oblique forms, often stressed.

2. Neuter forms (pronouns)

	Stressed that, this	Unstressed	Early forms that	this
NS	(*i*)*ço, ce*	*ce*	(*i*)*cel*	(*i*)*cest*
OS	(*i*)*ço, ce*	*ce*	(*i*)*cel*	(*i*)*cest*

3. Demonstrative pronouns are often used instead of personal pronouns:

> *Cil dormi et cele veilla.* (Er.2475)
> He slept and she lay awake.

4. Demonstrative adjectives are at times used for dramatic effect instead of the definite article, itself essentially a demonstrative:

> *Cez paiens fierent sor cez vermeilles targes.* (Or.1064)
> They strike these infidels on these scarlet shields.

5. The special oblique forms *celui, celi, cestui, cesti* appear mainly in stressed positions, i.e. as pronouns:

> *Celui ne tocherai.* (Ad.150)
> That one I will not touch.

> *Si bon ami come cestui.* (Yv.6749)
> As good a friend as this.

They are sometimes used as stressed subjects (cf. §80.5):

> *N'estes vos celui qui ...* Are you not he who ... (Gr.117)

59. Neuter demonstratives

These are all pronouns, the most common being *ço* and *ce*. *Cel* and *cest* are rare, and seldom found after the twelfth century. Unstressed *ce* is elided to *c'* before vowels.

1. They are used to introduce the real subject, or to refer to a sentence or a clause.

> *Ce est folie, ce me semble.* (F.11.205)
> This is folly, it seems to me.

2. They can replace the neuter pronouns *il, le* (it) as subject or object of a verb (cf. §58.3; see also §83).

> *Ce fu en mai.* It was in May. (Or.39)
> *Quant il voit ce.* When he sees it. (Gr.48)

3. They are often used pleonastically:
to duplicate a sentence or clause:

> *Ço sent Rollant que la mort li est pres.* (Rol.2259)
> Roland feels that death is near to him.

after prepositions, to introduce a clause:

> *por ce que . . .* for this (reason) that . . .

to anticipate or recall spoken words:

> *'Frere,' ce dit la pucele . . .* (Ay.2454)
> 'Brother,' says the young girl . . .

60. Demonstrative adverbs

1. Common demonstrative adverbs are *(i)ci* (here) and *la* (there):

> *Que fais tu ci?* What are you doing here? (F.10.267)
> *Traiez vos la!* Withdraw there! (Er.4013)

2. Other demonstrative adverbs are *ça*, 'here', 'to here', usually implying movement, and *(i)luec, (i)lueque*, etc., 'there':

> *Sire niés, ça venez!* Sir nephew, come here! (Or.54)
> *Iluec fu granz li desconforz.* (F.1.18)
> There the distress was great.

3. *Çaenz, çaienz, ceanz*, etc. (in here), and *laenz, laienz, leanz*, etc. (in there), are compounds of *ça, la* and the adverb *enz* (within):

> *Ceanz est paradis!* In here is paradise! (Or.688)
> *Leanz en la cité.* There in the city. (Cl.95)

61. The demonstrative particle *es*

Es is a common demonstrative particle, also spelt *ez*, *ais*, *e*, etc., meaning:
See! Look! Here is . . . There was . . ., etc. It is followed by a word in the
oblique case, referring to the person or thing observed:

> *Es la reïne qui revient.*   (Cl.105)
> See the queen who returns!

Es is usually accompanied by an indirect pronoun (normally *vos*, used
expletively) referring to the interested person or persons:

> *Es vos Renart le pelerin.*   (Ren.1483)
> Here you have Renard the pilgrim.

It is fairly often preceded by *a tant* (thereupon, then, now, etc.):

> *A tant ez vos un paien.*   (Or.746)
> Now there was a certain infidel (§31).

Confusion with the verb *estre*, 'to be' (*tu es*, *vos estes*) led at times to
estes being used with *vos* instead of *es*:

> *Estes vos le borjois.*   (F.10.560)
> Here is the bourgeois.

VOCABULARY

Class III (M)

NS *compaing*, OS *compaignon*,
  companion
NS *enfes*, OS *enfant*, child, youth
NS *niés*, OS *nevo* (<*nevoţ*),
  nephew
NS (*h*)*om*, OS (*h*)*ome*, man
on, the unstressed NS form of
  ome, usually means (some)one.

Class I (F)

bataille, battle
espee, sword
folie, folly

Class II (F)

amor, love
merci (<*mercit*), mercy
mort, death

Class III (F)

NS *niece*, OS *nieçain*, niece

Other

E! Ah!
(*tu*) *es*, you are (sing.)
(*vos*) *estes*, you are (plur.)
mort (Cl.I adj.), dead
ne, not
ne > *n'* before a word beginning
  with a vowel.

TEST YOURSELF

(Later 12th c. forms to be used)

(a) Give the nominative singular of:

    1. *Cel saintisme home.*
    2. *La soe seror Evain.*
    3. *Lor nevo chaitif et fol.*
    4. *Cest bel travail.*
    5. *S'amor, ceste graignor folie.*
    6. *Nostre povre fil, ton compaignon.*

(b) In what cases could the following phrases be? Give their oblique plural.

    1. *Li vostre nom.*
    2. *Icil lonc jor.*
    3. *Ta grant merciz.*
    4. *Li tuen fort poing.*
    5. *Cele bataille mortel.*
    6. *Mi enfant trové.*
    7. *Nostre vieil duc loial.*
    8. *La toe amie ocise.*

(c) Translate the following, then give the corresponding feminine:

    1. *Es vos son frere, cel roi vaillant e franc!*
    2. *Cil a trové le suen vieil pere.*
    3. *Veez cez seignors enfers et las.*
    4. *Morz est ses niés.*

(d) Translate:

    1. *Si ami e li mien.* (Per.4783)
    2. *E! gentis cuens, vaillanz hom!* (cf. Rol.2045)
    3. *La citez est moie!* (Ay.938)
    4. *Bernarz mes frere, li chenuz et li blans.* (Or.1092)
    5. *Les flors sont vermeilles del sanc de noz barons.* (cf. Rol.2871-2)

5
Verbs: basic patterns

62. Verb classes

OFr verbs fall into three classes, and can be grouped according to their infinitive endings, namely:

Class Ia: Infinitives in *-er*, e.g. *chanter*.
Most verbs belong to this class (well over 1000 in the twelfth century).

Class Ib: Infinitives in *-ier*, e.g. *laissier*.
These are fairly numerous (well over 500 in the twelfth century). They are conjugated like Class Ia verbs, except for a diphthong *ie* instead of *e* in the infinitive and in five other verb forms.

Class II: Infinitives in *-ir*, present participle with the infix *-iss-*, e.g. *florir*, *flor-iss-ant*.
This class contains a few score verbs in the twelfth century, but the number slowly increases with the absorption of *-ir* verbs from Class III.

Class III: Infinitives in *-ir*, *-re*, and *-eir > oir*, e.g. *servir*, *dire*, *deveir > devoir*.
Nearly 200 verbs belong to this class in the twelfth century, and many show irregular forms. Some of the *-ir* verbs however gradually adopt the infix *-iss-* and are absorbed into Class II (§68.2).

63. Conjugations

Tense endings of all verb classes are given in Table 5. A sample verb from each class is conjugated in Table 6 and the verb *boivre* has been added as an example of vocalic alternation (§§65, 76). For the auxiliary verbs *avoir* (to have) and *estre* (to be) see Tables 7 and 8.

Early twelfth-century endings which provide more information are shown in Table 5, but standard twelfth-century forms (after 1150) are used in Table 6 for comparison.

Table 5. *Verb endings (early 12th c.)*

A. *Present Stem Tenses*

Class	Ia	Ib	II	III
Infinitive	er	ier	ir (-iss-)	ir, re, eir (> oir)
Pres.Ind.				
PI.1	-*		is	-*
2	es		is	s*
3	eț		ist	t*
4	ons		iss ons	ons
5	ez	iez	iss ez	ez
6	ent		iss ent	ent
Pres.Subj.				
PS.1	-*		iss e	e
2	s*		iss es	es
3	t*		iss eț	eț
4	ons		iss ons	ons
5	ez	iez	iss ez	ez
6	ent		iss ent	ent
Imperative				
I've 2	e		is	-*
4	ons		iss ons	ons
5	ez	iez	iss ez	ez
Pres.Part.	ant		iss ant	ant
Impf.Ind.				
Impf.1	eie		iss eie	eie
2	eies		iss eies	eies
3	eit		iss eit	eit
4	iiens		iss iiens	iiens
5	iiez		iss iiez	iiez
6	eient		iss eient	eient
Perfect	Wk/a	Wk/a²	Wk/i	All types except Wk/a and Wk/a².

* Allow for consonant changes and supporting vowels (§§71-4, 78).

B. *Weak and Strong Perfects*

Perfect type	Wk/a	Wk/a²	Wk/i	Wk/i²	St/i
P.1	ai		i		-
2	as		is		is
3	aţ		iţ	iéţ	t
4	ames		imes		imes
5	astes		istes		istes
6	erent	ierent	irent	ierent	(d)rent
Past Part.	éţ	iéţ	iţ	uţ	uţ

Impf.Subj.

IS.1	as se		is se
2	as ses		is ses
3	as t		is t
4	is sons		is sons
	is siens		is siens
5	is seiz		is seiz
	is sez		is sez
	is siez		is siez
6	as sent		is sent

Perfect type	Wk/u	St/s	St/u	
P.1	ui	s	oi	ui
2	us	şis	e üs	e üs
3	uţ	st	ot	ut
4	umes	şimes	e ümes	e ümes
5	ustes	şistes	e üstes	e üstes
6	urent	strent	orent	urent
Past Part.	uţ	s, t	e üţ	

Impf.Subj.

IS.1	us se	şis se	e üs se
2	us ses	şis ses	e üs ses
3	us t	şis t	e üs t
4	us sons	şis sons	e üs sons
	etc.	etc.	etc.

For (*d*) in the St/i perfect see §69.1, and for ş in the St/s verbs §69.2.

C. *Other Tenses*

For all classes

Future		Conditional		Pres. Subjunctive	
Infinitive (sec §66.7) plus:				in -*ge* (§68.6)	
F.1	*ai*	C.1	*eie*	PS.1	*ge*
2	*as*	2	*eies*	2	*ges*
3	*at*	3	*eit*	3	*get*
4	*ons*	4	*iiens*	4	*giens, jons*
5	*eiz, ez*	5	*iiez*	5	*giez, gez*
6	*ont*	6	*eient*	6	*gent*

Class 1: Alternative Imperfect Ind.

Western dialects		Eastern dialects	
Early 12th c. -*oue*		Class 1a -*eve*	
Later 12th c. -*oe*		Class 1b -*ieve*	
Impf.1	*o(u)e*	Impf.1	*(i)eve*
2	*o(u)es*	2	*(i)eves*
3	*o(u)t*	3	*(i)evet*
4	*iiens*	4	*iiens*
5	*iiez*	5	*iiez*
6	*o(u)ent*	6	*(i)event*

Notes to Table 5:
1. *t* disappears early, and *ei* soon becomes *oi* in all positions (Inf.; Impf.1,2,3,6; Cond.1,2,3,6; IS.5 and F.5) but see §212.2.
2. In the later 12th c. *ii* > *i* in Impf.4,5 and Cond.4,5 (§15).
3. Note the similarity in endings. Standard Impf. and Cond. endings are the same throughout; Class II flexions in Table 5.A are the same as those for Class III, except that final *ss* (+*s*) > *s*, *ss*+*t* > *st*; perfect endings have regular variations and the Impf.Subj. can always be derived from P.2.
4. For alternatives see §§68 and 69.

Abbreviations have been added in Table 5 for easy reference, thus P.6 = the third person plural of the perfect tense, and IS.3 = the third person singular of the imperfect subjunctive. For other abbreviations, such as PP for the past participle, see p. xi.

For the meaning of verbs in this chapter see the vocabulary or the glossary. Irregular verbs are listed in Appendix E.

64. Weak and strong perfects

The term 'perfect' refers here to the simple past tense, at times called the past definite or past historic.

Old French perfects can be sub-divided into eight types, of which five are classed as weak, since the stem is never accented, and three as strong, since the stress falls at times on the stem.

These eight types are discussed below, and their endings are shown in Table 5.B. A classified list of weak and strong perfects is given in Appendix C.

1. Weak/a perfect

This is the most common perfect, used for all Class Ia verbs.

2. Weak/a² perfect

This, used for all Class Ib verbs, is like the Weak/a perfect except for *ie* instead of *e* in P.6.

3. Weak/i perfect

All Class II verbs and most Class III -*ir* verbs share this perfect (over 100 altogether).

Exceptions among Class III -*ir* verbs are *morir* (Wk/*u*), *venir*, *tenir* (St/i) and *plaisir*, *taisir*, *gesir*, *loisir*, *nuisir* (St/u).

4. Weak/i² perfect

This perfect is at times used instead of the Weak/i perfect by about 20 Class III verbs with infinitives in consonant (usually *d, t*)+-*re*, the only difference being the diphthong *ie* instead of *e* in P.3 and P.6. These verbs however gradually extend their use of the Weak/i perfect, which is generalised in the early thirteenth century, although they retain their distinctive past participle in -*u*.

5. Weak/u perfect

This perfect is used for about 10 Class III verbs.

6. Strong/i perfect

Only the 4 Class III verbs *tenir, venir, veoir and voloir* use this perfect.

Table 6. *Conjugations (later 12th c.)*

Class	Ia	II	III	III (VA)
Inf.	*son er*	*fen ir*	*cor re*	*boiv re*
Pres.Ind.				
PI.1	*son*	*fen is*	*cor*	S *boiǰ*
2	*son es*	*fen is*	*cor s*	S *boi s*
3	*son e*	*fen ist*	*cor t*	S *boi t*
4	*son ons*	*fen iss ons*	*cor ons*	U *bev ons*
5	*son ez*	*fen iss ez*	*cor ez*	U *bev ez*
6	*son ent*	*fen iss ent*	*cor ent*	S *boiv ent*
Pres.Subj.				
PS.1	*son*	*fen iss e*	*cor e*	S *boiv e*
2	*son s*	*fen iss es*	*cor es*	S *boiv es*
3	*son t*	*fen iss e*	*cor e*	S *boiv e*
4	*son ons*	*fen iss ons*	*cor ons*	U *bev ons*
5	*son ez*	*fen iss ez*	*cor ez*	U *bev ez*
6	*son ent*	*fen iss ent*	*cor ent*	S *boiv ent*
Imperative				
I've 2	*son e*	*fen is*	*cor*	S *boif*
4	*son ons*	*fen iss ons*	*cor ons*	U *bev ons*
5	*son ez*	*fen iss ez*	*cor ez*	U *bev ez*
Pres.Part.				
	son ant	*fen iss ant*	*cor ant*	U *bev ant*
Impf.Ind.				
Impf.1	*son oie*	*fen iss oie*	*cor oie*	U *bev oie*
2	*son oies*	*fen iss oies*	*cor oies*	U *bev oies*
3	*son oit*	*fen iss oit*	*cor oit*	U *bev oit*
4	*son iiens*	*fen iss iiens*	*cor iiens*	U *bev iiens*
5	*son iiez*	*fen iss iiez*	*cor iiez*	U *bev iiez*
6	*son oient*	*fen iss oient*	*cor oient*	U *bev oient*

Class	Ia	II	III		III (VA)
Inf.	*son er*	*fen ir*	*cor re*		*boiv re*
Perf.	Wk/a	Wk/i	Wk/u		St/u
P.1	*son ai*	*fen i*	*cor ui*	S	*bui*
2	*son as*	*fen is*	*cor us*	U	*be üs*
3	*son a*	*fen i*	*cor u*	S	*but*
4	*son ames*	*fen imes*	*cor umes*	U	*be ümes*
5	*son astes*	*fen istes*	*cor ustes*	U	*be üstes*
6	*son erent*	*fen irent*	*cor urent*	S	*burent*

Past Part.

PP	*son é*	*fen i*	*cor u*	U	*be ü*

Impf.Subj.

IS.1	*son asse*	*fen isse*	*cor usse*	U	*be üsse*
2	*son asses*	*fen isses*	*cor usses*	U	*be üsses*
3	*son ast*	*fen ist*	*cor ust*	U	*be üst*
4	*son issons*	*fen issons*	*cor ussons*	U	*be üssons*
	son issiens	*fen issiens*	*cor ussiens*		*be üssiens*
5	*son issoiz*	*fen issoiz*	*cor ussoiz*	U	*be üssoiz*
	son issez	*fen issez*	*cor ussez*		*be üssez*
	son issiez	*fen issiez*	*cor ussiez*		*be üssiez*
6	*son assent*	*fen issent*	*cor ussent*	U	*be üssent*

Future

F.1	*soner ai*	*fenir ai*	*corr ai*	U	*bevr ai*
2	*soner as*	*fenir as*	*corr as*	U	*bevr as*
3	*soner a*	*fenir a*	*corr a*	U	*bevr a*
4	*soner ons*	*fenir ons*	*corr ons*	U	*bevr ons*
5	*soner oiz*	*fenir oiz*	*corr oiz*	U	*bevr oiz*
	soner ez	*fenir ez*	*corr ez*	U	*bevr ez*
6	*soner ont*	*fenir ont*	*corr ont*	U	*bevr ont*

Conditional

C.1	*soner oie*	*fenir oie*	*corr oie*	U	*bevr oie*
2	*soner oies*	*fenir oies*	*corr oies*	U	*bevr oies*
3	*soner oit*	*fenir oit*	*corr oit*	U	*bevr oit*
4	*soner iiens*	*fenir iiens*	*corr iiens*	U	*bevr iiens*
5	*soner iiez*	*fenir iiez*	*corr iiez*	U	*bevr iiez*
6	*soner oient*	*fenir oient*	*corr oient*	U	*bevr oient*

Table 7. *Avoir (early and later 12th c. forms)*

Pres.Ind.			Imperative	
1 *ai*			2 *aies*	
2 *as*			4 *aiiens*	
3 *aṭ*			*aions*	
4 *avons*			5 *aiiez*	
5 *avez*				
6 *ont*			Pres.Part. *aiant*	

Pres.Subj.			Impf.Ind.	
1 *aie*			1 *aveie > avoie* etc.	
2 *aies*			2 *aveies*	
3 *aieṭ, ait*			3 *aveit*	
4 *aiiens*			4 *aviiens*	
aions			*avions*	
5 *aiiez*			5 *aviiez*	
6 *aient*			6 *aveient*	

Perfect			Future	
1 *oi*	*oi*		1 *avrai*	*arai*
2 *eüs*	*oüs*		2 *avras*	*aras*
3 *ot*	*ot, out*		3 *avraṭ*	*araṭ*
4 *eümes*	*oümes*		4 *avrons*	*arons*
5 *eüstes*	etc.		5 *avreiz*	*areiz*
6 *orent*			*avrez*	*arez*
			6 *avront*	*aront*

Past Part. *eüṭ, oüṭ*

			Conditional	
Impf.Subj.			1 *avreie*	*areie*
1 *eüsse*	*oüsse*		*> avroie*	*> aroie* etc.
2 *eüsses*	etc.		2 *avreies*	*areies*
3 *eüst*			3 *avreit*	*areit*
4 *eüssons, -iens*			4 *avriiens*	*ariiens*
5 *eüsseiz*			*avrions*	*arions*
eüssez, -iez			5 *avriiez*	*ariiez*
6 *eüssent*			6 *avreient*	*areient*

1. The early infinitive of *avoir* was *aveir*.
2. For the perfect in *oi/oüs* see §69.4.
3. The alternative Fut. and Cond. *arai*, *areie*, etc., originally Picard forms, were also current in Francien (cf. *savrai* or *sarai* etc. in the verb *savoir*).
4. *ṭ* disappeared early and *ei* soon became *oi* in all positions. In the later 12th c. *ii > i* throughout.

Table 8. *Estre (early and later 12th c. forms)*

Pres.Ind.	Imperative	
1 *sui*	2 *seies* > *soies* etc.	
2 *es, ies*	4 *seiiens*	
3 *est*	*seions*	
4 *somes, esmes*	5 *seiiez*	
5 *estes*		
6 *sont*	Pres.Part. *estant*	

Pres.Subj.	Impf.Ind.	
1 *seie* > *soie* etc.	1 *(i)ere*	*esteie* > *estoie* etc.
2 *seies*	2 *(i)eres*	*esteies*
3 *seit*	3 *(i)ereṭ, (i)ert*	*esteit*
4 *seiiens*	4 *eriiens*	*estiiens*
seions	*erions*	*estions*
5 *seiiez*	5 *eriiez*	*estiiez*
6 *seient*	6 *(i)erent*	*esteient*

Perfect	Future		
1 *fui*	1 *(i)er*	*serai*	*estrai*
2 *fus*	2 *(i)ers*	*seras*	*estras*
3 *fuṭ*	3 *(i)ert*	*seraṭ*	*estraṭ*
4 *fumes*	4 *(i)ermes*	*serons*	*estrons*
5 *fustes*	5 —	*sereiz*	*estreiz*
6 *furent*		*serez*	*estrez*
Past Part. *estéṭ*	6 *(i)erent*	*seront*	*estront*

Impf.Subj.	Conditional	
1 *fusse*	1 *sereie*	*estreie*
2 *fusses*	> *seroie*	> *estroie* etc.
3 *fust*	2 *sereies*	*estreies*
4 *fussons, -iens*	3 *sereit*	*estreit*
5 *fusseiz*	4 *seriiens*	*estriiens*
fussez, -iez	*serions*	*estrions*
6 *fussent*	5 *seriiez*	*estriiez*
	6 *sereient*	*estreient*

1. Varying VL stems led to OFr forms like *est*, *sont*, *ert* and *fui*. The Impf. and Fut. in *est-* use the infinitive stem, which is modified, with the *t*-glide omitted, in the Fut. *serai*, etc.
2. The Impf. and Fut. in *er-* had stressed doublets in *ier-* (§18.3), but by the 12th c. they were interchangeable.
3. *ṭ* disappeared early and *ei* soon became *oi* in all positions. In the later 12th c. *ii* > *i* throughout.

7. Strong/s perfect

This is shared by about 50 Class III verbs in -*re* and a few others. They fall into two groups (see Appendix C):

(a) those with vocalic stems in the perfect, e.g. *dire*, P.1 *di-s*;

(b) those with consonant stems in the perfect, including vowel+*i* (formerly a consonant), e.g. *tordre*, P.1 *tor-s*; *traire*, P.1 *trai-s*.

8. Strong/u perfect

This perfect is used for about two dozen Class III verbs. Here the ending has fused with the stem vowel to form a P.1 in either -*oi* or -*ui*, and both forms are shown in Table 5.B. Verbs belonging to each sub-section are listed in Appendix C.

65. Vocalic alternation in strong perfects

In weak perfects the stress always falls on the ending, while in strong perfects the stress falls on the stem in P.1, P.3 and P.6. The perfect of *doner*, for instance, is weak, while that of *tordre* is strong (see Table 9.1).

Since stressed and unstressed vowels often developed differently (§16), this change of accent in strong perfects led in about half the cases to vocalic alternation in the stem (see Table 9.2).

The stressed and unstressed stems can be found from P.1 and P.2 respectively; both forms are listed in Appendix C in the case of vocalic alternation. The weak stem vowel in the perfect is usually *e*.

St/s perfects of group (a) have vocalic stems and normally undergo vocalic alternation, but those of group (b) end or formerly ended in a consonant, which prevented vocalic alternation.

All St/u perfects show vocalic alternation, but the endings -*ui*, -*ut*, -*urent* of P.1,3,6 have merged with the stressed stem vowels *o* or *u*, though the unstressed stem vowel *e* is still found in P.2,4,5. This will be clear from Table 6, where the Perf. and Imp.Subj. of *boivre* (St/u) and *corre* (Wk/u) should be compared.

66. Tense formation

1. **The present stem** can be derived from the infinitive, except in the case of some Class III verbs. It can always be obtained, however, from PI.4; thus the PI.4 of *son-er*, *flor-ir*, *boiv-re* is *son-ons*, *flor-iss-ons*, *bev-ons*, with stems *son-*, *flor-*, *bev-*.

Change of stress in present stems led in over 100 cases to vocalic alternation, resulting in two stem forms (§76). In this case the unstressed stem is found in PI.4 and the stressed stem in PI.6.

Table 9. *Weak and strong perfects*

1. Stress patterns in weak and strong perfects.

	doner (Wk/a)		*tordre* (St/s)	Stem*
P.1	doˈnai	P.1	ˈtors	S
2	doˈnas	2	torˈsis	U
3	doˈna	3	ˈtorst	S
4	doˈnames	4	torˈsimes	U
5	doˈnastes	5	torˈsistes	U
6	doˈnerent	6	ˈtorstrent	S

2. Vocalic alternation in strong perfects.

	veoir (St/i)	*dire* (St/s)	*devoir* (St/u)	Stem*
P.1	ˈvi	ˈdi-s	ˈdui	S
2	ve-ˈis	de-ˈsis	de-ˈus	U
3	ˈvi-t	ˈdi-st	ˈdut	S
4	ve-ˈimes	de-ˈsimes	de-ˈumes	U
5	ve-ˈistes	de-ˈsistes	de-ˈustes	U
6	ˈvi-rent	ˈdi-strent	ˈdurent	S

* The abbreviations S and U refer to stressed and unstressed stems respectively.

2. **The present tenses** (present indicative and subjunctive, imperative, present participle and imperfect) are basically derived by adding the endings given in Table 5.A to the present stem, but standard modifications are discussed in Chapter 6. In the case of vocalic alternation the imperfect and the present participle use the unstressed stem.

3. **The perfect stem** of weak verbs is the same as the present stem, and is unstressed, since the accent falls on the ending (e.g. *soner*, stem *son-*, PI.4 soˈnons, P.1 soˈnai). In strong perfects, however, the stem often differs from the present stem, and change of stress can lead to vocalic alternation between stressed stems in P.1,3,6 and unstressed stems in P.2,4,5 (§65).

4. **The perfect** is formed by adding the endings given in Table 5.B to the perfect stem, and allowing for vocalic alternation. The P.1 of strong perfects (and the P.2 where there is vocalic alternation) can be found in Appendix C.

5. **Past participles** usually have stressed vocalic endings affixed to the unstressed perfect stem found in P.2; thus P.2 *chant-as*, *ven-is*, *e-üs*, PP *chant-é*, *ven-u*, *e-ü*; the past participles of St/s verbs, however, add *s* or *t* to the stressed stem found in P.1 (see Appendix C); thus v. *metre*, *dire*: P.1 *mi-s*, *di-s*, PP *mi-s*, *di-t*.

6. **The imperfect subjunctive** can always be derived by adding the endings *-se, -ses, -t*, etc., to P.2 (which ends in *-as, -is*, etc., according to type) and by changing *-as* to *-is* in Class I verbs in IS.4 and 5.

7. **The future and conditional** endings shown in Table 5.C are the same for all classes; they are added to the infinitive, which is modified as follows:

(a) In Class Ia, *-rer, -ner* are often contracted to *-rr* and *-nr* (or *-rr*) respectively; thus *plorer*, F.1 *plorr-ai*; *doner*, F.1 *donr-ai* or *dorr-ai*.

(b) In Class Ib, *-ier > er*, e.g. *aidier*, F.1 *aider-ai*.

(c) In Class III verbs, *-re > r* (e.g. *rire*, F.1 *rir-ai*), while the final vowels of *-oir* infinitives and of some *-ir* infinitives drop, often leading to consonant changes (§75); thus *venir*, F.1 *vendr-ai*; *voloir*, F.1 *voldr-ai > voudr-ai*. After stems in *-fr, -vr*, e.g. *covrir*, *-ir > er*, hence F.1 *covrer-ai*.

8. **Compound tenses** are formed with the auxiliaries *avoir* and *estre* (Tables 7, 8).

67. Palatalised stems

Class Ib verbs differ from those of Class Ia in that their stem ended in Gallo-Roman with a palatalised consonant. In the twelfth century, due to subsequent development, Class Ib verbs usually have stems ending in *-ill, -gn, -g, -c, -ch*, or diphthongal stems ending in *-i, -id, -ir, -is, -isn, -iss*, or *-it* (see examples in Appendix C).

Class III verbs with these stems also take *-iez* in PI.5, PS.5 and I've 5; in addition they usually have a diphthongal flexion *-iens* in PS.4. At times Class II verbs use *-iens* and *-iez* in these positions after their palatalised infix *-iss-*.

For further information on palatalised stems see Technical Terms, p. xv.

68. Alternative forms: general

1. Class III verbs sometimes have alternative forms for infinitives (e.g. *plaisir* or *plaire*), for tense types (e.g. *lire*, St/u or St/s) or for persons (e.g. *dire*, PI.4 *dimes, dions* or *disons*).

2. The following Class III verbs can adopt Class II forms: *bolir, convertir, emplir, englotir, foïr* (to dig), *guerpir, haïr, joïr, partir* (to divide), *resplendir*, and their compounds. All except *bolir* and *partir* are later absorbed into Class II.

3. From the twelfth century onwards analogical forms in *-e* were gradually introduced in PI.1 and PS.1 in Class I, while analogical forms in *-z* or *-s* are occasionally found in PI.1 and I've 2 in Class III.

4. Alternative flexions for 1st person plurals in *-ons* are *-omes*, *-oms*, *-om*, *-on* (or *-um(s)*, *-un(s)* in Anglo-Norman).

5. For 2nd person plurals in *-iez* see §67.

Although $z > s$ in the thirteenth century (§7.3) 2nd person plurals usually retain the graphy *-(i)ez* and only occasionally change to *-(i)és* (see e.g. §212.15).

6. Alternative present subjunctives in *-ge* are common in west French dialects (*-che* and *-ce* in the north and east) for verbs with stems in *-l*, *-n*, *-r* (e.g. *doner*, PS.1 *don-ge*). These forms have been added in Table 5.C.

7. Alternative subjunctive flexions sometimes found are PS.5 in *-eiz* > *oiz* for Class I verbs, also PS.4 in *-iens*, mainly in verbs with palatal stems (§67), but extended in the later thirteenth century to other verbs.

8. The ending *-ions* was introduced in Impf.4 and Cond.4 in the twelfth century ≠ PI.4 in *-ons* and generalised in the thirteenth, although *-iens* was still current in northern and eastern dialects.

9. The ending *-ions* was introduced in PS.4 and IS.4 in the later thirteenth century ≠ current PS.4 and IS.4 flexions in *-ons* and *-iens*.

10. Class I imperfects in *-o(u)e* and *-(i)eve* found in dialects are shown in Table 5.C.

11. Although the final t of the P.3 in weak perfects dropped well before 1150, forms in *-it* and *-ut* were gradually reintroduced in the thirteenth century ≠ strong perfects. Similarly, in the perfect of *estre*, *fut* > *fu*, then *fut*.

69. Alternative forms: strong perfects

1. In St/i perfects a glide consonant, shown as (*d*), appeared in the P.6 of *venir*, *tenir* and *voloir* (*vindrent*, *tindrent*, *voldrent*) (cf. §75) but was omitted in north and north-western dialects.

2. In St/s perfects the initial *s* of the ending in P.2,4,5 (shown as *ş* in Table 5.B) followed one of three courses (reflected in the corresponding Impf.Subj. as well):

(i) It gradually disappeared from the late twelfth century onwards in many group-(a) verbs with vocalic stems (e.g. *metre*, P.2 *me-sis* > *meïs*). Here *s* between vowels = [z] (§7.1).

(ii) It was retained in all group-(b) verbs where the stem ended in a consonant in OFr (e.g. *criembre*, P.2 *cren-sis*). Here *s* after a consonant = [s].

(iii) It was often doubled in group-(b) verbs where the OFr stem ended in a vowel + *i* (formerly a consonant) to indicate an alternative

pronunciation in [s] (§7.1) (e.g. *conduire*, P.2 *condui-sis* or *condui-ssis*).

3. Some St/s perfects had an early P.6 in *-sdrent*. Later forms at times end in *-rent*, e.g. v. *faire*, P.6 *fi-rent*. A dialectal P.6 in *-sent*, *-ssent* is found in the north and north-east.

4. All St/u perfects in *-oi* had an early P.3 and 6 in *-out*, *-ourent*. Together with most St/u perfects in *-ui* they sometimes use *oü* instead of *eü*, giving an alternative P.2,4,5 in *-oüs*, *-oümes*, *-oüstes*, IS in *-oüsse*, etc., and PP in *-oüt* (see *avoir*, Table 7). Note: *-out* = 1 syllable, *-oüs* = 2 syllables, etc.

5. In St/u perfects the weak *e* in hiatus in *eü* began to disappear in pronunciation in the thirteenth century, though it was usually retained in the spelling. The imperfect subjunctive and past participle were also occasionally affected.

VOCABULARY

Class Ia (Wk/a)

amer, love
chanter, sing
doner, give
durer, last
plorer, weep
soner, ring

Class Ib (Wk/a²)

aidier, help
laissier, leave, let
noncier, announce
otroiier, grant

Class II (Wk/i)

choisir, see, choose
fenir, finish
florir, bloom
garir, save, heal

Class III (Wk/i)

covrir, cover
ferir, PP *feru*, strike
oïr (< *oḍir*), hear
servir, serve

Class III (Wk/i²)

perdre, lose
respondre, reply

Class III (Wk/u)

corre, run
doloir, suffer

Class III (St/i)

tenir (*tin*/*tenis*, PP *tenu*), hold
venir (*vin*/*venis*, PP *venu*), come
veoir (< *veḍeir*) (*vi*/*veïs*, PP *veü*), see

Class III (St/s)

(a) Vocalic perfect stems
dire (*dis*/*deṣis*, PP *dit*), say
metre (*mis*/*meṣis*, PP *mis*), put
rire (< *riḍre*) (*ris*/*reṣis*, PP *ris*), laugh
(b) Consonant perfect stems
conduire (*conduis*, PP *conduit*), lead
criembre (*crens*, PP *crient*), fear
tordre (*tors*, PP *tors*, *tort*), twist
traire (*trais*, PP *trait*), pull

Class III (St/u)

(a) P.1 in *-oi*
savoir (soi/seüs, PP *seü),* know

(b) P.1 in *-ui*
boivre (*< beivre*) (*bui/beüs,* PP
beü), drink
devoir (dui/deüs, PP *deü),* should

Early twelfth-century infinitives with stems in *ḍ* have been added above. In verbs with strong perfects, the P.1 has been given in brackets (and the P.2 where there is vocalic alternation) followed by the past participle. Many of the above verbs have modified forms (see Chapter 6 and Appendix E), but the forms needed in the exercises below are regular, although vocalic alternation in strong perfects should be taken into account.

For further meanings of the above verbs see the glossary or an OFr dictionary.

TEST YOURSELF

Omit the pronoun subject, and use later 12th c. forms, unless early forms are requested.

The present stem, where needed below, can be derived from the infinitive (*dur-er, flor-ir, trai-re, laiss-ier,* etc.).

(a) 1. Conjugate in full the present indicative, present subjunctive and imperative of: *durer, florir, traire* (§67).
  2. Add the early 12th c. forms that would differ from the above.
  3. Give the Pres.Ind.5, Pres.Subj.5 and I've 5 of *laissier* and *otroiier.*

(b) 1. Give the present participle of *plorer* and *choisir.*
  2. Give the early and later 12th c. imperfect indicative of *garir* and *veoir* (*< veḍeir*).
  3. Add the alternative present subjunctive in *-ge* (§68.6) of *venir* (*venge,* etc.).

(c) 1. Give the perfect tense of the following verbs (§66.3,4): *amer, aidier, oïr, perdre, doloir, venir, metre, criembre, savoir, devoir.*
     Add their perfect type (Wk/a etc.) and their past participle.
  2. Give the 13th c. perfect tense of *dire,* without *s* (§69.2).
  3. Give the imperfect subjunctive of : *aidier, choisir, doloir, metre, devoir.*

(d) 1. Give the future of *noncier* and *dire* (§66.7).
  2. Add the early and later 12th c. conditional of *dire.*

(e) 1. Give four alternative forms for the Fut.1 of *estre,* three for the Impf.2 of *estre,* and two for the Fut.5 of *avoir.*
  2. Add the later 12th c. present subjunctive of *estre.*
  3. Which imperfect forms of *estre* are identical with forms for the same persons in the future of this verb?

6
Verbs: standard modifications

70. General

The basic patterns of OFr verbs were given in Chapter 5. Several factors however influence the conjugations of individual verbs. The most important, discussed below, affect only the present indicative, the present subjunctive and the imperative, except for features mentioned in §§74,75.

See the vocabularies on pp. 54 and 61 for the meaning of verbs in this chapter.

71. Supporting vowels

Verbs in Class I and Class III with a stem ending in -g, -ch or consonant + r, l (but not ll) have a weak e as a supporting vowel when the normal ending is -, -s or -t. The verb forms affected are asterisked in Table 5.

Thus *entrer*: PS.1,2,3 *entre, entres, entret*. Similarly the PS.1 of *jugier, sachier = juge, sache*, while the PI.1 of *emplir, ofrir = emple, ofre*.

Note that the 3rd person singular ends in -et > e due to the supporting vowel, while the regular form ends in -t.

72. Uninflected stems

Voiced stem consonants become unvoiced when final (see Technical Terms). This affects Class I: PI.1, PS.1, also Class III: PI.1, I've 2.

Thus: $v > f$ *servir / serf*
        $b > p$ *gaber / gap*
        $d > t$ *tordre / tort*
        $ḍ > ṭ$ *riḍre / riṭ*

Occasionally a phonetic change is not reflected in the spelling:

        [z] > [s]   *taisir / tais*

A stem consonant may be spelt differently when final (§7.1).

Thus: [ts] *noncier | nonz*
      [l'] *faillir | fail*
      [n'] *deignier | deing*
      [s] *laissier | lais*

73. Stems + *s, t*

Final stem consonants disappear or are modified before -*s* and -*t*. This affects Class I: PS.2,3, also Class III: PI.2,3.

For modifications due to flexional -*s* see §§38, 39. Changes due to -*t* are similar but simpler, namely:

1. *p*, *b*, *v* disappear before -*t*.
2. *t*, *d*, *ḍ* combine with -*t* to form *t*.
3. After a vowel *m*+*t* becomes *nt*.
4. *rm*+*t* becomes *rt*.
5. *rn*+*t* becomes *rt*.
6. *n'*+*t* becomes *nt*.
7. *el*+t becomes *eaut*.
8. *l*, *l'* become *u* before -*t*, but disappear after *i*, *u*.

Thus:

Verb	Tense	2nd sing.	3rd sing.	Rule for -*s*, -*t*
servir	PI	*sers*	*sert*	1
chanter	PS	*chanz*	*chant*	2
prendre	PI	*prenz*	*prent*	2
riḍre	PI	*riz*	*rit*	2
criem(b)re	PI	*criens*	*crient*	3
rompre	PI	*rons*	*ront*	1, 3
dormir	PI	*dors*	*dort*	4
torner	PS	*torz*	*tort*	5
deignier	PS	*deinz*	*deint*	6
apeler	PS	*apeaus*	*apeaut*	7
valoir	PI	*vaus*	*vaut*	8
conseillier	PS	*conseuz*	*conseut*	10 (-*s*), 8 (-*t*)

Also: *laissier* PS *lais* *laist* See §7.1 for [s].

Here *ss*+*s* > *s* when final, while *ss* > *s* before a consonant.

Verbs are not found with stems in -*f*. The stem of *signifier*, for example, is *signifi*-.

Note that -*z* is the normal ending in Class I PS.2 and Class III PI.2 for verbs with stems in *t*, *d*, *ḍ*, *l'*, *n'*, and *rn*. Even when -*z* was pronounced -*s* in the thirteenth century the spelling -*z* was often retained.

74. Stems in -c, -g

The final -*c* in verb stems is usually pronounced [ts], as in *noncier*, leading to the following consonant changes (see §7.1):

PI.1	*nonz*	[ts] is spelt *z* when final.
2	*nonz*	[ts]+*s* > [ts].
3	*nonzt*	[ts] is spelt *z* before a consonant.
4	*nonçons*	[ts] is nowadays represented by *ç* before *a, o, u*.
5	*nonciez*	[ts] is spelt *c* before *e, i*.
6	*noncent*	as for PI.5.

Veintre has a stem in [k], spelt *c* when final or before *a, o, u*; e.g. PI.1 *venc*, PI.4 *vencons*, PP *vencu*; *c* is replaced by *qu*, pronounced [k], before *e, i*, hence PI.6 *venquent*, P.1 *venqui*.

The final -*g* in verb stems is pronounced [dž], as in *jugier*, and needs a supporting vowel (§71). It is often replaced by *j* before *a, o, u*, but is pronounced [dž] here even if spelt *g*.

Thus: v. *jugier*, PI.1 *juge*, PI.4 *jujons* or *jugons*.

75. Stems in -l, -m, n- -s

Glide or intrusive consonants developed in Class III verbs between a final stem consonant *l, m, n, s* and a following -*r*, e.g. *pren(d)re*, stem *pren-*.
    Verb forms which can be affected are:

(a) the infinitive in -*re*, and the future and conditional based on it.
(b) the 3rd person plural in -*rent* of St/i perfects (§69.1),
(c) the future and conditional formed on infinitives in -*oir* or -*ir* contracted to -*r* (§66.7c).

The added consonant can modify the stem, thus *plaign-+re* > *plain(d)re* (cf. §73.6); it is not part of the stem, however, and does not normally appear elsewhere in the verb.

In the examples below stems in -*l* are shown before the vocalisation of *l*, ind the added consonant is bracketed. The stem is seen in PI.4.

Groups	Infinitive	PI.4	Fut.1	
l+r > ldr	*voloir*	*vol-ons*	*vol(d)rai*	
l'+r > l'dr	*coillir*	*coill-ons*	*coil(d)rai*	
m+r > mbr	*criem(b)re*	*crem-ons*	*cren(d)rai**	
n+r > ndr	*venir*	*ven-ons*	*ven(d)rai*	
n'+r > ndr	*plain(d)re*	*plaign-ons*	*plain(d)rai*	
s+r > sdr	*cos(d)re*	*cos-ons*	*cos(d)rai*	stem in [z]
ss+r > str	*nais(t)re*	*naiss-ons*	*nais(t)rai*	stem in [s]

Criembre uses an analogical future in -*ndr*-.

Table 10. *Vocalic alternation in present stems*

	amer	laver	veoir	proisier	Stem
VA	ai/a	e/a	ei > oi/e	i/ei > oi	
PI.1	aim	lef	voi	pris	S
2	aim-es	lev-es	voi-z	pris-es	S
3	aim-e	lev-e	voi-t	pris-e	S
4	am-ons	lav-ons	ve-ons	prois-ons	U
5	am-ez	lav-ez	ve-ez	prois-iez	U
6	aim-ent	lev-ent	voi-ent	pris-ent	S

	querre	movoir	apoiier	Stem
VA	ie/e	ue/o	ui/oi	
PI.1	quier	muef	apui	S
2	quier-s	mue-s	apui-es	S
3	quier-t	mue-t	apui-e	S
4	quer-ons	mov-ons	apoi-ons	U
5	quer-ez	mov-ez	apoi-iez	U
6	quier-ent	muev-ent	apui-ent	S

	amer	movoir				Stem
PS.1	aim	muev-e	I've			S
2	ain-s	muev-es	2	aim-e	muef	S
3	ain-t	muev-e				S
4	am-ons	mov-ons	4	am-ons	mov-ons	U
5	am-ez	mov-ez	5	am-ez	mov-ez	U
6	aim-ent	muev-ent				S

76. Vocalic alternation in present stems

In the present indicative, present subjunctive and imperative the stress falls on the ending in the 1st and 2nd persons plural and on the stem in all other cases, e.g. *soner*: PI 'son, 'sones, 'sone, so'nons, so'nez, 'sonent. In over 100 Class I and Class III verbs this change of stress led to vocalic alternation in the stem.

The present indicative of seven verbs showing vocalic alternation is given in Table 10, and the subjunctive and imperative of *amer* and *movoir* have been added to illustrate the stem changes in these tenses as well.

Where the VA type is indicated the stressed stem vowel is given first, following by the unstressed stem vowel, e.g. VA e/a. Where *ei > oi* the later form is used in the table. Consonant changes, as in PI.1 *lef*, are explained in §§72, 73.

The infinitive normally uses the unstressed stem (as do the present participle and the imperfect) but at times the stressed stem is adopted, e.g. *boivre*.

For a classified list of vocalic alternation types and verbs affected see Appendix D.

77. Syllabic alternation in present stems

In six common Class I verbs, originally with polysyllabic stems, change of stress in present-stem tenses led to the loss of a vowel in unstressed stems; this resulted in syllabic alternation in the present indicative, subjunctive and imperative, at times accompanied by further changes.

The PI.6 and PI.4 of these verbs are given in Table 11 to show the stressed and unstressed stems respectively, while the present indicative, subjunctive and imperative of *parler* are conjugated in full to illustrate the syllabic alternation.

The unstressed stem vowel also disappears in the infinitive, the present participle and the imperfect, hence *parler, parlant*, and Impf.1 *parloie*.

Table 11. *Syllabic alternation in present stems*

Infinitive	PI.6	PI.4	SA type	
aidier	*ai'uḍ-ent*	*ai$_\wedge$d-ons*	u/-	
disner	*des'jun-ent*	*dis$_\wedge$n-ons*	ju/-	
mangier	*man'ju-ent*	*manj$_\wedge$-ons*	u/-	
parler	*pa'rol-ent*	*par$_\wedge$l-ons*	o/-	
araisnier	*arai'son-ent*	*arais$_\wedge$n-ons*	o/-	
deraisnier	*derai'son-ent*	*derais$_\wedge$n-ons*	o/-	

Parler						Stem
PI.1	*parol*	PS.1	*parol*	I've		S
2	*parol-es*	2	*parou-s*	2	*parol-e*	S
3	*parol-e*	3	*parou-t*			S
4	*parl-ons*	4	*parl-ons*	4	*parl-ons*	U
5	*parl-ez*	5	*parl-ez*	5	*parl-ez*	U
6	*parol-ent*	6	*parol-ent*			S

78. Palatalised stem in PI.1

A fair number of Class III verbs have a palatalised stem (see Technical Terms) in PI.1 for etymological or analogical reasons. The same stem is usually found throughout the present subjunctive as well, in which case PS.5 is in *-iez* and PS.4 usually in *-iens* (§67); thus *manoir*, VA ai̲/a:

PI: *maing, mains, maint, manons, manez, mainent.*
PS: *maigne, maignes, maigne, maigniens, maigniez, maignent.*
Normal and palatalised stems are commonly paired as follows:

Stems in	Verb	PI.4	PI.1	Pres. Subj.
l / l'	*valoir*	*valons*	*vail*	*vaille*, etc.
n / n'	*doner*	*donons*	*doing*	*doigne*, etc.
nd / n'	*respondre*	*respondons*	*respoing*	*respoigne*, etc.
ḍ / i	*oḍir > oïr*	*oḍons*	*oi*	*oie*, etc.
ḍ / is	*poḍeir > pooir*	*poḍons*	*puis*	*puisse*, etc.
r / ir	*morir*	*morons*	*muir*	*muire*, etc.
v / i	*avoir*	*avons*	*ai*	*aie*, etc.
v / i, ch	*savoir*	*savons*	*sai*	*sache*, etc.
is / [ts]	*faire*	*faisons*	*faz*	*face*, etc.

Palatalisation can affect the stem vowel, e.g. *morir*, PI.1 *muir*. In the pair *is* / [ts] the normal stem is also palatalised.

Some verbs have more than one stem for PI.1 or for the present subjunctive (see Appendix E).

VOCABULARY

Class Ia (Wk/a)

apeler, call
disner, dine
entrer, enter
gaber, joke
laver, wash
parler, speak
torner, turn

Class Ib (Wk/a²)

apoiier, lean
araisnier, address
comencier, begin
conseillier, advise
deignier, deign
deraisnier, argue
jugier, judge
mangier, eat
proisier (< *preisier*), value
sachier, pull

Class III (Wk/i)

coillir, gather
dormir, sleep
emplir, fill
faillir, fail
ofrir, offer

Class III (Wk/i²)

cosdre, sew
naistre, be born
rompre, break
veintre, conquer

Class III (Wk/u)

morir (PP *mort*), die
valoir, be worth

Class III (St/i)

voloir, wish

Class III (St/s)

(a) *faire*, do, make
    manoir, stay
    prendre, take
    querre, seek
(b) *joindre*, join
    plaindre, complain
    soudre (< *soldre*), pay for

Class III (St/u)

(a) *pooir* (< *poḍeir*), be able
    taisir, be silent
(b) *conoistre*, know
    movoir, move
    reçoivre (< *receivre*), receive

For the perfect stem of the above verbs, and for their vocalic alternation type (where applicable) see Appendices C and D. Some verbs show irregular forms, and these are given in Appendix E. For further meanings of the above verbs see the glossary or an OFr dictionary.

TEST YOURSELF

(Later 12th c. forms to be used)

(a) Explain the apparent irregularities in the present indicative of the following verbs:

    1. *boivre* : PI *boif, bois, boit, bevons, bevez, boivent.*

    2. *soudre* : PI *soil, sous, sout, solons, solez, solent.*

    3. *conoistre* : PI *conois, conois, conoist, conoissons, conoissiez, conoissent.*

    4. *pooir* : PI *puis, puez, puet, poons, poez, pueent.*

    5. *coillir* : PI *cueil, cueuz, cueut, coillons, coilliez, cueillent.*

(b) Comment briefly on the form of the infinitive, and add the PS.1 and PS.5 you would expect for each of the five verbs above.

(c) Give the PI.1,2,3 and 5 of:

    perdre, doloir (VA <u>ue</u>/o), *joindre* (PI.4 *joignons*).

(d) Give the present subjunctive of:

    lever (VA <u>ie</u>/e), *comencier,*

    and the imperative of:

    covrir (VA <u>ue</u>/o), *reçoivre* (VA <u>ei</u> > oi/e), *mangier* (SA <u>u</u>/-).

7
Personal pronouns

79. General

Personal pronouns agree in gender, number and case with the noun they replace. Declensions are given in Table 12. In some cases pronouns developed two forms, depending on whether they were pronounced with or without a stress, e.g. moi / me (§18). In other cases, e.g. nos, a single form was retained, whether stressed or not.

Forms which are stressed, unstressed, or which can be either are differentiated in the table and in their use below, although differentiation in the use of subject pronouns is at times only tentative.

The pronominal adverbs en and i were never stressed.

Table 12. *Personal pronouns*

			Singular			
Persons	1st	2nd	3rd (M)	3rd (F)	3rd Neut.	3rd Refl.
	I	you	he	she	it	him/her/
	me		him	her		itself
NS	jo, je	tu	il	ele	il	—
OS dir. ⎫			le	la		
⎬ moi me	toi te	lui	li	le	soi se
OS ind. ⎭			li	li		

			Plural			
Persons	1st	2nd	3rd (M)	3rd (F)		3rd Refl.
	we	you	they	they		them-
			them	them		selves
NP	nos	vos	il	eles		—
OP dir. ⎫			eus les	eles les		
⎬ nos	vos				soi se
OP ind. ⎭			lor	lor		

tu = stressed or unstressed; toi = stressed; te = unstressed, etc.

80. The pronoun subject

1. The pronoun subject was originally omitted, unless stressed. Its use slowly increases during the twelfth century, especially in the case of the 1st person singular *je*, *ge* (pronounced [džé] when stressed), though it is still usually omitted in inversions:

> *Or chanterai* ʌ .   Now I will sing.   (See §35)

2. It is occasionally used with the imperative:

> **Tu** *m'escoute!*   You listen to me!

3. When stressed, it can be separated from its verb, or used on its own:

> **Jo** *del mien ferai ma volenté.*   (Ad.617)
> I will do my will with mine.

> **Ge,** *por quoi?*   I, what for?   (F.9.682)

4. *Il* is often used pleonastically, duplicating an existing subject:

> *Li niés Marsilie,* **il** *est venuz.*   (Rol.860)
> The nephew of Marsile has come.

5. Since there is usually only a tonal distinction between stressed and unstressed pronoun subjects, the stressed oblique forms **moi, toi, lui, li** and **eus** are occasionally used as subjects for special emphasis:

> **Moi** *et* **vos,** *oncles, i somes oblié.*   (Ch.N.39)
> You and I, uncle, are forgotten there.

81. Direct and indirect objects

These are only differentiated in the 3rd person (M) and (F). Here unstressed forms differ in the singular:

> *Raous* **la** *voit* (direct) *et* **li** *done la letre* (indirect).
> Raoul sees her and gives her the letter.

while both stressed and unstressed forms differ in the plural:

> *Dieus beneïe* **eus** *et* **eles** (direct, stressed).
> God bless them (M) and them (F).

> *Car* **les lor** *donez!* (direct, indirect unstressed).
> Do give them to them!

As a rule the stressed direct object is used after prepositions:

> *Sans* **eus.**   Without them (M).
> *Vers* **eles.**   Towards them (F).

but occasionally a preposition is followed by *lor*:

> *Entre* **lor.**   Between themselves.

82. Reflexive pronouns

The normal oblique forms serve as reflexive pronouns, except for the 3rd person, which has a distinctive reflexive *se*, *soi*. The stressed 3rd person forms **lui**, **li**, **eus**, **eles** are also used as reflexives, particularly after prepositions:

> **Je** *me deport.* I amuse myself.
>
> **Il** **se** *deportent.* They amuse themselves.

but: *Por* eus *deporter.* To amuse themselves.

At times *se* expresses reciprocal action:

> *Granz cous se donent.* (Cl.92)
> They give each other great blows.

Some verbs can be used with or without a reflexive pronoun (§187), thus *dormir* or *se dormir*, 'to sleep'. Where the object pronoun, as in this case, merely reflects the personal involvement of the subject, it need not be translated.

83. Neuter pronouns

Il is used as a subject to impersonal verbs, though often omitted, e.g. *estuet*, 'it is necessary', and *(il) i a* or *(i) a*, 'there is', 'there are' (§188.5):

> *Meillor i a de* **vos.** (Gr.13)
> There is a better (knight) than you.

Il or *le* can refer to a phrase or clause, often pleonastically:

> *Quant Charles l'ot que* ... When Charles hears that ...

Since there is no stressed oblique form, unstressed *le* is used in strong positions, though it can be replaced by the neuter demonstrative *ço*, *ce* (§59.2):

> *por l'oïr, por ce oïr,* to hear it.

84. *En* and *i*

The pronominal adverbs *en* and *i* are used as unstressed equivalents of *de*+pronoun (of him, of it, etc.) and *a*+pronoun (to him, to it, etc.) respectively, and can refer to persons as well as to things or clauses:

> *Gauvains en ocit un.* Gawain kills one of them. (Gr.53)
>
> *Dit Nostre Sire: 'G'i irai.'* (F.7.110)
> Our Lord says: 'I will go to him.'

En and *i* are also used adverbially, meaning 'from there' and 'there' respectively (see examples in §83). For the use of *en* with verbs of movement, e.g. *s'en torner*, see §194.1.

85. Elision

The final vowel of *je* can be elided before a following vowel, e.g. *j'ai*. If there is no elision (je *ai*) a stress or half stress seems implied.

If the pronouns *me, te, se, le, l*a precede a verb, the vowel is always elided:

> **Tu** *l'as ocis.*   You have killed him.   (Ad.732)

If they follow a verb, elision is optional:

> *Laissiez m'aler!*   or   *Laissiez me aler!*
> Let me go!   (Cf. §88.2b)

Unstressed *li* can become *l'* before *en*:

> **Il** *l'en dist la verité.*   (Gr.53)
> He told him the truth about it.

86. Unstressed oblique pronouns

These are used in weak positions, namely:
1. Before a finite verb (but see §87.3):

> *Or le me dites!*   Now tell it to me!   (Yv.1995)
> **Il** *en but.*   He drank of it.   (Tr.1415)

2. Before an infinitive used as an imperative:

> *Ne te haster!*   Do not hurry yourself!   (Tr.1023)

3. Before *en* and *i* after a finite verb:

> *Fui t'en de ci!*   Get yourself away from here!   (Gr.131)
> but: *Fui toi de ci!*   Be gone from here!   (Ad.195)

4. In general before a word which carries a stress:

> *Veez me ci!*   Here I am!   (Rol.308)

87. Stressed oblique pronouns

These are used in strong positions, namely:
1. After a preposition (even if this governs a following infinitive):

> *Vers* li.   Towards her.
> *Por* eles *parer.*   To adorn themselves.   (Ch.V.702)

2. After a finite verb, where they are often placed for added distinction or emphasis:

> Il *m'ama et* je *haï* **lui**. (Per.8935)
> He loved me and I hated him.

3. Often before or after impersonal verbs:

> *Quant* **lui** *plaira*.   When it pleases him.
> *Ce poise* **moi**.   It grieves me.

4. When separated from their governing verb:

> *Feri la pucele et* **moi**. (Er.1021)
> He struck the maiden and me.   (Two objects.)

> **Lui** *serf et aime*. (Ad.37)
> Serve and love him.   (Two governing verbs.)

> *Cil fiert Erec, et Erec* **lui**. (Er.968)
> He strikes Erec, and Erec him.   (Verb omitted.)

5. When used in an absolute sense:

> **Lui** *oiant*.   Him hearing (= in his hearing).   (§185.3b)
> **Soi** *quart*.   Himself the fourth (of a group).   (§177.3)

6. In any position where special stress is required:

> *Mon cheval prist et* **moi** *laissa*.   (Yv.544)
> He took my horse and me he left.

88. Stressed and unstressed pronouns after verbs

1. (a) If the subject is omitted, or if it follows the verb in a question or inversion, oblique pronouns are placed after the verb to avoid unstressed pronouns in a strong initial position:

> *Porpense* **soi**.   He bethinks himself.
> *Creras* **me** *tu?*   Will you believe me?
> *Ot* **le** *Guillelmes*.   William hears it.

In this case, as the above examples show, 1st, 2nd and reflexive pronouns are stressed (unless followed by a pronoun subject which carries the stress), while 3rd person pronouns (*le, la, li, les, lor*) are unstressed.

(b) Oblique pronouns remain before the verb, however, if the sentence starts with a word or phrase which takes the stress:

> *Si* **se** *porpense*.   And he bethinks himself.   (Gr.61)
> *Que* **te** *voloit?*   What did he want from you?   (Ad.278)
> *Ou* **l'**as tu *mis?*   Where have you put him?   (Ad.731)

2. (a) Oblique pronouns follow an imperative (to avoid unstressed introductory pronouns) unless the imperative phrase begins with an adverb (*ne, car, or, si,* etc.), an adverbial phrase, the conjunctions *et* or *si,* etc.:

> *Dites* moi ...   *Or me dites* ...   Tell me ...

(b) After an imperative (even with a dependent infinitive) 1st, 2nd and reflexive pronouns are usually stressed (except before *en* or *i,* or in the Picard dialect); 3rd person pronouns are unstressed:

> *Garissiez les moi!*   Cure them for me!   (Fb.13.310)

but: *Laissiez m'aler!*   (Er.4017)
> Let me go!   (Dialectal influence.)

89. Word order

1. In a series of oblique pronouns, the direct object precedes the indirect object, while *en,* then *i,* come last:

> *Car le me pardonez!*   lit: Do forgive it to me!   (cf. Rol.2005)
> *Alez vos en!*   Go away!   (Ren.4447)
> *Trop en i a.*   There are too many of them.   (Fb.13.312)

2. In a sequence of unstressed 3rd person pronouns, the direct object (*le, la, les*) is often dropped before the indirect object (*li, lor*):

> *Demande ses armes, et l'on ˰ li aporte*
> (= *les li aporte*).   (Gr.51)
> He asks for his arms, and someone brings them to him.

3. Oblique pronouns precede the finite verb, even if there is a dependent past participle or infinitive (but see §§ 88 and 89.4 for inversions):

> *Ne la vos puis doner.*   (Ch.N.514)
> I cannot give it to you.

4. Oblique pronouns precede the subject in inversions, even if a dependent past participle or infinitive follows:

> *Amis, savroiz le me vos dire?*   (Er.5332)
> Friend, could you tell it to me?

90. Special uses

1. The indirect object is often used as an 'ethic dative', referring to the person or persons concerned; it frequently replaces a possessive adjective:

> *L'escuṭ li fraint.*   (Rol.1270)
> He shatters him the shield (= his shield).

2. When a 3rd person plural pronoun refers to nouns of both genders, the masculine form is used.

3. The plural pronoun *vos* is often used with a plural verb in a singular sense:

> *Par foi, dame! vos dites voir.* (Yv.1819)
> Faith, lady! you speak the truth.

Singular and plural forms of address are often used indiscriminately in the same text, sometimes even in the same sentence:

> **Vos** *estes oncle* (NS) *et* **il** *tes niés.* (Tr.1104)
> You are (his) uncle and he your nephew.

4. There is a certain confusion between stressed **lui** and **li** in the thirteenth century, with a growing tendency to use **lui** for **li**, and even (with weakened stress) for unstressed *li*.

5. *Meïsme* (*mesme*, etc.), meaning 'self', 'in person' (§46.2), is sometimes added to a stressed pronoun for extra emphasis:

> **Ge** *meïsme sui si confus.* (F.7.108)
> I myself am so embarrassed.

6. *De* plus a stressed pronoun sometimes replaces a possessive adjective for added emphasis:

> *Sor l'ame de* **moi** (= *sor m'ame*). Upon my soul.

7. A personal pronoun is sometimes replaced by a periphrase, like *mon cors* (my body), *ta charn* (your flesh), etc.:

> *Por lor cors deporter.* To amuse themselves. (Ch.N.26)

8. The stressed pronoun subject was originally used in negative or affirmative phrases with *non* or *o*; thus:

> *o* **je**, that I am, that I did, etc.
> *non* **je**, not I; *non* **tu**, not you, etc.

The most common forms *o* il > *oïl* > *oui* and *non* il > *nenil* > *neni* were generalised to mean 'yes' and 'no'.

91. Enclitic forms

The unstressed pronouns *le* and *les* could be reduced to *-l* and *-s* respectively before a following consonant after many common monosyllabic words ending in a vowel, such as *jo, je, ne, se, qui, que, si, ja*; thus: **je** *le croi* > *jel croi*. A final *-l* could then be vocalised, e.g. *jel* > *jeu, ju*.

The unstressed pronouns *me*, *te*, *se* and *en* were also occasionally affected and lost their vowel, e.g. **tu** *me* > **tum**.

A list of fairly common twelfth-century enclitic forms is given in Appendix B.

92. Alternative forms

The early twelfth-century forms of **moi**, **toi**, **soi** and **eus** were **mei**, **tei**, **sei** and **els** respectively. Forms in *-ei* were retained in many dialects, including Anglo-Norman (§212.2). *Lo* is an early or dialectal form of *le*.

Je could be written *ge*. Stressed forms sometimes found are **gié**, **jeo***, **jeu***, **jou*** and **ju***.

Lei* or **lié*** are sometimes found for stressed (F) **li**, and *el** for *ele* or for the neuter nominative *il*. In Picard *la* > *le* (§212.17).

In the thirteenth century *nos*, *vos* > *nous*, *vous*, and *lor* > *leur*.

* These are dialect forms.

TEST YOURSELF

(a) Give fairly literal translations of the following, using the glossary:

1. *Paien s'adobent . . . por eus defendre.*   (Ch.N.1408–10)
2. *Quant messire Gavains l'esgarde*
   D'aler contre li ne se tarde
   Si la salue et ele lui.   (Per.8111–13)
3. *Si com moi semble.*   (Yv.6027)
4. *Sor le perron . . Tristran* (NS) *s'apuie . . .*
   Demente soi a lui tot sol.   (Tr.235–7)
5. *Et cil respont: 'Gavains, tais t'en.'*   (Per.7085)
6. *Si dist: 'Vassal* (NS), *feru m'avez.'*
   – 'Voire, fait il, feru t'ai gié.'   (Per.7030–1)
7. *. . . Si com il firent moi.*   (cf. Yv.213)
8. *'Rendez les nos, jel vos demant.'*   (cf. Er.4388)
9. *Yvains lor voit cheoir des lermes,*
   Vient contre eles si les salue.   (cf. Yv.5242–4)
10. *'Merci! Ne m'ocire tu pas!'*   (Er.990)
11. *Vien toi reposer!*   (Gr.113)
12. *Et li dus errant li demande . . .*
    Qu'ele ʌ *li die maintenant.*   (Ver.111–13)
13. *'Est il armez?' – 'Par foi, oïl.'*
    – 'G'irai a lui parler.'   (Per.4227–8)
14. *L'elme li fraint.*   (Rol.1326)
15. *'Volez le me vos faire avoir*
    A force?' – 'Nenil voir, amie.'   (Omb.802–3)

(b) The above phrases illustrate most points covered in this chapter. For extra practice: check your translation, then identify the personal pronouns in these

phrases, giving the person, number and, for 3rd persons only, the gender where possible, or type (M, F, neut., refl.). Add their case (subject, direct or indirect object). State and explain their position and their form (stressed, unstressed) by brief references to the indications given in this chapter. Mention if they are elided or enclitic.

e.g. *Que te voloit?* What did he want from you?

te : 2 sing., ind.obj., placed before verb despite §88.1a since the phrase starts with *que* (§88.1b); unstressed (§86.1). (No key.)

8

Relatives and interrogatives

93. General

Declensions of relative and interrogative pronouns are almost the same. In each case singular and plural forms are identical; the neuter, however, is only found in the singular.

(a) Relatives (who, whom, whose, which, etc.):

Sing./Pl.	Persons	Things	Neuter uses	
Nom.	*qui*	*qui*	NS	*que*
Obl. dir.	*que*	*que*	OS dir.	*que*
Obl. dir.	*cui (quoi)*	*quoi (cui)*	OS dir.	*quoi*
Obl. ind.	*cui*			

(b) Interrogatives (who, whom, whose, which, what, etc.):

Sing./Pl.	Persons	Things	Neuter uses	
Nom.	*qui*	*qui*	NS	*que, quoi*
Obl. dir.	—	*que*	OS dir.	*que*
Obl. dir.	*cui*	*quoi*	OS dir.	*quoi*
Obl. ind.	*cui*			

Note: *cui, quoi* = stressed; *qui, que* = stressed or unstressed (the direct interrogative is usually stressed).

Interrogative pronouns, adjectives or adverbs can be used:

> for direct questions (§201.2): *Que ferai je?*
> for indirect questions: *Savez vos quele aventure ce est?* (Gr. 36)
> or where no question is implied: *Ne sai que faire.*

Interrogatives frequently function as subordinating conjunctions introducing a noun clause:

> *Or me dites, fet Galaad, que li cors senefie.* (Gr.38)
> Now tell me, says Galahad, what the body means.

94. Functions of *qui*

1. *Qui* (subject) refers to persons or things:

(a) Relatives:

> *Hector, qui mout fu sages.*   (R.Tr.49)
> Hector, who was very wise.

> *L'aigle d'or, qui reluist.*   (Or.462)
> The golden eagle, which shone.

Que sometimes replaces the relative *qui*, especially in dialects:

> *Agamenon, que lor princes estoit.*   (R.Tr.70)
> Agamemnon, who was their prince.

(b) Interrogatives:

> *Qui est cil chevaliers?*   Who is that knight?   (Er.753)

> *Qui est tel vile?*   What town is that?   (Ay.195)

2. *Qui* is often used in an absolute sense (see §103.1).

95. Functions of *que*

1. *Que* (subject) is used as a neuter, mainly as the subject of an impersonal verb:

(a) As a relative, e.g. after the neuter antecedent *ce*:

> *Ce que lui plot.*   That which pleased him.   (F.6.59)

(b) As an interrogative:

> *Que me chaut?*   What does it matter to me?

Que is also used as an anticipatory subject before *estre*, *devenir*, etc., with the real subject at times omitted:

> *Qu'est mes sens devenuz?*   (F.11.333)
> What has become of my reason?

Qui (relative or interrogative) is at times found as a neuter subject:

(a)   *Lors li conte ... tout ce qui li estoit avenu.*   (Gr.44)
      Then he tells him all that which had happened to him.

(b)   *Et qui vous meine?*   (Fb.15.205)
      And what brings you (here)?

2. *Que* (direct object) is used throughout, except for persons in the interrogative:

(a) Relatives:

> *La pucele que il feri.*   The maiden whom he struck.   (Per.4477)

> *Les pechiez que il avoient faiz.*   (Cl.257)
> The sins which they had committed.

> *Vos dirai ce que je vi.*   (Yv.174)
> I will tell you that which I saw.

(b) Interrogatives, mainly found as neuters:

> *Et que tint?*   And what did she hold?   (Per.3566)

> *Que diras tu?*   What will you say?   (F.12.153)

96. Functions of *cui*

1. *Cui* (stressed direct object) refers to persons, and is also used after prepositions:

(a) Relatives:

> *Mes sire, cui je doi tant amer.*   (Cl.329)
> My lord, whom I must love so much.

> *Je sui li sire a cui volez parler.*   (Ay.4041)
> I am the lord to whom you wish to speak.

Occasionally the relative *cui* refers to things.

(b) Interrogatives:

> *Un romanz, ne sai de cui.*   (Yv.5366)
> A romance, I don't know about whom.

> *A cui estes vos?*   To whom do you belong?   (Fb.11.147)

2. *Cui* (stressed indirect object) only refers to persons (to whom), and is sometimes even used as a genitive, indicating the possessor, source, etc. (of whom, whose):

(a) Relatives:

> *Au seignor cui Nerbonois apant.*   (Ay.759)
> Of the lord to whom the land of Narbonne belongs.

> *Artus, la cui proesce ...*   (Yv.1–2)
> Arthur, the valour of whom (whose valour) ...

(b) Interrogatives:

> *Cui chaut ?*   To whom does it matter?   (Yv. 5354)
>
> *Il ne set . . . cui filz il fu.*   (Gr.20)
> He does not know whose son he was.

97. Functions of *quoi*

1. *Quoi* (stressed subject) is sometimes found as a neuter interrogative:

> *Que est amors? Ge ne sai quoi.*   (En.7890)
> What is love? I do not know what (it is).

2. *Quoi* (stressed direct object) refers to things or functions as a neuter; it is also used after prepositions:

(a) Relatives:

> *Li chevaus sor quoi il seoit.*   (Gr.29)
> The horse on which he sat.
>
> *N'orent cure de ces argumens, de quoi li reis fu mout liez.* (R.Tr.56)
> They took no notice of these arguments, because of which the king was very pleased.

(b) Interrogatives:

> *Quoi dites vos, Alein, que est ?*   (F.5.104)
> What do you say, Alan, that it is?
>
> *Por quoi as tu cest moine mort ?*   (§187) (F.9.635)
> What have you killed this monk for?   (cf. §103.2)

98. Variations in usage

1. *Que* (and occasionally *qui*) can become *qu'* before a vowel:

(a)   *Vez de cest home qu'est morz ci!*   (Fb.2.20)
       Look at this man who is dead here!

(b)   *Qu'avez vos fait ?*   What have you done?   (F.9.59)

2. *Que* sometimes replaces *quoi* after prepositions, especially before a vowel, when it becomes *qu'*:

(a)   *A faire chose de qu'on rie* (= *de quoi*).   (Fb.11.2)
       To produce something over which one could laugh.

(b)   *Guillaumes, por qu'as tu ce fait ?*   (F.9.356)
       William, what have you done this for?

3. Confusion between *qui* and *cui* occurs in the twelfth century already, and increases during the thirteenth, owing to the similarity between *qui*, [ki], and *cui*, [küi > kŵi > ki], the more frequent error being that *qui* is used for *cui*:

(a)   *Cil qui (=cui) Amors a pris au laz.*   (F.12.244)
        He whom Love has ensnared.

(b)   *Qui (=cui) as tu donc aamé?*   (En.8497)
        Whom then have you begun to love?

99. Omission of relatives

1. *Qui* is often omitted after a negative phrase in the context: 'There is not one, who . . .' (+*ne*+subjunctive):

> *N'i a celui ∧ n'ait brisiée sa lance.*   (Ay.1823)
> There is not one, who has not broken his lance.

> *Nen aḍ remes paien ∧ ne seit ocis.*   (Rol.101–2)
> There is no infidel left, who is not killed.

2. *Qui* (occasionally even *que*) can be omitted after *tel*, or other indefinite pronouns or adjectives:

> *Tel i ara ∧ ferai dolent (=que ferai dolent).*   (Tr. 1244)
> I will make someone suffer (see §118).
> lit. There will be someone whom I will make unhappy.

3. A relative can be omitted in the second of two relative clauses, even if its function differs:

> *Celui cui j'amoie et ∧ trahie m'a (=qui trahie m'a).*
> He whom I loved and who betrayed me.   (Ver.738–9)

100. Omission of antecedents

1. The antecedent can be separated from the relative pronoun:

> *Ce m'est mout grief, que vos me comandez a faire.*
> That which you order me to do is very distressing to me.
> (Yv. 142–3)

or even omitted:

> *Je ne truis ∧ qui m'en defende.*   (Yv.3605)
> I do not find anyone who may protect me.

2. The antecedent *ce* is thus often omitted before the neuter pronoun *que*:

> *Or escoutez ∧ que ge ferai.*   (F.9.196)
> Now listen to what (=to that which) I will do.

3. For *qui*, often found without an antecedent meaning 'he who', 'whoever', etc., see §103.1.

101. The multipurpose *que*

Que is often used in the twelfth century as a relative adverb (when, where, etc.):

> *La nuit que la lune fu pleine.* (Ren.1076)
> The night when the moon was full.

Its use is extended in the thirteenth century, when it can replace any other relative, even those governed by prepositions:

> *Ce est icel escu meïsmes que je vos cont.* (Gr.34)
> It is that very shield of which I am telling you.

For *que* used as a versatile conjunction, see §155.

102. Other relatives and interrogatives

1. *O, ou* (rel./interr. adv.) indicates place or time (where, in which, in whom; when, etc.) and sometimes refers to persons as well as to things:

(a) *La chose ou il a grant senefiance.* (Gr.37)
     The matter in which there is a deep meaning.

     La pucele . . . ou cil avait mise s'entente. (F.10.63-4)
     The maiden, on whom he had fixed his interest.

(b) *Ou est il alés?* Where has it gone? (R.Tr.144)

2. *Dont* (rel./interr. pron./adv.) is often used instead of *de + ou* (whence, where from, etc.) or *de + cui, de + quoi* (whose, of whom, of which, of what, with which, etc.), and can refer to a whole phrase:

(a) *Ces douces herbes, dont orent a plenté.* (Or.414)
     These sweet herbs, of which there were plenty.

     Vos m'avez fait chevalier, dont j'ai si grant joie. (Gr.40)
     You made me a knight, because of which I am so happy.

(b) *Sire niés, dont venez?* (Ch.N.32)
     Sir nephew, where do you come from?

Note: *Dont* is also a variant of *donc* (then).

3. *Quel* (interr. pron./adj. Cl.III): which one, which, what. In the later twelfth century a feminine form in -*e* is introduced ≠ Class I (F) adjectives:

> *Quel la ferons?* (F.9.578)
> What shall we do now? (lit. there)

'*Noveles vos aport molt merveilleuses.*' '*Queles?*' *fet li rois.*   (Gr.5)
'I bring you most wondrous tidings.' 'What (tidings)?' says the king.

Lors li demande Perceval dont il est et de quel terre.   (Gr.100)
Then Percival asks him whence he is and from what land.

4. *Lequel, laquel* (rel./interr. pron./adj.) was used in the early twelfth century as an interrogative pronoun and later as a relative pronoun (who, whom, which), and occasionally also as an adjective. Often still written *le quel*, it is declined as a combination of *quel* (see above) and the definite article, and can be preceded by prepositions. It has a slight demonstrative stress (cf. §30):

(a)   *Calcas de Troie, dou quel* (= *de* + *le quel*) *vos orrez.*   (R.Tr.71)
      Calchas of Troy, of whom you will hear.

      Vilenie, la quel chose je ne vosisse.   (R.Tr.136)
      Villainy, which thing I would not like.

(b)   *Mostre moi li quels est li rois.*   (Per.919)
      Show me which is the king.

5. *Com, come,* etc., *comment* (rel./interr. adv.): how:

      Com a nom la cité?   How is the city named?   (Ay.259)
      Coment fustes vos si cruëls?   (R.Tr.144)
      How were you so cruel?

6. *Quant* (interr. pron./adj. Cl.1): how much, how many:

      Quantes en i covient il donques?   (F.11.145)
      How many (women) are there needed then?

      S'est ne sai quantes foiz seigniez.   (F.9.633)
      He crossed himself I don't know how many times.

7. *Enne, en* (= *et* + *ne*) and *donc ne* (*dont ne, don ne, don,* etc.) introduce questions to which an affirmative answer is expected:

      '*Enne me conissiés vos?*' '*Oïl.*'   (Auc.22)
      'Don't you know me?' 'Yes.'

      '*Don ne porroit ce estre?*' '*Oïl.*'   (Yv.3612)
      'Could this not happen?' 'Yes.'

103. Absolute uses

Relatives and interrogatives are frequently used in an absolute sense.

1. The relative pronoun *qui* is often found on its own, meaning 'he who', 'whoever' (see §128). For its use as 'if one', or in an exclamation ('you should have . . .' etc.) see §§128 and 182.4d.

2. The interrogative expressions *por quoi* and *que* often mean 'why':

> *Por quoi m'esparng? Que ne me tu?* (Yv.3547)
> Why do I spare myself? Why don't I kill myself?

3. Stressed interrogatives can stand on their own:

> *Qui? Nostre chiens?* Who? Our dog? (Fb.3.58)
>
> *Et mostiers, quoi?* And a church, what (is that)? (Per.577)
>
> *Joie? La ques?* (§104) Joy? Which (joy)? (Yv.3555)

4. Interrogatives are commonly used in exclamations, often meaning 'what':

> *Cui? fet il, vassax, qui es tu?* (Er.840)
> What? he says, vassal, who are you?
>
> *Quel pesans aventure!* (R.Tr.156)
> What a tragic situation!
>
> *Comment? Por Dé!* What? In God's name! (Yv.3617)

104. Alternative forms

In the early twelfth century *quoi* was *quei*, or *queid* before a vowel. The form *quei* was retained in many dialects, including Anglo-Norman.

Ki, qi = qui; ke, qe = que; k', c', q' = qu'; koi, coi, qoi = quoi.

Dont (sometimes *don* before a consonant) could be spelt *dons, dom,* etc.

The inflected form of *quel* could be *quels, queus, quieus, quex, ques,* etc. (§39.9). The same applies to *lequel.*

TEST YOURSELF

Give fairly literal translations of the following, using the glossary:

1. '*Qui les ocist?*' *fet Galaad.* (Gr.51)
2. *Quier* (Pl.1) *ce, que trover ne puis.* (Yv.359)
3. *Ne set mais cui la doie doner.* (Ay.554)
4. *Troye, dont Laomedon* (NS) *estoit rois.* (R.Tr.9)
5. *Ge ne truis* ʌ *qui me die que est amors.* (En.7900-1)

6. *Je te demant | d'une cité que je voi la*
   Cui ele est et quel nom ele a. (Per.8618–20)
7. *Cassandre . . . de la quelle nos avons parlé.* (R.Tr.65)
8. *Ge sui Guillelmes, cui la barbe as tiree.* (Ch.N.1349)
9. *Il orront* ⋀ *dont il seront dolant.* (Or.644)
10. *Je hé l'ore que je sui vive.* (Ren.320)
11. *N'i a celui* ⋀ *n'ait chastel ou cité.* (Ay.4238)
12. *Dex! que ferai? Por coi vif tant?*
    La morz que demore, qu'atant? (Er.4617–18)

9
Indefinite pronouns and adjectives

105. General

The main indefinite pronouns and adjectives are listed below. A few are also used as adverbs.

Where adjective declension classes are given, pronouns are also declined according to these classes and have corresponding feminine and neuter forms where applicable; thus:

nul (Cl.I): NS pronouns *nus* (M), *nule* (F), *nul* (N).

All pronouns or adjectives ending in *-un* (*chascun, nesun, nun*, etc.) are compounds of *un* and are declined in the same way.

Paragraphs 130 to 133 list an important series of pronouns, adjectives and adverbs composed of an interrogative followed by *que*. These usually introduce concessive clauses, with the verb in the subjunctive (see §181.4b). When used in a general sense, however, they take the indicative.

Words beginning with *au-* (*autre*, etc.) were still found with *al-* (*altre*, etc.) in the early twelfth century.

For asterisked forms see §§136 and 137.

106. *Un**

(Pron./adj. Cl.I), normally used with the definite article: someone, one, etc.:

> *L'une respont.*   One (of them) replied.   (Yv.5250)

> *L'une partie fu vermeille.*   (Per.642)
> One part (of the tent) was crimson.

107. *Autre**

(Pron./adj. Cl.II), stressed OS *autrui***: other, another, etc.:

> *Donez la autre.*   Give it to someone else.   (Ay.355)

> *Autre terre, sire, ne vos demant.*   (Ch.N.500)
> I ask of you, sir, no other land.

L'autre (pron.) is often used in conjunction with *l'un* (pron.):

> *Li un sont mort et li autre navré.*   (Ay.910)
> Some are dead and the rest wounded.

108. *Chascun*

(Pron./adj. Cl.1), later also *chasque* (adj.): each:

> *Chascuns de cez maus.*   Each of these evils.   (Fb.3.13)

> *Chascune dame ou damoiselle.*   (Gr.19)
> Each lady or damsel.

Chascun (pron.) can be reinforced by *un: un chascun*, each one.

109. *Negun, nun*

(Pron./adj. Cl.1), rare: not one, none, etc., mainly used to reinforce a negative:

> *Nuns nel peüst el lit tenir.*   (Fb.10.48)
> No one could have kept him in bed.

> *Ne criement negun asalt.*   (En.442)
> They fear not a single assault.

Negun and its contracted form *nun* are occasionally used without *ne* in a positive sense:

> *Foloié ai, s'onques nuns foloia.*   (Rutebeuf)
> I have acted foolishly, if ever anyone was foolish.

110. *Nesun*

(Pron./adj. Cl.1), at times still *neïs* (not even) + *un*: not even one, not one, etc.:

> *En ceste eve a neïs un pont.*   (Per.3015)
> Across this river there is not even a bridge.

Nesun is sometimes used to reinforce a negative:

> *A vos ne s'en prent nes une.*   (Er.833)
> Not one can compare herself to you.

> *Si n'avez home nesun.*   (Ay.226)
> And you have not even one man.

111. *Aucun**

(Pron./adj. Cl.1), rare: someone, some, anyone, any:

> *S'aucuns envers toi s'umelie*
> *Respon orgueil.*   (Th.262–3)
> If someone humbles himself towards you,
> reply with pride.

> *Escu vos envoiera Diex d'aucune part.*   (Gr.12)
> God will send you a shield from somewhere.

112. *Nul*

(Pron./adj. Cl.1), stressed OS *nului***: someone, some, anyone, any:

> *Savoit nus fors vous dui ceste oevre?*   (Ver.346)
> Did anyone besides you two know of this affair?

> *Sanz nule doute.*   Without any doubt.   (Ver.263)

Note: *Nul*, originally a negative reinforcing *ne* (cf. *negun, nun,* §109), had acquired a positive meaning in OFr when used on its own.
    For *nul . . . ne* (no one, none) see §138.

113. *Rien(s)*

A Class II (F) noun used in an indefinite sense, at times with OS in -*s*: someone, something, anyone, anything:

> *As tu riens fait?*   Have you done anything?   (Th.205)

often reinforced by *nul*, which usually agrees in gender:

> *Ne vos movez por nule rien.*   (Yv.1310)
> Don't move for anyone.

> *De rien nule ne mentez.*   (Er.1151)
> You aren't lying about anything.

    For *rien . . . ne* (no one, nothing) see §138.

114. *Chose*

A Class I (F) noun used in an indefinite sense: something:

> *Fet m'avez chose, qui m'enuie.*   (Yv.506)
> You have done something to me, which annoys me.

115. *Auques*

(Adv., pronominal use), rare: somewhat, some, something:

> *Auques des meillors barons.* (Er.1667)
> Some of the finest barons.

> *Or pueent dire auques de lor talent.* (Or.675)
> Now they can speak something of their mind.

116. *El*

(Neuter pron.): something else, etc.:

> *Que fereient il el?* (Rol.1185)
> What else could they do?

> *Assez i truevent pain et el.* (Ren.9092)
> There they find plenty of bread and other things.

117. *On**

(Pron.), unstressed NS form of the Class III noun *ome* (sometimes spelt *en*, *an*): one, someone, etc.:

> *Or dira l'on ...* Now one will say ... (F.9.456)

On is only used as a subject, and is often better rendered by 'they' or a passive construction:

> *On me desrobe en votre terre.* (Fb.11.191–2)
> They are robbing me / I am being robbed in your land.

118. *(I)tel*

(Pron./adj. Cl.III, adv.), inflected forms: *tels, teus, tieus, tex, tes* (§39.9), stressed OS *telui***: such a one, such, etc.:

> *Tel li dona qu'il l'abat.* (Ay.926)
> He gave him such (a blow) that he strikes him down.

> *Une tel tanpeste* (§21.9). Such a storm. (Yv.397)
> *Itex bestes neissent en Inde.* (Er.6738)
> Such animals are born in India.

Tel i a: someone (= 'there is such a one', treated as a unit).
Tes i a: some:

> *Anuia molt a teus i ot.* (Per.4273)
> It greatly annoyed some.

For *tel* (adj.) followed by a number, see §175.6.

119. *Autel**

(Pron./adj. Cl.III, adv.), rare, sometimes reinforced by *tot*: similar, like, the like, etc.:

> *Cherche boites et armoires et les autex.* (F.9.271–2)
> He looks for boxes and chests and the like.
>
> *Une autel porte.* A similar door. (Yv.956)
>
> *Et tout autel faisait dame Elaine.* (R.Tr.156)
> And lady Helen did just the same.

120. *Autretel*

(Pron./adj. Cl.III, adv.), rare, sometimes reinforced by *tot*: similar, the same, etc.:

> *Tout autretel respondi Hercullès.* (R.Tr.11)
> Hercules replied in just the same way.
>
> *Firent tout autretel veu com messires*
> *Gauvains avoit fet.* (Gr.16)
> They swore the very same vow that
> Sir Gawain had sworn.

121. *Auquant**

(NP pron./adj. Cl.III), rare: some, several, a certain number, etc.:

> *Li auquant traient les espees.* (Er.4691)
> Several draw their swords.
>
> *Prent i chastels e alquantes citez.* (Rol. 2611)
> There he takes castles and several cities.

122. *Plusor**

(NP pron./adj. Cl.IV): several, many:

> *Fu de plusors blasmé.* (Fb.1.66)
> He was blamed by many.
>
> *De plusors choses i parlerent.* (F.10.194.v.)
> There they spoke of several things.

Li plusor: the majority; *tuit li plusor*: the vast majority (cf. Rol.995):

> *Li plusor ont la chanson oïe.* (Ay.4664)
> The majority have heard the song.

123. *Plus**

(Adv., pronominal use), rare: the majority, most, more:

> *Li meillor des chevaliers et toz li plus.*   (Yv.2692–3)
> The best of the knights and the vast majority (NS).

124. *Maint*

(Pron./adj. Cl.1), often found in the singular in a plural sense: many,
many a:

> *Maint en ocient.*   They kill many of them.   (Ay.1142)

> *J'ai oï avantures maintes.*   (Fb.3.68)
> I have heard many stories.

> *Mainte lance ont brisiée.*   (Ay.4452)
> They broke many a lance.

125. *Tant*

(Adj. Cl.1, adv., pronominal use): so many, so much, such a number,
many a, etc.:

> *Tantes proeces.*   So many noble deeds.   (Ay.34)

> *Ne vos esmaiez tant.*   (Ay.2043)
> Don't be so discouraged.

> *De mon avoir vos ferai tant doner.*   (Ch.N.1167)
> I will give you so much of my merchandise.

Tant is sometimes found in the singular in a plural sense:

> *Voit . . . tante lance, et tant hiaume jemé.*   (Ay.2005–7)
> He sees so many lances, and so many jewelled helmets.

Tant is at times uninflected:

> *Onques . . . ne vit nus tant rois, tant contes.*   (Er.6845–6)
> No one ever saw so many kings, so many counts.

126. *Tot*

(Pron./adj. Cl.1 irreg., adv.): everyone, everything, every, all, quite:

> *Tuit li sont failli.*   All have failed him.   (Ay.581)

> *Ja n'iert tot dit.*   All will never be said.   (Yv.788)

The adjective is sometimes used with a qualifying word, like an article or a possessive or demonstrative adjective:

> *Tote la corz.*   The whole court.   (Yv.674)

127. *Trestot*

Tot (§126) reinforced by *tres*: absolutely everyone / everything / every, etc.:

> *Trestuit s'arment.*   (Ay.1059)
> One and all arm themselves.

> *Trestote ma puissance.*   All the force I have.   (Yv.531)

128. *Qui*

(Pron.), oblique form *cui*, referring to persons: whoever, he who, etc.:

> *Qui merci crie avra pardon.*   (Ren.8862)
> He who begs for mercy will be forgiven.

> *Cui il consivent, morz est sanz demorance.*   (Ay.1825)
> Whomever they pursue is slain without delay.

Qui often duplicates a personal pronoun which can precede or follow:

> *Qui trop despent, il s'endete.*   (Fb.10.56)
> He who spends too much, he falls into debt.

Qui (+ conditional or subjunctive) can mean 'if one':

> *Qui me donroit tot l'or de .X. citez . . .*   (Ay.3318)
> If one were to give me all the gold of ten cities.

Qui (+ imperfect subjunctive) is used in an exclamatory sense:

> *Qui dont oïst Sarrazins gramoier!*   (Ay.1144)
> If one had then heard = Then you should have heard the Saracens lament!

For further examples, see §182.4d.

129. *Qui . . . qui*

(Distributive pronouns): one . . . another, etc.:

> *Qui porte hache, qui maçue.*   (Ren.654)
> One carries an axe, another a club.

130. *Qui que*

(Pron.), also *cui que, que que, quoi que, quel que*: whoever, whomever, whatever, etc. This compound pronoun is declined and used like an interrogative pronoun followed by *que* (see Chapter 8). It usually introduces a concessive clause, with the verb in the subjunctive:

> *Qui que s'en aut, je remendrai ici.* (Ay.601)
> Whoever leaves, I will stay here.

> *Par cui que soit.* By whomever it may be. (Yv.3611)

> *Je sai bien, que que nus die . . .* (Ren.89)
> I well know, whatever anyone may say . . .

> *Quoi que j'aie fait, or sui ci.* (Th.603)
> Whatever I may have done, now I am here.

The second element is occasionally declined like a relative pronoun, e.g. *qui qui s'en aille*, whoever leaves.

Confusion between *qui and cui* (see §98.3) is fairly common:

> *Qui que* (= *cui que*) *il poist ne cui il griet.* (Fb.3.30)
> Whomever it may trouble or whomever it may annoy.

Qui que and *quel que* are often used (and later fused) with the adverb *onque(s)*, 'ever', and can take the indicative:

> *Qui que* + *onques, quiconque* (pron.): whosoever.

> *Quelconque* (pron.): whatsoever.

131. *Quel. . .que, quel que. . .que, quelque. . .que*

(Conjunctive adj.): whichever, whatever, etc. Here the interrogative adjective *quel* is combined with *que*, usually functioning with concessive force followed by the subjunctive (cf. §130). *Quel* is normally not declined, and often qualifies a word like *lieu*, 'place', *hore*, 'hour', etc., in which case the whole phrase can mean 'wherever', 'whenever', etc.:

> *Quel part qu'il tort* (§73). (F.9.766)
> Whichever way (= wherever) he may go.

> *Quel que hore qu'il i venist.* (Per.3390)
> Whatever hour (= whenever) he might arrive there.

> *De quelque terre que il fussent.* (Cl.266)
> From whatever land they might have been.

Quel que (adj.) is often used or fused with the adverb *onque(s)* (cf. §130):

> *Quel que* + *onques . . . que, quelconque . . . que*: whatsoever.

132. *Ou que*

(Conjunctive adv., usually + subj.): wherever:

> *Ou que vos ailliez.*   Wherever you may go.   (Per.619)

133. *Comment que*

(Conjunctive adv., usually + subj.): however:

> *Coment que je me desespoir.*   (Cou.9)
> However I may despair.

134. *Quant que, quanque*

(Pron.): all that, as much as, etc.:

> *M'est legier quant que est grief.*   (R.Tr.18)
> All that is difficult is easy for me.
>
> *Vit quanque il vost veoir.*   (Yv.801)
> He saw as much as he wanted to see.

135. *Quelque*

(Adj.): a certain, some, etc.:

> *A quelque paine sus monterent.*   (Ren.9195)
> They climbed up with some difficulty.

*136. The definite article

Li etc. is frequently used with the pronouns *un, autre, aucun, on, autel, auquant, plusor, plus,* adding a slight demonstrative stress. Examples are included above.

**137. *Autrui, nului*

These pronouns, and the rare *telui,* are stressed masculine OS forms in *-ui,* formed ≠ *celui.* They are found as direct or indirect objects or after prepositions, and are sometimes used as genitives, indicating the possessor, source, etc., or as stressed subjects:

> *Je n'oserai nului veoir.*   (Th.39)
> I shall not dare see anyone.
>
> *Por moi fu dit, non por autrui.*   (Er.2518)
> It was said for me, not for another.

Tu ne criens autrui menace. (Ren.350)
You don't fear the threat of anyone else.

A commandé que nului (NS) *ne remaigne.* (Ver. 523–4)
He ordered that no one should stay (see § 138).

138. *Nul...ne, rien...ne,* etc.

1. Indefinite pronouns and adjectives with a positive meaning in OFr
(*rien, nul,* etc.) are frequently used with the negative particle *ne.* Often the
combination is best rendered by a negative pronoun or adjective; thus:

Renart l'oï, mais ne dist rien. (Ren.209)
Renard heard it, but did not say anything / but said nothing.

Il n'est chose que je n'en face. (Th.80)
There is not anything / There is nothing that I would not do.

Nus ne me voit. (Yv.3546)
Someone does not see me / No one sees me.

Riens nule n'est qui tant lor pleise. (Er.5202)
There is not anything / There is nothing which pleases them
so much.

2. This does not apply, however:
(a) where the negative particle is linked to a different section of the phrase:

A nul fuer je ne norriroie trahitor. (Ver. 123–4)
I would not keep a traitor at any price.

(b) or where *ne* is not a true negative, but:
an expletive *ne* (§148.6):

Ja Diex ne me puist tant haïr ...
que a nului riens (ne) *mesface!* (Ren. 1120–2)
May God never hate me so much
that I would do anything wrong to anyone.

or the conjunction *ne* replacing *et* or *ou* in a negative or hypothetical
phrase or in a query (§158):

Se tu as nul autre ami n'amie nule. (Per.2287–8)
If you have any other friend or any sweetheart.

TEST YOURSELF

Watch for spelling variations, and give fairly literal translations of the following,
using the glossary:

1. *Trestuit li oisel chantoient.* (Yv.465)
2. *Povretez fait maint home fol.* (Fb.3.25)

3. *A chascun, qui que il soit.* (Yv.619)
4. *Son tens pert qui felon sert.* (F.2.68)
5. *Autel diras a la reïne.* (Per.9126)
6. *Onques nului n'i esveilla.* (Per.2074)
7. *Molt lor plaist quanque il voient.* (Er.2040)
8. *Ge n'ai besoing d'autrui amer.* (En.1319)
9. *L'en n'i puet trover vïande.* (Ren.3451)
10. *Ge n'en sai el que dire.* (F.11.349)
11. *Nus ne demanda livraison*
    De rien nule, que que ce fust. (Er.2012–13)
12. *Alixandres, qui . . . a tanz princes monstra s'ire.* (F.11.61–2)
13. *Alquant ocis e li plusor neiét.* (cf. Rol.2477)
14. *Quel c'onques voie que je tiegne.* (Per.7016)
15. *La novele a tex i ot ne fu pas bele.* (Ren.487–8)
16. *Ki lui veïst l'un geter mort su l'altre!* (Rol.1341)

10
Adverbs

139. Types of adverbs

OFr has a wide variety of adverbs, expressing:

> time: *hui, ja, ore,* today, already, now, etc.,
> place: *enz, fors, soz, iluec,* inside, outside, below, there, etc.,
> manner: *com, si, bien,* as, so, well, etc.,
> degree: *tres, molt, tant, plus, trop,* very, much, so much, more, too much, etc.,
> and opinion: *non, ne,* no, not.

The above adverbs are etymologically simple, but there are many compound adverbs, e.g.:

> *amont, aval,* to the hill, to the valley = up, down,
> *oïl, nenil,* yes, no (§90.8), *oan,* this year,

in some of which the elements have fused, e.g.:

> *assez,* to enough = enough,
> *mar,* in an evil hour = unfortunately, etc.,
> *buer,* in a favourable hour = fortunately, etc.

Adverbial phrases are common, often condensed into one word:

> *isnel le pas,* rapid the step = quickly,
> *doresanavant* (< *d'ores en avant*), from now on.

Demonstrative adverbs, *(i)ci, la, ça, (i)luec, çaenz, laenz,* are discussed in §60, and relative and interrogative adverbs, *ou, dont, com,* etc., in §102. For the pronominal adverbs *en, i* see §84. Words not translated in this chapter will be found in the glossary.

140. Adjectives used as adverbs

Neuter adjectives (*soef, voir, bel, cler,* etc.) are frequently used as adverbs:

> *Li ostes molt bel les reçut.* (Er.3197)
> The host received them very well.

Adjectives used as adverbs can agree with the adjective or participle they modify. This agreement is usual in the case of *tot*:

> *Unes armes totes dorees.* (Per.4106)
> A suit of armour, all gilded.

The adverbs in *-es*, *certes*, *primes*, *longes* (indeed, at first, for a long time), were originally feminine plural adjectives.

141. The adverbial suffix *-ment*

The suffix *-ment*, meaning 'in a . . . spirit', 'in a . . . manner', was added to the feminine singular of adjectives or participles to create numerous new adverbs; thus:

> *fierement, freschement* (<Cl.I adjs. *fier, frais*),
> *tendrement* (<*tendre*: Cl.II),
> *fortment, loialment* (<*fort, loial*: Cl.III),
> *iriedement, celeement* (<early and later PPs *iriét, celé*).

This adverbial suffix was occasionally added to nouns (*vassal, vassaument*) or even to adverbs (*alsi, alsiment*).

Note: *-mant* is a variant of *-ment* (§21.9).

142. Stem changes before *-ment*

All common Class III (F) adjectives end in *t, f, nt* or *l* (App. A.7) and are usually modified as follows before *-ment*:

> *t, f* soon disappear: *fortment > forment,*
> *briefment > briément > briment.*
> *nt > n*, then *m*: *grantment > granment > gramment,*
> *prudentment > prudenment > prudemment.*
> *l > u*, or disappears after *i*: *loialment > loiaument,*
> *sotilment > sotiment.*

When Class III adjectives are absorbed into Class I, some develop adverbial doublets, e.g. *fortement, brievement*.

143. Adverbial *-s*

Many OFr adverbs end in *-s*, e.g. *tres, plus, jus, certes, fors, enz* ($z = ts$). This characteristic *-s* was added by analogy to other adverbs as well.

At times the *-s* form prevails, e.g. *tandis*; usually, however, double forms are found, often in the same texts; thus:

> *encore(s), gaire(s), meïsme(s), loing / loinz,*

but additions leading to awkward modifications (e.g. *onc + s*) are usually avoided.

144. Adverbial doublets

Five kinds of adverbial doublets are found in OFr:

1. Those of the type *forment* / *fortement* (§142).

2. Those with or without adverbial -*s*, e.g. *gaire(s)*.

3. Those reinforced by the prefix *de*:

   soz / *desoz* (below),   *fors* / *defors* (outside).

4. Those due in rare cases to stressed and unstressed forms of adverbs, or adjectives used as adverbs; thus:

   ¹*non* / *nen, ne* (not),   ¹*buen* / *bon* (good).

5. Those with or without a final -*e*. These doublets first arose when several common adverbs in -*e* (*arriere, deriere, encore, mare, onque, ore, sore*) dropped this weak *e* before a vowel (§19). By the twelfth century, however, this distinction was lost, as in the following four-syllable phrases:

   Or me dites... (Ver.344)   *Ore issez hors*... (Ad.491)

Due to the addition of adverbial -*s*, these adverbs developed triple or even quadruple forms:

   onc / *onque(s)*,   *lor(s)* / *lore(s)*.

By an inverse process, *iluec* and *donc* acquired the doublets *ilueque(s)* and *donque(s)* ≠ *onc* / *onque(s)*.

145. Comparison of adverbs

The neuter adjectival comparatives (*moins, mieuz, pis*, etc.) are used adverbially as well.

Normally the adverb *plus* serves to indicate a comparative, and *le plus* or *au plus* a superlative:

   plus tost, sooner,   *au plus tost*, at the earliest.

Absolute superlatives are expressed by the use of adverbs like *molt, assez, tres, trop*, all meaning 'very' (cf. §52):

   Molt volentiers le prist. (F.9.518)
   He took it very willingly.

146. Negation

Negation was expressed in the early twelfth century by the stressed adverb *non*, and by its unstressed or half-stressed counterpart *nen*, which

had contracted to *ne* before consonants, and usually even to *n'* before vowels:

> *Vueillent ou non.*   Whether they wish or not.   (Ay.1966)

> *Cel nen i aḍ ki ne crieṭ: 'Marsilie!'* (*nen, ne*)
> There is not one who does not cry: 'Marsile!'   (Rol.1661)

> *N'est gueres granz ne trop nen est petiz.*   (*n'est, nen est*)
> He is not very tall and (§158) he is not too short.   (Rol.3822)

N' soon became the normal form before vowels, even though *nen* was still used in this position in the thirteenth century.

147. The stressed adverb *non*

1. *Non*, being stressed, can appear on its own:

> *Nel feras? – Non.*   You won't do it? – No.   (Ad.171)

> *Les uns barbez, les autres non.*   (Per.7567)
> Some bearded, the others not.

2. *Non* is frequently found after *se*, forming a split conjunction meaning 'except', etc. (§159.2):

> *Ne . . . nus, se Dieus non.*   (VP.1052–3)
> No one, except God.

3. *Non* is used in contradictions, either with *avoir* or *estre*, repeating the previous verb:

> *Tu es traïtres tot provez. – Certes, non sui.*   (Ad.682–3)
> You are a proven traitor. – Indeed, I am not.

or with *faire*, which can follow any verb (cf. §150.1):

> e.g. *Non ferai!*   (That) I will not!

148. Unstressed *ne*

1. *Ne*, being weak, is often reinforced by nouns used adverbially which add little to the meaning, e.g. *pas, mie, mot, gote, point* (step, crumb, word, drop, point):

> *Mot n'en sait.*   (Yv.5658)
> He doesn't know (a word) about it.

> *Morir ne voldroie je mie.*   (Yv.1556)
> I should not like to die.

Point is at times still used as a noun, followed by *de*:

> *N'a point d'oscur en la clarté.*   (VP.671)
> There is not a spot of shadow in the radiance.

2. *Ne* can be linked to nouns, pronouns or adjectives used in an indefinite sense, meaning 'someone', 'anyone', 'anything', etc. (e.g. *rien, nul, chose, ame*), the combination often meaning 'no one', 'nothing':

> *Il ne veut faire nule rien.* (Fb.13.151)
> He does not want to do anything.
>
> *Nus ne vit sa pareille.* (F.12.114)
> Someone did not see = No one saw her equal.

For further examples, see § 109, 110, 112, 113, 138.

3. *Ne* is frequently reinforced by adverbs (*onques, mais, ja, plus, gaire,* etc.) which can modify the meaning:

> *Ne creire ja le traïtor.* (Ad.280)
> Don't ever believe the traitor.
>
> *Je n'i os plus demorer.* (Yv.1081)
> I dare not stay longer here.
>
> *Li tans gaires ne dura.* (Yv.452)
> The storm did not last long.

See § 149 for further examples.

4. *Ne* is used in an absolute sense, followed by a stressed pronoun, in the expressions *ne je > naie, nen il > nenil,* etc., meaning 'no' (§90.8).

5. *Ne* is combined with other adverbs in the compounds *neporquant* and *neporuec,* meaning 'nevertheless', etc. The combination *ne mais* can be used in an absolute sense, meaning 'except':

> *Ne mais Rollant.*   Except Roland.   (Rol.382)

6. An expletive *ne* often precedes the verb in subordinate clauses dependent on verbs of fearing, forbidding, etc., or in expressed or implied comparisons:

> *Crient que la vieille n'oublit.* (F.10.322)
> He fears that the old woman may forget.
>
> *Plus fresche que n'est rose.* (Ad.228)
> Fresher than a rose is.

149. *Onques, mais, ja*

These are common adverbs of time, often accompanying a negative. In this case the combination is at times best rendered by 'never' (cf. §138), but only when *ne* is the negative particle, and not an expletive *ne* (§148.6) or the conjunction *ne* replacing *et* or *ou* (§158):

1. *Onques*: ever, etc. (usually referring to the past):

> *Onques dormir ne pot.* (Ver.145)
> He could not sleep at all.

2. *Mais*: more, any more, ever, before, again, etc. (referring to past or future):

> *N'en parlez mais.* (Rol.273)
> Don't speak about it again.

3. *Ja*: formerly, already, now, soon, ever, etc. (referring to past or future):

> *Ja orroiz verité.* (Ch.N.33)
> Now you'll hear the truth.

Ja is sometimes merely an affirmative particle:

> *Ja me fait bien.* (Ad.260)
> It certainly does me good.

4. Combinations are common, often reinforcing or modifying the negative, e.g. *ja mais (ne)*, (n)ever again; *onques mais (ne)* or *onques devant (ne)*, (n)ever before; *onques puis (ne)*, (n)ever again:

> *Onques mais n'ot joie graignor.* (F.8.272)
> She had not ever before had a greater joy.

150. *Si, car, espoir, ainz, ainc*

1. *Si*: thus, so, as, etc.

> *Si est en si grant desconfort.* (Ver. 188)
> He is thus in so great a distress.

Si is often used as an affirmative particle in contradictions, either with *avoir* or *estre*, echoing the previous verb:

> *N'ai point de m'espee. – Si as.* (Tr.1009–10)
> I have not my sword. – Yes, you have.

> *Vos n'estes mie tuit venu. – Si somes.* (Fb.14.63–5)
> You are not all here. – Yes, we are.

or with *faire* (cf. §147.3):

> *Vos n'en gouterïez. – Si feroie. – Non ferïez.*
> You wouldn't eat any. – Thus I would do.
> (= Yes, I would.) – No, you wouldn't. (Ren.823–4)

Elision is optional in the case of *si*. For the conjunction *si*, see §157.1.

2. *Car*, a conjunction, is often used adverbially to stress a wish (+sub-junctive) or an invitation or request (+imperative):

> *Quar fusse ge en Babiloine!*   (F.9.352)
> If only I were in Babylon!

> *Car me secorez!*   Please help me! / Do help me!   (Cl.112)

3. *Espoir*, 'I hope', used adverbially means: perhaps, probably, about, etc.:

> *Mieuz vos ira, espoir, que ne pensez.*   (Ay.4027)
> It will go better for you, perhaps,
> than you think.   (§148.6)

4. *Ainz*, before, and *ainc*, ever (in the past), tend to be confused by scribes.

151. Adverbial expressions

Words or phrases in the oblique case without an introductory preposition are often used as adverbial expressions of time, manner, place, etc. (§29.7); thus: *lonc tens*, for a long time; *les galos*, at a galop; *tot le chemin*, all along the path, etc.

A poi, por poi (*que*), *a bien petit* (*que*), followed in each case by an expletive *ne*, are common adverbial expressions for 'nearly', 'almost':

> . . . *Pur poi d'ire ne fent;*
> *A ben petit que il ne pert le sens.*   (Rol.304-5)
> He nearly bursts with rage; he almost loses his sanity.

Que (+an adjective or noun in the nominative case) can form an adverbial phrase of manner (cf. *faire que*, §192):

> *Or as que bris parlé.*   (Ch.N.895)
> Now you have spoken like a fool.

152. Syntax

The place of adverbs is very flexible in OFr, and adverbs can even appear far from the word they modify:

> *Trop lui avoit duré petit.*   (§140) (Ver.482)
> lit. (The night) had lasted too little for him.

Ne, however, is normally placed before the verb, from which it can only be separated by pronouns, although *non* can be used on its own (see examples in §§146-9).

Adverbs at the head of a phrase usually cause the inversion of subject

and verb, especially in the main clause. *Certes, onques* and *ne* with its compounds (§148.5) are exceptions.

> *Lors sont venu li chevalier.* (F.12.451)
> Then the knights came.

> *Certes on te devroit tüer.* (F.10.46)
> Certainly one should kill you.

TEST YOURSELF

(a) Translate:

1. **Ore** *s'en rit Rollant* (NS). (Rol.303)
2. **Isnelement** *est retornez* **arrier.*** (Al.903)
3. **Encore** *avront Orenge ma cité.* (Al.803)
4. **Or** *est,* **espoir,** *li vilains ivres.* (F.10.283)
5. *Les chevaliers fait* **arriers** *traire.* (Er.3624)
6. *Cil aime* **plus** **bassement.** (Ver.660)
7. *Sainz Pierres . . . s'en torna* **isnelepas.** (F.7.44–5)
8. *Guillelmes, quar seez.* – *Non ferai, sire.* (Ch.N.59–60)
9. **Jamais** *n'ert jor que Carles ne se plaignet* (§181.3b). (Rol.915)
10. *Sa drue / qui molt li sera chier* **vendue.*** (F.9.305–6)
11. **Onques** *Tristans . . .* si *coraument n'ama.* (Cou.3v)
12. **Defores** *a un chevalier armé.* (Al.1534)
13. *Espee traite est venuz au mostier.*** (Cl.134)
14. **Or** *sui je venuz* **trop matin?*** (Th.204)
15. *S'est . . . couchiee* **trestote** *nue.*** (F.8.275–6)
16. *Ot le Guillelmes,* **a poi** *n'est forsenez.* (Ch.N.79)

* For the use of *estre* as an auxiliary verb, see §189.

(b) Check your translation, then comment on the words in bold type (form, use, etc.). (No key.)

I I

Conjunctions

153. Types of conjunctions

OFr makes use of:

> a few true conjunctions: *e(t)*, *o(u)*, *ne*, *se*, *quant*, *que*,
> a few adverbs used as conjunctions: *ainz*, *mais*, *si*, *com*, *donc* / *donque(s)*,
> and well over a hundred conjunctive phrases ending with *que* (sometimes *com*), e.g. *lors que*, 'when', *de ce que*, 'because', in which the elements have occasionally fused, e.g. *endementiers que*, *entresque*, 'while'.

Note: The broad meaning of conjunctions is indicated below. For variations in meaning see the glossary or an OFr dictionary.

154. Functions

1. Co-ordinating conjunctions are few in number, with four functions: cumulative (*et*, *si*, *ne*), alternative (*ou*), adversative (*ainz*, *mais*) and inferential (*donc*, *car*, *que*).

2. *Que* is the chief subordinating conjunction used before a noun clause:

> *Je cuit que tu m'as enchanté.*   (Fb.5.223)
> I think that you have bewitched me.

Interrogatives can also function as subordinating conjunctions introducing a noun clause (see Chapter 8).

3. There are numerous subordinating conjunctions introducing adverb clauses, e.g.:

> Cause: *que*, *quant*, *por ce que* (+ ind.).
> Purpose: *que* (+ subj.), *por ce que* (+ subj.).
> Result: *que*, *si que*, *tant que*, *tel que*.
> Condition: *se*, *por que*, *par si que*.

Concession, restriction: *que, que que* (+subj.), *com bien que, comment que.*
Comparison:
    equality: *si com, ainsi com, tant com.*
    inequality: *mieuz que, plus que, moins que.*
Time (particularly numerous):
    before: *ainz que, ainçois que, devant que.*
    until: *jusque, tres que, tant que.*
    as soon as: *des que, lues que, tantost que.*
    as, when, while: *quant, que que* (+ind.).
    after, since: *puis que.*

Many conjunctions (*que, quant, por ce que,* etc.) can have more than one function, sometimes reflected in the tense used (as indicated above). Their meaning will depend on the context. For conjunctions followed by the subjunctive, see §181.4.

Note: *Com* (also spelt *con, come, conme, comme*) normally replaces *que* in comparisons of equality (§50).

155. Uses of the conjunction *que*

1. *Que* introduces subordinate noun clauses (§154.2), at times anticipated in the main clause by a neuter demonstrative pronoun, e.g. *ço, ce* (§59.3):

> Ço dit li reis que sa guere out finee. (Rol.705)
> Thus says the king that he had finished his war.

2. *Que* can introduce many adverb clauses on its own (see §154.3):

> ... Riens ne vaut;
> Que ge crïerai ja si haut (cause)
> Que tost sera ci acorue (result)
> Tote la gent de ceste rue. (F.10.373–6)
> It avails nothing; for I will immediately
> shout so loudly that soon everyone
> in this street will have run here.

3. *Que* is at times repeated before a noun clause after an insertion:

> Raison me semble que, quant l'on voit home
> d'estrange païs, que l'on parole a lui. (R.Tr.14)
> It seems reasonable to me *that*, when one sees a man
> from a foreign country, *that* one talks to him.

Note: For *que* as a relative or interrogative pronoun or a relative adverb, see Chapter 8.

156. Omission of *que*

It is helpful to realise that the conjunction *que* can be omitted in the
following cases:

1. Before a noun clause, especially:

(a) after a negative main clause:

> *Li arcevesque ne poet müer ∧ n'en plurt.*   (Rol.2193)
> The archbishop cannot help (that) he weeps.

(b) after verbs such as:

> *criembre, garder, ne laissier* (cf. §181.2b):
> *Gardez ∧ sans lui ne retornez.*   (Ren. 950)
> See (that) you don't return without him.
> *cuidier, croire, penser, sembler* (cf. §181.2c):
> *Cuida ∧ ce fust son compaing.*   (Fb.3.97)
> He thought (that) it was his companion.
> *savoir, voloir, prometre, jurer*, etc.
> *Renart set bien ∧ ce est li ors.*   (Ren.513)
> Renard knows well (that) it is the bear.

(c) after *mieuz . . . que, plus . . . que,* to avoid a double *que*:

> *Asez est mielz qu'il i perdent les testes*
> *Que ∧ nus perduns clere Espaigne.*   (Rol.58–9)
> It is much better that they lose their heads there
> Than (that) we lose fair Spain.

(d) before the second of two noun clauses:

> *Quant ce voit Charles que tuit li sont failli,*
> *∧ Ne vuelent estre de Nerbone saisi . . .*   (Ay.581–2)
> When Charles sees that all have failed him,
> (That) they do not want to be granted Narbonne.

2. Before adverbial clauses of result (after *si, tant, tel*), of concession and
occasionally of comparison:

> *Tel duel en a ∧ le sens cuide changier.*   (Cl.134)
> He has such grief (that) he thinks he will lose his wits.

Note: *Que* is not used to introduce a main clause with the verb in the
subjunctive:

> *Deus ait merci de l'anme!*   (Rol.3721)
> May God have pity on her soul!

157. The conjunctions *si* and *et*

1. *Si* as a conjunction has a wide variety of meanings: and, so, since, yet, but, etc.

Si can reinforce *et* (*et si*) or form a stylistic alternative to *et*:

> *Et si s'en va.*   And (so) he leaves.   (Fb.5.123)

> *Va, si te couche.*   Go and lie down.   (F.10.351)

Si often introduces and stresses a main clause after a subordinate clause (for two further examples see §180):

> *Quant il i vinrent, si ont joie menee.*   (Ch.N.1474)
> When they came there, they rejoiced.

Si is frequently expletive, and its use must be deduced from the context.

Note: *Si*, or its common dialectal form *se*, should not be confused with *se*, meaning 'if'.

For the adverb *si*, see §150.1.

2. *Et*, like *si*, can introduce and stress a main clause after a subordinate clause:

> *Que qu'Isengrin se dementoit*
> *et Renart trestoz coiz estoit.*   (Ren.3485–6)
> While Isengrin lost his temper
> Renard stayed quite quiet.

The correlatives *et* . . . *et* (or *entre* . . . *et*) mean 'both . . . and':

> *En irons . . . entre moi et toi.*   (F.10.426–7)
> Both you and I will go.

158. The conjunction *ne*

Ne, meaning 'and', 'or', normally replaces *et* or *ou* in negative or hypothetical phrases or in queries:

> *Je n'os Dieu reclamer ne ses sainz.*   (Th.424)
> I dare not call on God or his saints.

> *Dont estes vos, ne que querez?* (Fb.13.127)
> Where are you from, and what do you want?

While *ou* . . . *ou* means 'either . . . or', *ne* . . . *ne* can therefore mean 'either . . . or' or 'neither . . . nor', depending on the context:

> *Se vos volez ne chastel ne cité* . . .   (Ch.N.471)
> If you desire either castle or city . . .

Avez vos ne coc ne geline? (Ren.818)
Have you either a cock or a hen?

Il n'avait ne buef ne vache. (Ren.855)
He had neither ox nor cow.

159. *Quant, se...non*

1. *Quant* (*qant*, etc.) can mean 'when', 'if' or 'since':

Quant vit le roi.   When he saw the king. (Ay.702)

Quant Deu plaira.   If it please God. (Ay.737)

Il vaut grant argent, quant latin parole. (Fb.7.111–12)
It is worth a lot of money, since it speaks Latin.

2. *Se ... non* (if not, except, unless) is often used in a restrictive sense after a negative main clause; the combination *ne ... se ... non* can at times be rendered by 'only':

On ne parloit se de lui non. (F.8.10)
One did not speak except of him /
One only spoke of him.

160. Elision

Elision is optional in the case of the conjunctions *si*, *se*, *ne*, *que* and compounds of *que*.

In the following eight-syllable line the second *que* is thus elided, but not the first:

Et que il vit qu'il ne vivra ... (Fb.12.13)
And that he saw that he would not live ...

The negative particle *ne*, however, always becomes *n'* before a vowel (§146).

12
Prepositions

161. Types of prepositions

OFr prepositions express relations of time and place, also cause, means, manner and purpose, etc. They can b⟨ ·

simple: *a, de, en, o, vers,*
compound, sometimes still written in two words: *envers, desus, parmi* or *par mi,*
adverbs (occasionally nouns or adjectives) used as prepositions: *soz, enz, lez* (side, beside), *lonc* (long, along),
or prepositional phrases: *en aval de* (below).

Note: *Oḍ,* and even *aḍ,* the early forms of *o* and *a,* are still found in the early twelfth century, especially before vowels.

162. Reinforcement

The need for extra stress or greater precision encouraged compounds and prepositional phrases:

Atot le moine. (F.9.381)
With / Together with the monk.

Et lor dites de par moi . . . (Gr.8)
And tell them from me on my behalf.

   This tendency led to several forms with the same or similar meanings, e.g. *a, tresqu'a entresqu'a* (to, up to, right up to).

163. Extended functions

Many OFr words are etymologically both adverb and preposition (e.g. *sus, sor*) and retain their double function. In other cases adverbs and adverbial compounds were soon used as prepositions also (e.g. the compounds *desus, devant, deriere*). Thus by the twelfth century all elements in a reinforced series like *soz, desoz, par desoz* (under, below) can function as either prepositions or adverbs.

While most prepositions are restricted in their use, several have extended functions in OFr, particularly the common prepositions *a, de, par, por* and *en*. Their chief uses are indicated below.

Examples in §§164–9 have mainly been drawn from the *Charroi de Nîmes, Yvain* and the *Prise d'Orange.*

164. Functions of *a*

1. *A* can introduce adverbial phrases expressing:

> place (to, at, from): *au mostier vait* (to); *as fenestres au vent* (at, in); *penduz as forches* (from).
> time: *a ceste fois* (this time); *chevaucherai au soir* (by).
> means, instrument: *as mains se prenent* (by the hand); *a ceste espee* (with).
> manner: *a si grant bruit* (with); *a vo plaisir* (according to).
> measure: *a milliers et a cenz* (by).
> state: *livré a torment* (to); *a seürté* (in safety, safe).
> purpose: *as armes cort* (to arms = to arm himself); *l'espousa a moillier* (he took her to wife).
> association: *vient . . . a quatre bués, alez donc a Dé* (with).
> opposition: *jostai a lui* (I fought against him).

2. *A* is also used to indicate:

> possession: *filz sont a contes* (of).
> an attribute: *.C.M. as espees, Guillelme au cort nés* (with).
> the indirect object: *vorroie a vos parler* (to).
> the passive agent: *escorcier les fet au bacheler* (by).

165. Functions of *de*

1. *De* can introduce adverbial phrases expressing:

> the point of departure: *de la vile issent* (of); *de cest jor en avant, garis mon cors de mort* (from).
> means, instrument: *se fierent des espees* (with).
> manner: *afublee d'un mantel* (dressed in); *de gré* (willingly).
> cause, origin: *de peor* (through); *de Deu de gloire* (on behalf of).

2. *De* also indicates:

> the source or possessor: *trente de mes pers, le seignor de la meison, el ventre del poisson* (of).
> the type or material: *chevalier de vostre pris, chauces de soie* (of).
> the topic: *del soper vos dirai* (about).
> apposition: *la cité de Nymes* (of).
> comparison (§50): *plus de quatorze, plus grant de moi* (than).

a partitive (§32): *des navrez et des morz* (some).
the passive agent: *de la lance fu feruz* (by).

3. *De* can reinforce other prepositions: *delez, desoz,* etc. (see §169). It is elided before a vowel.

166. Functions of *par*

1. *Par* can introduce adverbial phrases expressing:

> motion: *par la fenestre* (through); *m'envoia par mer* (by).
> time, weather: *ne puis dormir par nuit, par mal tens* (by).
> means, instrument: *(il) le sesi par l'estrier* (by).
> manner: *par force* (by); *par amor* (through); *par lui* (by himself, within himself).
> measure: *par un et un* (one by one); *par trois fois* (three times).
> cause: *par ce* (because of this); *par molt grant amistié* (out of).
> in the name of, on behalf of: *par Mahomet, par ma foi, de par Jhesu.*

2. *Par* is used for the passive agent: *escuz n'en fu par toi portez* (by).

3. *Par* can reinforce other prepositions, e.g. *par delez, par desoz,* etc. (see §169); it is frequently used with *mi* (middle): *par mi la sale* (in the middle of); *par mi la vile* (throughout); *par mi le cors* (right through).

167. Functions of *por*

Por is mainly found in adverbial phrases of cause or purpose:

> because of: *por ce, por la gent paienor.*
> for the sake of: *por amor Deu.*
> in exchange for: *por nule rien, por tot l'or desoz ciel.*
> in order to: *por dormir, por son seignor secorre.*
> (See also §194.3.)

168. Functions of *en*

En is mainly used for adverbial phrases expressing:

> motion towards: *fu entrez en la vile* (into); *en piez sailli li vilains* (to); *es chevaus montent* (onto).
> position in space or time: *en cest bois, en France, en son poing* (in); *en ses piez* (on); *en mai, en la fin* (in).
> state: *en lermes, en sa baillie* (in).

En can be combined with other prepositions: *en mi la sale* (in the middle of); *enz el col* (into, right into).

169. Other prepositions

These mainly express relations of time and place (literal or figurative). They can be grouped for convenience as follows:

1. Near, next to:

>Lez, delez, par delez: *lez la fontaine, par delez lui* (next to).
>Joste, de joste, par dejoste: *dejoste lui, joste les autres* (next to).
>Lonc, selonc: *un chastel ci selonc* (near here); *lonc, selonc la costume* (according to).
>Entre: *entre mes pers* (among).
>Entor, environ: *entor lui, tot environ moi* (around).
>Endroit: *endroit le vespre* (about); *endroit moi* (as regards).

2. Inclusion and exclusion:

>O, avuec, ensemble, ensemble o, a tot: *o sa maisniee, avuec moi, ensemble o moi, atote sa couture* (with).
>Enz, deenz, dedenz, par dedenz: *remest dedanz la sale, fu mort par dedenz ta grant tor* (in).
>Fors, fors de, defors: *defors la porte* (outside); *n'i a fors vos* (except).
>Sans: *vinrent sens demorer* (without).

3. Before or after:

>Avant, devant, dedavant: *devant moi, devant set anz* (before).
>Ainz: *ainz midi* (before).
>Puis: *puis cele eure* (since).
>Deriere: *deriere un grant chesne* (behind).
>Apres, enpres: *apres moi vien, apres soper, l'un enpres l'autre* (after).

4. Above, on, below:

>Sor, desor, par desor: *sor le pont* (on); *vint sor eus* (upon); *dessor un tronc* (onto); *dessor le perron* (over); *sor tote gent* (above).
>Sus, desus, par desus: alternatives to *sor*, etc.
>Soz, desoz, par desoz, dedesoz: *desoz les murs* (below); *soz cest arbre* (under).

5. Towards, against:

>Vers, devers, dedevers, par devers, envers: *droit vers Orenge, par devers la mer, se vos avez vers moi mespris* (towards); *envers moi entendez* (to); *combati vers Corsolt* (against).
>Contre, encontre: *en piez contre lui saillirent, encontre s'est levez* (before, in front of); *contre la mïe nuit* (towards); *le devez... contre toz homes secorre* (against).

6. Up to, from here to:

> *Tresque, dusque, jusque, trusque* (+ *a*): *tresqu'a la sale, tresqu'a un an, jusqu'a la fontaine, trusqu'au palais* (up to).
> *Deci, deci que* (+ *a, en, vers*): *deci a Moncontor, de si en Normandie, desi que en Pavie* (from here to).

170. Syntax

Words governed by prepositions are normally in the oblique case, although *fors* (*hors*) can take the nominative as well. Prepositions are followed by stressed pronouns, as a rule in the direct oblique case (*por eus, vers eles*).

For prepositions used with verbs, see §§185.3a and 191. For the omission of prepositions (*li fiz ∧ Marie, donez la ∧ autre, il va ∧ le grant chemin*) see §§29.3, 4, 7, and §§137, 151.

171. Conclusion

There is often no clear distinction in OFr between adverbs, conjunctions and prepositions. Prepositions are also found with or without -*e*, e.g. *sor(e)*, or with an adverbial -*s*, e.g. *jusque(s), avueque(s)*, and at times the same word (*puis, devant*, etc.) can be adverb or preposition, or even conjunction when followed by *que*.

An awareness of the varied and imaginative construction of these parts of speech, however, as either words or phrases, will help towards the understanding and enjoyment of OFr texts.

13
Numerals

172. Notation

Numbers could be written in words, or in large or small Roman numerals, often inserted between stops:

> .*XXXI. furent au conte Savari,*
> *Et .xxxij. a Gaion le hardi.* (=31, 32) (Ay.1517–18)

The two methods were frequently combined:

> *Mil CCIIII*ˣˣ *et dis et ouit.* (=1298) (SB.75)

The following examples from Aymeri show some of the variations found in practice:

> .*I. Alemant ; prent .j. destrier ; huit jorz ;*
> .*iiij*ᶜ. *chevalier ; .V*ᶜ. *Lonbarz ; .m. loges ;*
> .*x. mile en a ; .xx*ᵐ. *paien ; .XX*ᵐ. *Turs.* (Ay.)
> (1, 1, 8, 400, 500, 1000, 10 000, 20 000, 20 000)

Roman numerals are often replaced by words in edited texts.

173. Cardinal numbers

1–10: *un, dous* or *deus, trois, quatre, cinc, sis, set, uit, nuef, diz*. 11–20: *onze, doze, treze, quatorze, quinze, seze, diz et set, diz et uit, diz et nuef, vint.* 30–100: *trente, quarante, cinquante, seissante, setante, uitante, nonante, cent.* 1000: *mil, milie, mile.*

Treis is an early or dialectal form of *trois*.

Twenty or multiples of twenty can be used as a base, up to nineteen times twenty, e.g. *vint et doze* (32), *dous vinz et diz* (50); thus:

> *Dis et sept vinz livres.* £(17 × 20) = £340. (SB.50a)

Mil is more often used for the singular, especially in dates (see examples below), and *milie* or *mile*, usually uninflected, for plurals. There is no fixed rule, however, hence *plus de vint mile* (Ch.N.268), but *plus de .XX. mil* (Rol.2578).

Multiples of 100 can also be used for numbers over 1000, e.g. *seze cenz livres* (SB.39).

Numbers can be linked by *et*, particularly the final unit, but usage varies, as in the following dates:

> *mil et dous cenz et sexante et dix.*   1270.   (SB.43)
> *mil dous cenz septante et six.*   1276.   (SB.43e)
> *mil deuz cenz et cinquante un.*   1251.   (SB.37)

174. Cardinals: declensions

	Two	Three	Twenty	Hundred
(M) NP	*dui*	*troi*	*vint*	*cent*
(M) OP	*dous, deus*	*trois*	*vinz*	*cenz*
(F) NP/OP	*dous, deus, does*	*trois*	*vinz*	*cenz*

Ambe(s), meaning 'both', is often used to reinforce *dui*, and many variations are found, e.g. *ambedui, andui, andoi, endui*, with inflected forms *an(s)dous*, etc., the compound also meaning 'both':

> *Molt sont fier andui li vassal.*   (Er.957)

> *'Sire, bien soiez vos levez',*
> *Font les reïnes ambesdeus.*   (Per.8296–7)

Sometimes the masculine NP forms *dui, andui*, etc., serve for the feminine NP as well:

> *Andui les puceles ploroient.*   (Er. 890)

175. Cardinals: usage

1. When used as numbers, *un, deus* and *trois* are in the oblique case; when used as adjectives or pronouns, however, *un* and *dui* are declined, and usually also *trois*. Other cardinals, apart from *vint* and *cent*, are not declined:

> *Il se sont assis tuit troi.*   (Er.481)
> *Trois ne cinc armez ne dote.*   (Er.3109)

2. *Vint* and *cent* are not inflected, but their multiples are often declined:

> *Vint chevaliers. Quatre vinz chevaliers.*

3. After numerals ending in *un* or *une* the noun is normally left in the singular:

> *Voit vint et un chevalier.*

4. A cardinal can be treated as a noun and followed by *de*:

thus: *.XX. milie Francs.*   (Rol.587)
or: *.XV. milie de Francs.*   (Rol.3019)

5. A number referring to a portion of a whole is preceded by the definite article:

> *Veant moi a les deus ocis,*
> *Et demain ocirra les quatre.*   (Yv.3866–7)
> In front of me he killed two (of my six sons),
> And tomorrow he will kill the (other) four.

6. *Tel* + a numeral can mean 'about', 'some':

> *Tels .IIII. cenz s'en asemblent.* Some 400.   (Rol.2120)
>
> *Dames i ot tes nonante.* About ninety ladies.   (Yv.2443)

7. The feminine suffix *-aine* is frequently added to cardinals to form collectives, e.g. *une dozaine*, a dozen. These are used in a precise sense, thus *une quarantaine* means 'a group of forty', not 'about forty'.

The collective form of *mil* is *un millier*.

8. There is often no elision before a numeral beginning with a vowel.

176. Ordinal numbers

1st: *prim, premier, premerain.* 2nd: *autre, secont.* 3rd–10th: *tierz, quart, quint, siste, se(t)me, ui(t)me, nue(f)me, disme.* 11th–20th: *onzisme, dozisme, trezisme, quatorzisme, quinzisme, sezisme, diz et se(t)me, diz et ui(t)me, diz et nue(f)me, vintisme,* 30th–1000th: *trentisme, quarantisme,* etc., *centisme,* etc., *milesisme* (rare).

Note that from the later twelfth century *s* was silent in the ending *-isme* (§7.1) and at times omitted in the spelling. From this time onwards ordinals up to ten were supplemented by analogical forms in *-i(s)me*: *troisisme, quatrisme, cinquisme, sisisme, setisme, uitisme, nuevisme, disisme,* which were then extended to higher numbers, e.g. the seventeenth: *le diz (et) setisme. Unisme* and *deusisme,* however, were only used in compounds, e.g. the twenty-first: *le vintisme premier* or *le vint (et) unisme.*

A suffix *-ie(s)me* was taken over from dialects, especially from the thirteenth century onwards:

> *Raoul li semes, li huitiemes Braier.*   (Ay.1494)
> Raoul the seventh, the eighth Braier.

The masculine suffix *-ain* was at times used for ordinals, thus *le quartain, le disain, le quarantain,* the fourth, the tenth, the fortieth.

Variations in spelling are common, and *et* can be omitted, hence *le diz et uitisme, le disuitime, le desoitime* or *le desotime* = the eighteenth.

177. Ordinals: usage

1. Ordinals are declined like Class I adjectives and agree with the nouns to which they refer. *Autre,* however, belongs to Class II. Other numbers up to *quint* end in a consonant and take *-e* in the feminine, with *secont* and *tierz* modified to *seconde* and *tierce* (§48).

(M) NS: *Gauvains li premiers, | li seconz Erec.*
Gawain the first, the second Erec.   (Er.1672–3)

(F) NS: *La premere est des jaianz de Malprose,*
L'altre est de Hums e la terce de Hungres,
Et la quarte est de Baldise.   (Rol.3253–5)
The first, second, third and fourth (battalion).

2. Ordinals are used for dates of the month, or for successive kings, counts, etc., of the same name:

Le desotime jur de octobre.   (SB.80)
Henri quatorzime.   (SB.81)

3. A stressed personal pronoun + an ordinal can form an adverbial phrase indicating the total number of persons involved:

Toi tiers seras fet chevaliers.   (Tr.3408)
You the third of a group = you and two others.

Pinte, | qui avenoit a cort soi quinte.   (Ren.295–6)
Pinte, herself the fifth = with four others.

178. Multiplication and fractions

1. To double = *dobler,* from the adjective or (M) noun *doble. A doble* = twice as much; *a cinc dobles,* however, means 'five times as much', 'fivefold':

Diex . . . a cent doubles le vos rendra.   (Gui.d'A.161–2)
God will return it to you a hundredfold.

The terms *foiz* or *tens,* meaning 'times', are normally used for multiplication, e.g. *deus foiz, trois tens*:

La comande a Deu cent foiz.   (Er.3415)
He commends her a hundred times to God.

2. Fractions are expressed by *le demi* (half), *le quartier* (quarter), or by the ordinals *le tierz, le quart,* etc., at times combined with *part* or *partie*: *demi son regne* (Ch.N.535), *la centiesme part* (Er.642), *la tierce partie* (Ay.1502).

De chevaliers i avoit tant . . .
que je n'en sai nomer le disme,
le treziesme ne le quinzisme.   (Er.1662–6)

La disme part was soon shortened to *la disme*, used concurrently with *le disme*:

> *Il ne l'aime pas la disme*
> *Qu'il fait s'amie.* (F.6.22–3)

Fractions are found with or without the article; they agree in gender with the relevant noun, which can be in the oblique singular:

> *Ge vos dorrai de France un quartier . . .*
> *Le quart chevalier, | Quart vavassor . . .*
> *Quarte pucele et la quarte moillier.* (Ch.N.384–9)
> I will give you a quarter of France, a quarter of
> the knights, lesser vassals, young girls and women.

179. Dates and times

The term 'A.D.' is rendered by phrases like *l'an de grace*, or *l'an nostre Seignor*; thus 'in 1270 A.D.' can become:

> *En l'an de l'incarnation nostre Seigneur Jhesu*
> *Crist mil et deus cenz et soixante et dis.* (SB.2)

Ordinals can be used for days of the month (§177.2) but dates are usually expressed by reference to the Church calendar:

> *Le lundi devant la feste Saint Dyonis.* (SB.76)
> *Le mardi apres la nativité Nostre Dame.* (SB.36)

Times of the day are indicated as follows:

> *Prime*, the 'first hour', = 6 a.m.
> *Tierce*, the 'third hour', = 9 a.m.
> *Mïedi* or *midi*, (from *mïe* or *mi* = middle),
>   the 'middle of the day', = noon.
> *None*, the 'ninth hour', = 3 p.m.
> *Mïenuit* or *minuit* = midnight.

All the above terms, except for compounds of *di* (day), are feminine.

14
Verb usage

180. The indicative

Indicative tenses express actual states or actions. The present occurs as a real or historic present, occasionally as a future, while the perfect is used for descriptions, even in dialogue, of people or events in the past:

> *Ge descendi, ele me tint l'estrier.* (Ch.N.557)

The imperfect, rare at first, but increasing in use, mainly expresses habitual action in the past:

> *Sovent aloit et venoit | a la cort.* (Ver.46-7)

and at times also continuous action, although this can be done by the perfect:

> *En mai estoie.* (Cl.190) *Ce fu en mai.* (Ch.N.14)

The present perfect, more often found in prose or dialogue than in narrative verse, expresses a completed action viewed from the present:

> *Or est Guillelmes dedenz Orenge entrez.* (Or.446)

The pluperfect is used for an action not yet fully completed when viewed from the past:

> *Sorent que Lancelot estoit venuz.* (Gr.2)
> (= he had come, and was still there.)

although this can also be expressed by the past perfect, which however usually reflects a completed action viewed from the past:

> *Quant il fu la venuz, si hurta a la porte.* (Gr.26)

The future has its normal use, but the rare future perfect is occasionally used in a past sense:

> *Or dira l'on devant l'abbé*
> *Qu'en trahison l'avrai murtri.* (F.9.456-7)
> Now one will say . . . that I killed him.

Tense usage is fairly free, however, and this can lead to a striking combination of present and past tenses to describe a sequence of past events:

> *En piez se drecet, si vint devant Carlun.* (Rol.218)
> He gets to his feet, and came before Charles.
>
> *Quant el le sent, si est saillie*
> *Fors du lit, et cil l'embraça.* (F.10.364–5)

181. The subjunctive

The subjunctive expresses uncertainty about a fact or action, or indicates that its future realisation is not assured. It thus often replaces the conditional (§182).

The subjunctive is used in this sense, for example:

1. In main clauses, for wishes, orders or exclamations (occasionally introduced by *que, si* or *se*):

> *Bien soiez vos venuz!*   Welcome! (Gr.7)
> *Si m'aït Dieus.*   So help me God. (Gr.28)

2. In noun clauses (usually introduced by *que*):

(a) after verbs of desire, command, preference, advice, consent or prohibition (e.g. *voloir, mander, loer, sofrir*):

> *Carles comandet que face sun servise.* (Rol.298)
> *Sofrez qu'il viegne.*   Allow him to come. (cf. Gr.3)

(b) after verbs of fear or prevention (e.g. *criembre, garder, ne laissier*), at times preceded by *ne* (§148.6):

> *Molt redoutent ₍ Looÿs ne la preigne.* (Or.198)
> They greatly fear that Louis may take it (the city).

(c) after verbs of opinion (e.g. *croire, penser, sembler*) implying uncertainty:

> *Sire, ce croi je bien | qu'ele soit morte.* (Ver.875–6)
> I well believe, Sir, that she is probably dead.

thus commonly after *ne savoir*:

> *La reïne ne set que face.* (Er.192)
> The queen does not know what she should do.

(d) after impersonal expressions of possibility or impossibility, doubt, negation or necessity:

> *Il covient qu'ele soit destruite.* (R.Tr.79)

3. In adjective clauses (usually introduced by a relative):

(a) to express an aim or intention:

> *Ne sai la contreḍe | ou t'alge querre.* (Alex.133–4)
> I know not the country where I should go to look for you.

(b) after a negative, interrogative or hypothetical main clause:

> *N'i a celui ₍ₙ₎ ne soit bleciez.* (Yv.6132)
> There is not one who is not wounded. (§99.1).

(c) to qualify a superlative or its equivalent (e.g. *le seul, le meillor*):

> *La plus bele que l'on puisse trover.* (Ch.N.523)

4. In adverb clauses (usually introduced by a conjunction):

(a) of purpose or prospective result:

> *Si reclaimeṭ Rollant, qu'il li aiut.* (Rol.2044)
> And he calls on Roland, that he may (= to) help him.

(b) of concession, in parenthetic phrases, e.g. with a double alternative, or introduced by expressions like *qui que, quel que, quoi que, ou que*, etc. (§§130–3):

> *Volsist ele ou non.* (Per.708)
> Whether she wished, or not.

> *Que que il me doive couster.* (F.10.41)
> Whatever it may cost me.

(c) of hypothetic or conditional comparison (after *si com, tant com, mieuz que, plus que*, etc.):

> *... Mot ne dist*
> *Ne plus qu'une beste feïst.* (Yv.323–4)
> He didn't say a word more than an animal would have done.

(d) of time, after conjunctions like *tant que, jusque, ainz que*, etc., with the event still unrealised:

> *Ainz que m'en aille en France.* (Ay.204)

5. In addition:

(a) For the extensive use of the imperfect subjunctive in conditional sentences, see §182.

(b) A subjunctive is sometimes induced by a previous subjunctive, usually in an 'if' clause, and even by analogy where the 'if' clause is in the imperfect (§182.2):

> *... Se mes peres savoit*
> *Que je vesquisse a si vil fuer.* (C.d'Arras 554–5)
> If my father knew that I am living
> in such a wretched way.

(c) Note that the imperfect subjunctive is often found where a present subjunctive would seem more logical:

> *Car m'eslisez un barun . . .*
> *Qui . . . me portast mun message.* (Rol.275–6)
> Please elect a baron to take my message.

182. Conditional sentences

These consist essentially of two parts: an 'if' clause introduced by *se*, and a 'result' clause.

1. To express possibility, the 'if' clause is in the indicative, with the 'result' clause in the indicative or conditional:

> *Se vos nel fetes, vos en repentirez.* (Ay.2408)
> If you don't do it, you will regret it.

2. To express mere supposition, the 'if' clause is in the past subjunctive, in the imperfect (or pluperfect) or in the conditional, with the 'result' clause in the past subjunctive or in the conditional.
A past subjunctive is often used for both clauses:

> *S'il poïst, il t'eüst mort.* (Yv.1770)
> If he could have, he would have killed you. (§187)

but an imperfect followed by a conditional is fairly common:

> *Se ge tenoie Guillelme . . .*
> *Tost seroit morz.* (Or.493–4)
> If I held William, he would soon be dead.

Many combinations, however, are possible.

3. Note that the imperfect subjunctive can be used with pluperfect force, since the compound pluperfect subjunctive (e.g. *eüst pu*) is comparatively rare. The meaning will depend on the context; thus:

> *Se Tristran les peüst prendre,*
> *Il les feïst as arbres pendre.* (Tr.1665–6)

Here two interpretations are possible: 'If Tristan could catch them he would hang them (§192) from trees', or: 'If he could have caught them, he would have hung them'. The context shows that the first interpretation is correct.

4. Note also:

(a) Either clause of a conditional sentence can be omitted:

> *Lors vosist estre a Chartres ou a Blois.* (Or.330)
> Then he would rather have been (elsewhere).

(b) *Se* can be omitted in an inversion:

> *Donissez li o char o pain | el le manjast.*
> If you gave her ... she would eat it.   (R.Thèbes 4289–90)

or in the second of two 'if' clauses, at times replaced by *que* + subjunctive. *Que* can, however, be omitted:

> *Se je muir et (qu')ele reviegne.*   (cf. Er.2722)
> If I die (PI.1) and she returns (PS.3).

(c) *Quant* sometimes has the function of *se*:

> *Et quant la pert, n'est rien qui me remaigne.*   (Tx.3.5)

(d) *Qui*, meaning 'if one', can replace *se*, either before a conditional:

> *Qui me donroit tot le tresor Pepin ...*   (Ay.396)
> If one were to give me ...

or before a past subjunctive in exclamations:

> *Qui lors veïst le lion braire!*   (Ren.737)

Here 'if one could have seen' = 'you should have seen ...!'
For further examples, see §128.

183. The imperative

The imperative can be accompanied by the pronoun subject:

> *Tu la governe par raison.*   (Ad.21)
> You rule her wisely.

The command can be stressed by words like *si*, *or*, or more commonly *car* (§150.2):

> *François, quar vos rendez!*   (Or.930)

The future is sometimes found as an imperative:

> *A Carlemagne irez.*   (Rol.70)

Third person present subjunctive forms are used to supplement normal imperatives (cf. §181.1):

> *Par force soit li assauz comenciez!*   (Or.890)

while the subjunctive second person singular is often used for negative orders:

> *Ja mais devant moi ne viegnes!*   (Yv.1715)

For the infinitive as an imperative see §184.2.

184. The infinitive

1. Apart from its normal use, the infinitive often appears as a Class 1 (M) verbal noun (corresponding to a gerund), with usual noun functions, but able also to take an object or complement (see also §194.3):

> *N'i ot que de l'avaler*
> *Le pont et del leissier aler.*   (Yv.4165–6)
> Nothing remained but the lowering
> of the drawbridge and letting him go.

2. The infinitive can be used as an imperative:

(a) negatively, with a singular subject expressed or implied:

> *Ne t'esmaier, oncles!*   Don't be alarmed!   (Or.1613)

sometimes as the complement of another verb, usually *garder*:

> *Garde, ne demorer tu pas!*   (Yv.734)
> Take care that you don't delay!

(b) positively, as a verbal noun, preceded by *or* + *de* + *le*, meaning 'now (let us) . . .', etc.:

> *Por Deu, or del haster!*   (Al.1533)
> For God's sake, hurry!

185. The present participle

1. The present participle is used with *estre* and especially with *aler* to form a continuous tense.

(a) With *estre* (occasionally with *sembler*, etc.) it is used as a verbal adjective (§43) agreeing with the subject:

> *Onques n'en fus fuianz.*   (Al.740)
> You never used to flee.

Estre + the present participle can correspond to a simple tense:

> *Par Mahomet, en cui je sui creant.*   (Or.492)
> By Mohammed, in whom I am believing
> = in whom I believe.

The flexion is at times omitted, as in the example above, owing to confusion with the uninflected *-ant* form.

(b) With *aler* (occasionally with *venir*, etc.) the present participle is un-inflected:

> *Qu'alons nos atendant?*   (Or.905)
> What are we waiting for?

Parmi le bois s'en va fuiant. (Ren.685)
He goes fleeing through the wood.

Aler + the present participle can correspond to a simple tense:

Ne se vont arrestant. They don't stop. (Or.1781)

2. When used as a verbal adjective, the present participle is inflected but retains its verbal function, since it can have an object or complement:

N'estïez mie estolz ne mal queranz. (Al.733)
You were not proud or evil-seeking.

Sometimes it replaces a past participle:

Sor sa poitrine tenoit ses mains croisanz. (Al.725)
On his breast he held his hands crossed.

A fair number of present participles, however, are mainly used as adjectives; thus *trenchant* (<*trenchier*), sharp; *joiant* (<*joïr*), joyful; *combatant* (<*combatre*), valiant; e.g. *cez trenchanz espiez* (Rol.2539), *le cuer joiant* (Or.79), *Garin le combatant* (Or.1093).
A few are also found as nouns:

.XX.M. combatant. 20 000 soldiers. (Or.1098)

3. The uninflected form of the present participle is used:

(a) to qualify a verb. It can then be preceded by a preposition, usually *en* (but also *a*, *sur*, *par*, etc.), and can take an object:

Plorant s'est endormie. (Cl.60)

Nimes conquist par le charroi menant. (Ay.4517)
He conquered Nîmes by leading the waggon train.

(b) to form an adverbial phrase in the case of *oiant* and *veant* (<*oïr*, *veoir*) meaning 'in front of', 'before', etc., with the real subject in the oblique case:

Lisiez le brief, oiant nos toz. (Tr.2547–8)
... us all hearing = in front of us all.

Desfi les ci, sire, vostre veiant. (Rol.326)
I challenge them here, my lord, in your sight = before you.

(c) to form other adverbial phrases, e.g.:

En estant. While standing. / Upright. (Gr.192)

Ainz ... le soleil couchant. Before sunset. (Or.102)

Par devant none sonant. Before 3 p.m. (§179) (Ren.722)

A l'aube aparant. At dawn. (cf. Ay.1011)

(d) The present participle of a few verbs (*vivre*, *dormir*, etc.) can be used as an OS verbal noun:

> *Tot mon vivant.*   All my life.   (Or.678)
>
> *En mon dormant.*   In my sleep.   (Gr.74)

186. The past participle

Initially regarded as a verbal adjective, the past participle is declined, when inflected, like a Class 1 adjective (§41):

> *Pinte la lasse . . . cheï pasmee.*   (Ren.352–3)
> The unhappy Pinte fell in a faint.

When used with an auxiliary, it agrees as follows:

1. With *estre*, it normally agrees with the subject, even in the case of pronominal verbs:

> *Sire, Tristran (NS) est eschapez!*   (Tr.1101)
>
> *Iseut fu au feu amenee.*   (Tr.1141)
>
> *Ne s'est pas arestez.*   (Ay.661)
>
> *Il est jugé que nos les ocirons.*   (cf. Rol.884)

If the past participle heads a phrase in an inversion, however, it is sometimes treated as a neuter and left uninflected:

> *Benoit soit l'eure* (F).   Blessed be the hour.   (Al.86)

2. With *avoir*, it usually agrees with a preceding direct object, and often also with a direct object which follows, even if the participle has a dependent infinitive:

> *La traïson qu'il a faite.*   (Ren.411)
>
> *Il a trovee la dame.*   (Yv.1952–3)

The past participle is occasionally used as a verbal noun:

> *Chascuns menra .XX.M. d'adobez.*   (Or.603)
> Each will bring 20 000 armed men.

187. Transitive, intransitive and pronominal verbs

Many verbs can be either transitive or intransitive (e.g. *esgarder*, *fenir*, *lever*, *plorer*, *prier*); thus compound tenses of *morir* are used transitively:

> *Ton frere as mort.*   (Ad.743)
> You have killed your brother.

Pronominal verbs (used with a personal pronoun) are common in OFr, and many intransitive verbs can be used pronominally as well, e.g. *(se) dormir*, *(se) merveillier*, *(se) partir*, *(se) rire*, *(se) seoir*, *(se) taisir*, etc., the practice often differing from that today:

> *Ele se parti de l'isle.*   (R.Tr.23)
>
> *Carles se dort.*   (Rol.724)
>
> *'Taisiez, mere!'*   (Per.390)

Often, in fact, the same verb can be used as a transitive, intransitive or pronominal verb, e.g. *apeler, arester, combatre, demorer, doter, escrier, ferir, garir, metre, movoir, plaindre, porpenser, prendre, recorder, sofrir*, and many others:

> *'Venue me sui de toi plaindre.'*   (Ren.348)

Here, contrary to modern usage, Pinte the hen uses *se venir* for *venir* and *plaindre* for *se plaindre*.

188. Impersonal verbs

These are used with a neuter subject *il* or *ce* (§83), either expressed or implied. They can be accompanied by an indirect personal pronoun, often in the stressed form when the subject is omitted:

> *Que chaut?*   What does it matter?
>
> *Il ne me chaut.* | *Moi ne chaut.*
> It does not matter to me.

Impersonal expressions include:

1. Those describing natural phenomena, i.e. either true impersonals or phrases formed by *faire* + a noun or neuter adjective; thus:

> *Il ajorne, il pluet.*   It dawns, it rains.
>
> *Il avesprit.*   It becomes evening.
>
> *Il fait mult cler.*   It is very fine.

2. A few other true impersonals:

> *chaut*, it matters; *loist*, it is permitted; *estuet*, it is necessary.

3. Many other verbs (mainly intransitives, occasionally passives) used as impersonals:

> *Il avient, il covient, ce semble, il est jugé.*
> It happens, it is necessary, it seems, it is decided.
>
> *Il li membre, ce li poise, il li plait.*
> It comes to his mind, it worries him, it pleases him.

4. Expressions formed by *estre*+a noun or neuter adjective:

> *Ce lor est vis.*   It seems to them.
>
> *Il li est bel.*   It pleases him.

5. Verbs (usually *il a*, *il est*) introducing the real subject, which is normally in the oblique case, except after *estre*:

> *Il ot plusors qui burent a outrage.*   (R.Tr.95)
> There were many who drank in excess.

189. Auxiliary verbs

Transitive verbs, most intransitives and all true impersonals are normally conjugated with *avoir*, while pronominal verbs and verbs in the passive voice take *estre*, as do a few intransitives expressing a change of place (e.g. *aler*, *venir*, *arriver*, *repairier*).

Many verbs, however, can be used in a transitive, intransitive or reflexive sense (§187), while several intransitive verbs (e.g. *entrer*, *partir*, *repartir*, *rester*, *sortir*, *tomber*) can take *avoir* to express the action or *estre* to reflect the state:

> *(Hercules) a tant alé qu'il encontra Laomedon.*   (R.Tr.33)

This led to a flexible use of auxiliaries in general; any of the combinations *je sui levez, je me suis levez, j'ai levé, je m'ai levé* are for instance possible for 'I got up'.

190. Agreement of verbs

The verb normally agrees in number and person with the subject. In the case of a singular collective subject, however, the verb is often in the plural:

> *Nule gent n'ont si grant pooir ... come vos.*   (Cl.258)

With two subjects, the verb is usually in the plural, with the first person placed first, and the second person before the third:

> *Moi et vos somes. Vos et lui estes. Ele et lui sont.*

Where several third person subjects are linked by *et*, *o* or *ne*, however, the verb can agree with the nearest:

> *De la sale ist lui et sa gent.*   (Cl.229)
> He and his people leave the hall.   (cf. §80.5)

If a verb used impersonally introduces the real subject (§188.5), the verb can agree with the latter:

> *Ce estes vos.*   It is you.
> but: *Il a isles ci pres.*   (Cl.261)

For a plural verb used in a singular sense, e.g. *Venez, sire!*, see §90.3.

191. Government of verbs

1. Transitive verbs normally take a direct object, sometimes only an indirect object governed by a preposition (usually *a* or *de*):

> *aidier a, dire a, penser de, se remembrer de,*
> *entendre a | envers,*

although *a* is sometimes omitted (§29.4):

> *De vos pensez.* Think of yourself.
>
> *Envers moi entendez.* Listen to me.
>
> *Di ton nevo ...* Say to your nephew ...

A few verbs take both a direct and indirect object:

> *Si priet Deu mercit.* (Rol.2383)
> And he begs mercy from God.

2. Some verbs take a direct infinitive (thus *aler, laissier, pooir, voloir*), others an infinitive preceded by *a* or *de* (*a*, contrary to modern practice, being more common):

> *comander a, comencier a, desirer a, faire a, oblier a,*
> *s'aprester de, s'esforcier de, penser de,* etc.

Usage is flexible, however, and many verbs, e.g. *doter* (*a*), *feindre* (*de*), *jurer* (*a*), *loer* (*a*), can take or omit a preposition before an infinitive.

3. An infinitive used as the real subject of a phrase can be introduced by *de* (sometimes with an article) or can stand on its own:

> *Laide chose est de menacier.* (R.Tr.12)

4. Dependent infinitives are usually linked to nouns by *de*, and to adjectives by *de* or *a*:

> *Il avoit grant volenté d'aler.* (R.Tr.8)
>
> *Merveilloses a entendre et a moi*
> *grevoses de raconter.* (R.Tr.13)

192. The verb *faire*

Faire has many uses in OFr. It is used to avoid repeating a verb (e.g. *Car seez! – Non ferai.*) and frequently replaces *dire*:

> *'Baron,' fet il, 'Mahomez vos aïe!'* (Ay.3478)

Faire + an infinitive or a noun can replace a normal tense:

> *Faites moi escouter.* Listen to me.
>
> *Faire joie.* To rejoice.

Faire a + an infinitive (often *loer, mercier, otroier, proisier*) is equivalent to 'should be', 'deserves to be' + the past participle:

> *Charles, qui tant fet a douter.*   (Ay.4088)
> Charles, who is greatly to be feared.

also, commonly:

> *Ce fait a otroier.*   This should be granted.

Faire que (+ an adjective or a noun in the nominative case) means 'to behave like', etc. (cf. §151):

> *Ge tres l'espee, fis que chevaleros.*   (Ch.N.196)
> I . . . behaved in a knightly way.

> *Je fis que fous.*   I acted like a fool.   (Cl.171)

193. The prefix *re*

Re, elided to *r'* before a vowel, is frequently affixed to verbs, where possible to the auxiliary, to express mainly:

repetition:

> *Quant ce ot dit, si replora.*
> She wept again.   (Ver.630)

reversion:

> *Raler me faut errant au marchié.*
> I must go back.   (Fb.7.71)

reciprocity:

> *Li chevaliers le feri . . .*
> *Et li vallés referi lui.*
> The youth hit him back.   (Per.1232–4)

correlation or contrast:

> *Tristran ont pris et lïé l'ont,*
> *Et lïee ront la roïne.*
> They have also bound the queen.   (Tr.806–7)

sequence (then, now, etc.):

> *Or me rofrez Nerbone.*
> Here you now offer me Narbonne.   (Ay.353)

Where *re* applies to a dependent infinitive, it can be prefixed to the main verb:

> *Une dolors . . . lor refait la joie oblier.*   (Yv.3818–19)
> A sorrow makes them forget the joy again.

194. Special uses

1. Adverbial *en*, 'from thence', is often used with verbs expressing a change of place, e.g. *(s')en aler, (s')en fuïr, (s')en issir, (s')en eschaper*;

thus: *torner, se torner, en torner, s'en torner.*

It normally adds little to the meaning.

2. *Ne laissier* or *ne laier* (+ *ne* + subjunctive) means 'not refrain from', 'not be slow to', 'not fail to', etc.:

> *Ne laira n'en face justise.*   (Tr.1127)
> He will not fail to mete out justice.

3. *Por* (+ infinitive or present participle) can mean 'for fear of', etc.:

> *Ja por murir ne guerpirunt bataille.*   (Rol.3041)
> Never, for fear of death, will they forsake a battle.

The infinitive or present participle can take an object, or be used in a passive sense:

> *Ge nel feroie por les membres perdant.*   (Or.1791)
> . . . even if I were to lose my limbs.

> *Ge ne leroie, por les membres tranchier,*
> *N'aille avec vos.*   (Or.387–8)
> I would not refrain from going with you,
> even if my limbs were to be severed.

4. The impersonal expressions *n'i est que de, n'i a* (*fors, mais*, etc.) *que de* mean 'the best is to', 'it only remains to', etc.:

> *N'i ot que de l'avaler le pont.*   (Yv.4165–6)
> It only remained to lower the drawbridge.   (§184.1)

5. *Prendre a* (+ infinitive) means 'to begin to', but the whole phrase can correspond to a simple tense:

> *Bele Doette li prist a demander . . .*   (Cl.329)
> She began to ask him = she asked him.

15
Word order and versification

195. Sentence patterns

Word order is fairly free in OFr, since the case system facilitates easy recognition of subject and object. Certain sentence patterns however predominate, and these are illustrated below.

For convenient analysis the sentence can be divided into subject, verb and complement, 'verb' referring to the finite verb, and 'complement' covering direct and indirect objects, predicative adjectives and nouns, adverbs or adverbial phrases, participles and infinitives.

Note that there can be more than one complement in a sentence, and that unstressed oblique pronouns, which only carry weight in a short phrase, are normally excluded in the analysis.

The patterns below are listed in order of frequency of occurrence.

196. Subject – verb – complement

This pattern is common in both prose and poetry. It is found in main clauses:

> *Li vilains apele son fil.*   (Fb.3.39)

and in subordinate clauses, especially those beginning with a conjunction:

> *Quant il sorent la novele . . .*   (R.Tr.68)

A pronoun subject, normally stressed at the head of a phrase, is at times omitted in a main clause (especially before *ne*) and more often in subordinate clauses:

> ʌ *Ne sai que* ʌ *puisse devenir.*   (VP.368)

197. Complement – verb – subject – (further complement)

This pattern is characteristic for OFr and should be noted. This inversion of subject and verb, common in prose but more so in poetry, is found chiefly in the main clause. It occurs whenever the sentence starts with the complement, which is usually:

1. a direct or indirect object:

> *Ses barons fist li rois venir.*   (Ren.1807)

2. an adverb or adverbial phrase (but see §152):

> *Par le bois vint uns forestiers.*   (Tr.1837)

3. a predicative adjective:

> *Clers fuṭ li jurz e bels fuṭ li soleilz.*   (Rol.1002)

4. or a phrase as the object of a verb like *dire* or *respondre*:

> *'Sire,' fet il, 'por Dieu merci!'*   (Ver.190)

A pronoun subject is usually omitted, except in the latter case, especially in verse:

> *De venoison ont ₋ grant plenté.*   (Tr.1773)

Once this pattern is grasped, it is easier to interpret a phrase to suit the context; thus:

> *Bons chevaliers ama ₋ sus toutes riens.*   (R.Tr.72)
> He loved good knights (OP) above all things.
> (not: A good knight (NS) loved . . .)

Note that there is no inversion in subordinate clauses after relative pronouns or conjunctions.

198. Subject – complement – verb – (further complement)

This pattern, in which the complement precedes the verb, is more usual in verse than in prose. It is sometimes found in the main clause:

> *Li rois Tristran menace.*   (Tr.770)

but more often in subordinate clauses, particularly with the relative pronoun *qui* as subject:

> *Li gars, qui le bacon ot pris.*   (F.9.573)

or after conjunctions, especially *quant, se, si . . . que,* and *que*:

> *Quant ele les escrins ouvri.*   (Fb.5.129)

A pronoun subject is at times omitted, particularly in subordinate clauses (cf. §196):

> *. . . Molt forment s'esbahi*
> *Quant ₋ les trois boçus morz trova.*   (Fb.5.130–1)

199. Complement – subject – verb – (further complement)

The subject and verb are usually inverted after an introductory complement (§197), but the above pattern is at times found in the main clause:

> *De cele amor Dieus me gart.*   (Ver.91)

It is the normal pattern, however, in adjective clauses where the relative pronoun forms the complement:

> *Veez ci l'aventure dont je vos parlai.*   (Gr.12)

200. Verb – complement – subject – (further complement)

This pattern occurs mainly in older texts, i.e. in verse, with verbs like *veoir*, *oïr* or *dire*, followed by noun subjects.

> *Voit le li rois.*   (Ch.N.58)
>
> *Ot le Guillelmes.*   (Or.630)

A variation of this pattern is found in a line like the following:

> *Dist Aymeris: 'Gloton, car vos seez!'*   (Ay.4026)

201. Interrogation

1. General interrogation is expressed by the inversion of subject and verb:

> *Veïstes vos cinc chevaliers?*   (Per.324)

At times the context or intonation would be sufficient to indicate a query:

> *'Sire, ne sai.' – 'Vos ne savez?'*   (Per.7511)

2. Specific interrogation can be expressed by:
the interrogative pronoun *qui* (no inversion):

> *Qui a ma toile? Qui la vit?*   (Fb.4.39)

or by other interrogatives, with inversion of the subject (cf. §197):

> *Que as tu fet? Ou l'as tu mis?*   (Ad.731)

although a pronoun subject can be omitted:

> *Que fais, Adam?*   (Ad.113)

For further examples, see Chapter 8.

202. Flexibility

Within the framework of the above patterns, word position is flexible; e.g.:

1. Direct or indirect objects can precede their verb (§§ 197–8); they can be placed between the auxiliary and the participle, between the verb and a dependent infinitive, or between a preposition and the infinitive it governs:

> *Li rois descent . . . por ceste merveille veoir.*   (Gr.5)

2. Similarly a relative can be separated from its antecedent (see § 100.1); the enlargement of an object can precede the object:

> *Je criem molt du chien le cri.*   (Tr.1600)

and the past participle can precede the auxiliary:

> *Enserré furent li messagier.*   (§ 197) (Ay.3100)

3. For the position of pronouns, see §§ 86–9, and § 152 for that of adverbs.

Throughout OFr, in fact, rhythmic or stylistic considerations could override the logical order of words.

203. Patterns, variations and verse

It is interesting to note that sentence patterns could become compositional aids in verse. Early epics, particularly, used many standard lines:

> *Sun cheval brochet | des esperuns d'or fin.*   (Rol.1245)
> *Sun cheval brochet | des esperuns d'or mier.*   (Rol.1549)

He spurs his horse with the spurs of fine / pure gold.

This line, constructed on the inverted pattern of § 197 with the subject omitted, has been neatly adapted to fit a new tirade by changing the final assonance.

It would have been fairly easy though to find suitable assonances or rhymes owing to the flexible position of words; in addition metrical accuracy was facilitated by the optional use of pronoun subjects and common words like *si* or *en*, by optional elisions (§ 19) and by double forms of many words like *(i)cest*, *(de)soz*, *arrier(es)*. This was perhaps fortunate, since French literature of the twelfth century was almost entirely in verse.

204. Verse structure

OFr verse is syllabic, lines of eight, ten and twelve syllables being the most common, although lyric poetry uses the whole range from one to twelve syllables per line.

For syllabic division see §3. Note that a final weak *e* is usually pronounced unless elided (§19);

thus: *J'aim vos-tre nie-ce de Ver-gi.*   8 sylls.   (Ver.342)

but: *Or vor-roi(e) es-tr(e) o mes bre-bis.*   8 sylls.   (Ren.9208)

A hiatus was always permitted, except in cases of compulsory elision:

A-ssez i ai o-ï e(t) es-cou-té.   10 sylls.   (Ch.N.35)

205. Rhythmic stress and the caesura

Added structure was given to OFr verse by a stress at the end of each line and by a regular mid-line stress in the longer lines. These stresses are fundamental, and any chant or melody used would probably have followed and reinforced this rhythm.

If there is a mid-line stress, the line falls into two hemistichs, each with an end stress. At the end of a line this stress is emphasised by assonance or rhyme, often followed by a slight pause if the phrase forms a unit; thus:

Creras me 'tu? | Guste del 'fruit!   8 sylls.   (Ad.169)

The rhythmic break or caesura after a mid-line stress does not necessarily entail a pause unless it coincides with a logical break, as above. In the following ten-syllable lines, for instance, the fourth and tenth syllables according to rule (§209.2) bear the stress:

'Dex,' dist li 'cuens, | 'beaus rois de Para'dis!'   (Or.1611)

Apres con'quist | Orenge la ci'té.   (Ch.N.7)

yet there need only be a pause at the caesura in the first case.

206. Epic and lyric caesuras

After a syllable that carried a rhythmic stress a weak *e* was probably only voiced faintly. This could therefore occur:

at the end of a line,
at the end of the first hemistich,

and a weak *e* in these positions does not enter the syllable count:

Ensemble 'fie(rent) | sor les barons de 'Fran(ce).   10 sylls.   (Ay.1834)

If endings or rhymes contain a weak *e* they are termed 'feminine'; otherwise, as in the following example, they are called 'masculine':

Laisse le 'mal, | e si te prend al 'bien.   10 sylls.   (Ad.69)

Caesuras after a feminine ending are known as 'epic caesuras' because they are normally only found in the ten- or twelve-syllable lines used for epic verse.

In lyric works the structure of the melodic line could override that of the phrase if the two did not coincide. As a result the regular melodic stress, repeated from verse to verse, could occasionally fall on a weak *e*:

Douce da'me, | *se me volez a'mer* ... 10 sylls. (Cou.11)

The caesura in this case is termed a 'lyric caesura'.

207. Assonances

Assonances require the repetition of the final stressed vowel (monophthong or diphthong) plus any following weak *e*. Masculine assonances end in a stressed vowel, e.g. *chef*, *aler*, *pensé* in *é*, *ciel*, *piez*, *pitié* in *ié*, or *tant*, *sens*, *anz* in [ã], while feminine assonances end in a weak *e*, e.g. *vie*, *dire*, *riches* in *i.e* and *brune*, *perdue*, *fustes* in *u.e*.

The stressed element of a diphthong could assonate with a single vowel, e.g. *fuit*, *plus* in *u*, or, in the early twelfth century, *Anjou*, *fort* in *o* (Rol.2945–6) before ['ou] > [u] (§12.2).

Note that assonances and rhymes were avoided between words ending in [é:], e.g. verbs in *-er*, *-ez*, *-é* or nouns in *-té*, and those in [è], like *herbe*, *cest*, *chastel* (see §11.2,3).

Since nasalisation was only gradually introduced (§13), *-on* still assonated with *-ó* in the mid-twelfth century and *-in* with *-i* at the end of the century.

208. Rhymes

Rhymes require the repetition of the final stressed vowel together with at least one following phoneme, excluding a weak *e*,

e.g. *jor* / *amor*, *saillent* / *travaillent*.

Rhymes like *moi* / *roi* or *espee* / *trovee*, although permitted, are really assonances.

If previous phonemes are repeated (*val* / *cheval*, *assez* / *lassez*) the rhyme is termed rich.

There was no rule that masculine and feminine rhymes should alternate (cf. Tx.1), and on the whole the older the text, the greater the proportion of masculine rhymes.

Symmetric verses in lyric poetry adopt a symmetric pattern of masculine and feminine rhymes (Tx.3).

209. Verse usage

1. Octosyllables were mainly used in a series of rhyming couplets (see Tx.1):

> Li clerc es¹toient gros et ¹gras,
> Quar molt man¹joient bien, sans ¹gas.   (Fb.6.13)

There is often a mid-line stress on the fourth syllable, as above, especially in early verse, but usually no fixed caesura.

2. Decasyllables were usually grouped into tirades or *laisses* of varying length, each with lines ending in the same assonance or rhyme. In the early *Chanson de Roland* these tirades average ten to twenty lines each, with an outer limit of five to thirty-five; in later epics their length increases to well over 100 lines at times. Occasionally each tirade ends with a half-line as a cadence. Some works consist of short stanzas of equal length with assonances or rhymes.

The mid-line stress is normally on the fourth syllable (occasionally on the sixth):

> Tere de ¹Fran(ce), | mult estes dulz pa¹ïs.   (Rol.1861)

3. Alexandrines get their name from the popular *Roman d'Alexandre* which used these twelve-syllable lines. They were usually grouped in assonated or monorhyme tirades of varying length; sometimes they are found in rhymed stanzas.

The mid-line stress is on the sixth syllable:

> Molt fu liez Ali¹xan(dres) | des noveles qu'il ¹ot.   (Rom. d'Alex)

4. Lyric poetry made use of a wide variety of rhyme and metre patterns. In lines of nine or eleven syllables the stress is usually on the fifth syllable, while lines of less than eight syllables have no regular stress.

16
Old French dialects

210. General

The Francien dialect has been accepted as standard OFr in this work
because it was the forerunner of ModFr. Around 1200, however, it was
only one of many competing dialects in northern France, for in the passage
from Latin to OFr local differences had developed, slight or more marked,
merging or overlapping into neighbouring regions, as shown in Table 13.

This table lists some conspicuous differences in pronunciation or graphy
between Francien and its surrounding dialects, and these are discussed in
§212. Additional comments on individual dialects follow in §§213 and 214.

Since few twelfth-century manuscripts have come down to us, the
traits noted have been drawn mainly from thirteenth-century texts,
especially from charters (see SB., p. 178) where the date and origin are
usually known, and which illustrate the dialects more accurately than
literary texts which often reflect the idiom of more than one scribe.

211. Dialectal regions

The dialects of the *Langue d'Oïl* are divided here into twelve regions.
The south (S) includes the dialects of Bourbonnais, Nivernais, Berry and
Orléans; the south-west (SW) covers the idioms of Angoumois, Saintonge,
Aunis and Poitou, while the west (W) includes those of Touraine, Anjou,
Maine and Brittany. These are followed by Norman (N) in Normandy,
then Anglo-Norman (AN) in England. Picard (P) was spoken in Picardy
and Artois; Walloon (Wn) follows in the north-east, then the dialects of
Lorraine (L), Franche-Comté (FC) and Burgundy (B), these last five
areas forming a crescent round Champagne (Ch). The final region, that
of Francien, lies roughly in the centre and includes Paris.

212. Common dialectal traits

The main areas where the following dialectal traits occurred are shown in
Table 13 and indicated below. Note however that these traits were also
found elsewhere, especially in neighbouring areas.

Examples, all drawn from texts, are clarified at times by the addition of the standard OFr equivalent in brackets.

1. Tonic [ó:] became [ö], spelt *eu*, in Francien and Picard in the thirteenth century (*neveu, seigneur*) but [u] in other dialects, spelt *u* in Anglo-Norman (§212.14) and *ou* or *o* elsewhere (S, SW, W, N, Wn, ½Ch, L, FC, B): *nevou, soulement, seignor*.

2. The diphthong *ei*, instead of becoming *oi* during the twelfth century, was lowered through [èi] to [è], spelt *ei, e* (S, SW, W, N, AN): *saveir, le rei, aveit, esteient, seret, la metié, la vee* (= *savoir, le roi, avoit, estoient, seroit, la moitié, la voie*).

3. Tonic [ié] > [é:] spelt *e* (½S, SW, W, ½N, AN): *chevaler, ben, cel, jugé, manere, la pere* (= *chevalier, bien, ciel, jugié, maniere, la pierre*).

4. Class I verbs at times used the imperfect in -*oue*, later -*oe* (see Table 5.C) together with the standard imperfect which was generalised during the thirteenth century (½S, ½SW, ½W, ½N, ½AN): *il resemblout, ele demandot, li un ploroent*.

5. Tonic *el, eu* (usually < VL al) appeared as *al, au*, especially in the south-west, where a final *l* could become *u* before the initial consonant of the following word (SW, ½W): *quaus, dau, tau, corporau* (= *quels > queus, del > du, tel, corporel*).

6. The endings -*om(s)*, -*on* were used instead of -*ons* for the first person plural of verbs (SW, W, N, ½AN): *aloms! cum nos disiom, nous voulon*.

7. [ẽ] (+ *n*) remained [ẽ], and was not lowered to [ã] (W, N, AN, P, Wn); thus *prent*, at times spelt *prant*, could rhyme with *avant* in Francien, but not, e.g., in Anglo-Norman.

8. *ei* or *e* (§212.2) were at times spelt *ai* (W): *trais, monaie, saient, otraierent* (= *trois, monoie, soient, otroierent*).

9. The endings -*um(s)*, -*un(s)* were used instead of -*ons* for the first person plural of verbs (½N, AN): *donum, volums, nus volun et comanduns*.

10. [k], spelt *c, k*, and [g], spelt *g*, replaced *ch* and *j* (½N, ½AN, P): *camp, castel, kemin, cose, escaper; gardin, goie* (= *champ, chastel, chemin, chose, eschaper; jardin, joie*).

11. *c* (+ *e, i*) > *ch* (½N, ½AN, P, ½Wn, ½Ch): *chil, chité, grache, merchi* (= *cil, cité, grace, merci*).

12. The triphthong *eau* > *iau* (½N, P, ½Wn): *biaus sire, les oisiax* (= *beaus sire, les oiseaus*).

13 Tonic [é:] > *ei* (½N, Wn, ½Ch, L, ½FC): *teil, doneir, son peire, sa bontey, l'assembleie* (= *tel, doner, son pere, sa bonté, l'assemblée*).

Table 13. *Distribution of common dialectal traits*

xx = common or fairly common in most texts.

x = common or fairly common in certain texts only, e.g. from a limited area, or occasional in many texts.

Traits noted below are at times found elsewhere, mainly in neighbouring dialects.

For abbreviations and comments, see §§ 211 and 212.

Characteristics	S	SW	W	N	AN	P	Wn	Ch	L	FC	B
1. [ó:] > ou, o	xx	xx	xx	xx	.	.	xx	x	xx	xx	xx
2. ei stays, or > e	xx	xx	xx	xx	xx	.	.	.	.	.	.
3. ie > e	x	xx	xx	x	xx	.	.	.	.	.	.
4. Cl.1 impf. in -oue, -oe	x	x	x	x	x	.	.	.	.	.	.
5. Tonic el, eu > al, au	.	xx	x	.	.	.	.	.	.	.	.
6. 1st p.pl. -om(s), -on	.	xx	xx	xx	x	.	.	.	.	.	.
7. [ẽ] (+n) stays [ẽ]	.	.	xx	xx	xx	xx	xx	.	.	.	.
8. Graphy ai for ei	.	.	xx	.	.	.	.	.	.	.	.
9. 1st p.pl. -um(s), -un(s)	.	.	.	x	xx	.	.	.	.	.	.
10. [k], [g] for ch, j	.	.	.	x	x	xx	.	.	.	.	.
11. c (+e, i) > ch	.	.	.	x	x	xx	x	x	.	.	.
12. eau > iau	.	.	.	x	.	xx	x	.	.	.	.
13. [é:] > ei	.	.	.	x	.	.	xx	x	xx	x	.
14. [ó:], [ó] > u	.	.	.	.	xx	.	.	.	.	.	.
15. Final z > s 12th c.	.	.	.	.	x	xx	.	.	.	.	.
16. Use of w	.	.	.	.	x	xx	xx	x	xx	.	.
17. la > le	.	.	.	.	.	xx	xx	.	.	.	.
18. Final t remains	.	.	.	.	.	xx	xx	x	x	.	.
19. Cl.1 impf. in -(i)eve	.	.	.	.	.	.	x	.	x	x	x
20. a > ai	.	.	.	.	.	.	x	xx	xx	x	.
21. Initial e > a	.	.	.	.	.	.	.	.	xx	x	.
22. lo, lou = le	.	.	.	.	.	.	.	.	xx	x	x
23. Tonic [è] > a	.	.	.	.	.	.	.	.	.	xx	x
24. al, able > aul, auble	.	.	.	.	.	.	.	.	.	x	xx
25. ei (+nasal) > oi	.	.	.	.	.	.	.	.	.	.	xx

14. Tonic [ó:], [ó] and initial [ó] became [u], spelt *u*, later also *ou* (AN): *duner, sun seignur, pur sue amur* (= *doner, son seignor, por soe amor*).

15. Final [ts], spelt *z*, soon became [s] (½AN, P): *assés, vaillans* (= *assez, vaillanz*). In Picard the graphy *z* was rare in the thirteenth century, and second person plural verbs ended in -(i)és: *se vos volés, vos disiés*.

16. Germanic initial *w* was retained instead of becoming *g* or *gu* ($\frac{1}{2}$AN, P, Wn, $\frac{1}{2}$Ch, L): *warder, wages, Willaume* (=*garder, gages, Guillaume*); *w* could replace an initial *v* or *vu* in these dialects, and was at times used as an intervocalic glide: *ju wel, il lowent, awoust* (=*je vuel, il loent, aoust*).

17. The feminine article and pronoun *la* became *le*, which was not contracted after *a, de. Li* could replace *le* in the nominative (P, Wn): *le contesse, a lequele, chil de le vile, li vostre amie.*

18. Final *t*, which became *ţ* and disappeared after a tonic vowel in Francien, was retained (P, Wn, $\frac{1}{2}$Ch, $\frac{1}{2}$L): *volentet, portet, tenut* (= *volenté, porté, tenu*). The ending *-eit* instead of *-eţ* > *é* was common in the east (§212.13): *la veriteit, il at Deu honoreit* (=*la verité, il a Deu honoré*).

19. Class 1a and 1b verbs at times used an imperfect in *-eve* or *-ieve* respectively (see Table 5.C) together with the standard imperfect which was generalised during the thirteenth century ($\frac{1}{2}$Wn, $\frac{1}{2}$L, $\frac{1}{2}$FC, $\frac{1}{2}$B): *il parlevent, il nuncieve.*

20. *a* > [è], especially before [tš], [dž] and *ţ*, and was written *ai*, at times *ei, e* ($\frac{1}{2}$Ch, L, FC, $\frac{1}{2}$B): *saiche, usaige, mairdi, il m'espousai, sa veche* (= *sache, usage, mardi, il m'espousa, sa vache*).

21. Initial *e* > *a* (L, $\frac{1}{2}$FC): *nos davons, il saront, l'avesque, lou chamin* (= *nos devons, il seront, l'evesque, le chemin*).

22. *Lo, lou* replaced *le* as the masculine OS article and pronoun (L, $\frac{1}{2}$FC, $\frac{1}{2}$B): *lo cuer, lou conte, crucifie lou!*

23. Tonic [è] > *a* (FC, $\frac{1}{2}$B): *bale, farme, ales, je promat* (=*bele, ferme eles, je promet*).

24. *al, able* > *aul, auble* ($\frac{1}{2}$FC, B): *especiaul, honorauble.*

25. *ei* > *oi*, even before a nasal (B): *soignor, poine* (=*seignor, peine*).

213. Additional characteristics

Additional dialectal traits found in a more restricted area are grouped below; some were of limited occurrence only. The regions are listed in the sequence given in the table, except for Anglo-Norman, discussed in §214.

1. Southern dialects (S)

These dialects, except for the Orléanais, made frequent use of inorganic consonants: *chosse, droist, lestre, hou* (=*chose, droit, letre, ou*).

Towards the south the graphy was influenced by Provençal, thus *lh, hl, nh, hn* could stand for *l', n'*, and *tz* for [ts]: *senhor, tesmohn, ffilha, totz* (= *seignor, tesmoing, fille, toz*).

Provençal influence occasionally showed in the form of words; thus a final *-a* could replace a weak *e*: *cesta letre, ma ffema* (=*ceste letre, ma feme*).

2. South-western dialects (SW)

St/u perfects could become Wk/i perfects in *-gui*, e.g. *avoir*: P.1 *ogui*, IS.3 *oguist* (= *oï, eüst*).

A final *-al* could be vocalised to *-au* before the initial consonant of the following word: *mau, avau* (= *mal, aval*).

Provençal influence showed occasionally, e.g. in Class I infinitives in *-ar*, such as *amar* for *amer*, and in *-a* for a final weak *e* : *en la vila*.

3. Western dialects (W)

Tonic [ò] from VL au became *ou*: *chouses, clous* (= *choses, clos*).

4. Norman (N)

Normandy as a whole shared dialectal features with the south-west, west and Anglo-Norman, but Upper Normandy also showed dialectal traits common to Picard and Walloon (see table).

Jen, cen were sometimes used for *je, ce*.

5. Picard (P)

Ma, ta, sa > *me, te, se* : *me dame, te maison*.

Mon, ton, son > *me(n), te(n), se(n)* : *men oncle, avuec se frere*.

No, vo appeared as possessive adjectives ≠ the OP *nos, vos*; they were inflected like Class III adjectives: *vos pere, de no vile* (= *votre pere, de notre vile*).

Jou and *çou* or *chou* were stressed forms of *je, ce*.

Tonic [è] > *ie* : *tierre, apiele, apries* (= *terre, apele, apres*).

Weak *e* was introduced between *f, v, t* or *d* and a following *r* (cf. §214.3): *il avera, il prenderoit*.

There was no glide between *lr, nr*: F.1 *volrai* or *vorrai* (= *voldrai*).

pl, bl > *ul* : *le pueule, le taule* (= *le pueple, la table*).

ie, ue > *i, u* before a weak *e* : *se maisnie* (= *sa maisniee*), *ele fut plus corocie* (= *corociee*), *il puent* (= *il pueent*).

ieu, ueu > *iu, u* : *Diu, liu* (= *Dieu, lieu*); *pule* (= *pueple* > *pueule*).

6. Walloon (Wn)

l' was spelt *lh, hl* : *conselh* (= *conseil*).

Il appeared as [il'], spelt *ilh, ihl* : *ilh avoient, ihl vivrat* (= *il avoient, il vivra*).

l, *l'* were not vocalised to *u*, but disappeared before a consonant: *atre*, *assi*, *mies* (= *autre*, *aussi*, *mieus*).

There was no glide between *lr*, *nr* : F.1 *venrai* (= *vendrai*).

ai, *oi*, *ui*, *ie* > *a*, *o*, *u*, *i* : *fare*, *soent*, *por lu*, *jugir* (= *faire*, *soient*, *por lui*, *jugier*).

Ju, and *çu*, *chu* were stressed forms of *je*, *ce*.

7. Champenois (Ch)

The speech of Champagne was relatively free from individual dialectal features. Tonic [ó:] could become [ö], spelt *eu*, as in Francien and Picard, or [u], spelt, *ou*, *o* (§212.1), while areas influenced by Picard, Walloon and Lorrainese at times adopted traits of these dialects, as shown in the table.

8. Lorrainese (L)

Jeu, *ceu* were stressed forms of *je*, *ce*.

9. Franc-Comtois (FC)

The symbol *h* was used between vowels in hiatus: *recehu*, *ahide*, *il s'esjohit* (= *receü*, *aïde*, *il s'esjoït*).

Class 1 verbs at times had PI.1 in -*ois* : *je amois*, *je delivrois* (= *je aim*, *je delivre*).

10. Burgundian (B)

Initial *h* was used before forms of the verb *avoir* : *havoir*, *hai*, *haye*, *havons*, *hont* (= *avoir*, *ai*, *aie*, *avons*, *ont*).

Tonic [è] could become *au*, *o*, in addition to *a* (§212.23): *aules*, *lotres*, *Martinot* (= *eles*, *letres*, *Martinet*).

214. Anglo-Norman (AN)

Separated from continental French and influenced by English, Anglo-Norman changed more rapidly, especially from the beginning of the thirteenth century. In addition to dialectal traits already noted, the following were common:

1. There was an early declension breakdown, leading to an incorrect use of forms and flexions, e.g. *tot li mond* for *toz li monz*. The article *le* was found for *li*; *li* could replace *lui*, and *que* was used for *qui*, etc.

2. *Je, ce* could be spelt *jeo, ceo. Jo, jou, gié* were stressed forms of *je.*

3. Weak *e* could disappear in all positions from the later twelfth century onward: *v'u, sir', f'ras, ferei', sei'nt, espe', 'spee, emper'ur.* Weak *e* could be added, however, between *f, v, t, d* or *i* and a following *r: les poveres, il metera, ociere* (= *les povres, il metra, ocire*).

4. Vowels in hiatus coalesced (*chaaine* > *chaine, saiete* > *seete* > *sete*) or were separated by *h, w,* [y]: *pohoms, nuwe, espeie* (= *poons, nue, espee*).

5. Vowels fell together and graphies were confused:

(a) [êı] (from *ai, ei* + nasal) and [iẽ] both became [ẽ] in Anglo-Norman by the later twelfth century. Since *ai* (§12.2) and even *ei* or *ie* could become *e* (§212.2,3), the graphies *ai, ei, ie, e* and even (≠ English) *ea, eo* could represent the sounds [ẽ], [è] or [é:]: *meis, bein, saver, emperiere, fet, feare, paint* (= *mais, bien, savoir, emperere, fait, faire, peint*).

(b) [eu] and usually [ue] and [ueu] became [ö] (§12.2), spelt *ue, eu, oe,* at times *o, eo: peuple, le soen, bof, il veolent* (= *pueple, le suen, buef, il vuelent*).

(c) [ü], [u], [üi], [ui], often [iu] and at times [ue] and [ueu] all became [u], with graphies that varied from *u* to *o, ou, ui, oi, iu, ue,* or *uo: pus, le froit, buf, sarcu* (= *puis, le fruit, buef, sarcueu*).

6. From the beginning of the thirteenth century *ast* > *aust, an* > *aun* and *on* > *oun: chaustel, graunt, saunz, nos countes et barouns* (= *chastel, grant, sanz, nos contes et barons*).

7. Vocalised *l* or *l'* were noted as *u* or *l,* or even omitted: *beaus, bels, beas* (= *beaus*); *filz* (= *fiz*).

8. Final *ţ, t* often appeared as *ḍ, d: il aḍ parléḍ, le mond, regard.*

9. Since [ts] > [s] during the twelfth century already (§212.15), the use of *s, ss, sc, c, z* and *x* was confused: *puise, blescé, fuce, auxi, vus ditez, les bonz amiz* (= *puisse, blecié, fusse, aussi, vos dites, les bons amis*).

10. There was a random addition of inorganic letters, like *s* or weak *e;* consonants were doubled and dropped consonants restored, while consonants no longer pronounced could be omitted or interchanged: *chaistif, le secunde, usetz, ferra, vifs, altres, tro, branc* (= *chaitif, le secont, usez, fera, vis, autres, trop, brant*).

For further information on OFr dialects and Anglo-Norman in particular, see M. K. Pope, *From Latin to Modern French,* Part v. (Details in Bibliography.)

Appendices

APPENDIX A. DECLENSION CLASSES

Standard twelfth-century forms (after the vocalisation of *l*) are listed below, except that early twelfth-century forms are given of words in which *ei* > *oi* and of words ending in *ḍ*, *ṭ* (which disappeared well before 1150) since the latter have inflected forms in -*z*.

For further meanings of these words see the glossary or an OFr dictionary.

Asterisks indicate a fairly complete list of words in the particular class or sub-section.

1. Class II (M) nouns*

(a) Persons

compere, friend, crony
eschipre, sailor
frere, brother
gendre, son-in-law
maistre, master
parastre, stepfather
pere, father

(b) Names

Alixandre

(c) Other

livre, book
vespre, evening

2. Class III (M) nouns
NS and OS forms

(a) Persons*

abes, *abét*, abbot
ancestre, *ancessor*, ancestor
ber, *baron*, lord, husband

bris, *bricon*, rogue, fool
compaing, *compaignon*, companion
cuens, *conte*, count
emperere, *empereor*, emperor
enfes, *enfant*, child, youth
garz, *garçon*, boy, servant
glot, *gloton*, glutton, wretch
NS (*h*)*om*, *on*, OS (*h*)*ome*, man
lerre, *larron*, thief
niés, *nevoṭ*, nephew
pastre, *pastor*, shepherd
prestre, *proveiḍre* > *provoire*, priest
prodom, *prodome*, worthy man
sire, *seignor*, lord
traître, *traitor*, traitor

(b) Names

Aymes, *Aymon*, Aymes
Charles, *Charlon*, Charles
Guenes, *Guenelon*, Ganelon
Gui(s), *Guion*, Guy
Hugues, *Hugon*, Hugh
Lazares, *Lazaron*, Lazarus
Pierre(s), *Perron*, Peter

(c) Agents

Suffixes: NS -(i)ere, OS -eor
 (< -(i)eḍre, -eḍor)

buvere, buveor, drinker
defendere, defendeor, defender
pechiere, pecheor, sinner
poigniere, poigneor, warrior
sauvere, sauveor, saviour
trovere, troveor, lyric poet
 and many more.

3. Class II (F) nouns

amor, love
citéṭ, city
clamor, clamour
color, colour
cort, court
dolor, sorrow
feiṭ > foi, faith
fin, end
flor, flower
gent, people
(h)onor, honour
lei > loi, law
main, hand
maison, house
mer, sea
merciṭ, mercy
mort, death
nef, ship
nuiṭ, night
paor, fear
pechiéṭ, sin
pitiéṭ, pity, piety
raison, speech
rien, thing, person
saison, season
tor, tower
traïson, treason
valor, worth
vertuṭ, force, virtue
volentéṭ, will

4. Class III (F) nouns

NS and OS forms

(a) Persons*

ante, antain, aunt
niece, nieçain, niece
none, nonain, nun
pute, putain, harlot
suer, seror, sister
taie, taiain, grandmother, great-
 aunt

(b) Names

Aude, Audain, Aude
Berte, Bertain, Bertha
Eve, Evain, Eve
Marie, Mariain, Mary

(c) Animals

Pinte, Pintain, the hen Pinte
Blere, Blerain, the cow Blere

(d) Rivers

Orne, Ornain, Orne

5. Indeclinable nouns

Class I (M)

bois, wood
braz, arm
cors, body
dos, back
pais, country
palais, palace
pas, step
pris, price
respons, reply
sens, sense
solaz, comfort
tens, time, weather
uis, door
vis, face, opinion
Ais, Aix
Alexis, Alexis

Class II (F)

croiz, cross
feiz > foiz, time
pais, peace
voiz, voice

6. Class II adjectives*

aigre, acid
aspre, rough
autre, other, another
destre, right
povre, poor
senestre, left
tendre, tender

7. Class III adjectives

(a) Monosyllabic*

brief, short
fol, foolish
fort, strong
grant, great
grief, grievous
quel, which
soëf, sweet
tel, such
vil, vile

(b) In -al, -el, -il

celestial, celestial
coral, cordial
egal, equal
infernal, infernal
leial > loial, loyal
reial > roial, royal
charnel, carnal
cruël, cruel
mortel, mortal
naturel, natural
gentil, noble
sotil, ingenious

(c) In -ant, -ent

avenant, attractive
corant, swift

luisant, bright
puissant, powerful
trenchant, sharp
vaillant, valiant
diligent, diligent
pacient, patient
prudent, prudent

8. Class IV adjectives*

(a) Adjectives
NS, OS

fel, felon, treacherous, cruel

(b) Comparatives
NS, OS, Neuter

graindre, graignor, –, greater
maire, maior, –, greater
mendre, menor, meins > moins,
  smaller
mieudre, meillor, mieuz, better
noaudre, noaillor, noauz, worse
pire, peior, pis, worse

(c) Rare comparatives, found in
the OS only

alçor, higher
belesor, more beautiful
forçor, stronger

9. Indeclinable adjectives

(a) Class I (M)**

corteis > cortois, courteous
douz, sweet
faus, false
franceis > françois, French
gros, large
ploros, tearful
precios, precious
tierz, third

** The feminine forms end in -e
and are declined.

(b) Class III (M/F)

viez, old, ancient

APPENDIX B. ENCLITIC FORMS

The following enclitic forms in general use in the twelfth century were retained in the thirteenth (see §37.2):

a le > al, au	*a les > as*
de le > del, deu, dou, du	*de les > des*
en le > el, eu, ou, u	*en les > es*

Most of the enclitic forms listed below, in which (i) *le, les,* or (ii) *me, te, se* or *en* are abbreviated, were fairly common in the twelfth century, though less frequently found in the thirteenth (see §§20, 91):

ja le > jal	*ne le > nel, nul,*	*que le > quel, queu*
ja me > jam	*nou, nu*	*que se > ques*
je le > jel, gel,	*ne les > nes*	*si le > sil, sel, seu*
jeu, ju	*ne me > nem*	*si les > sis, ses*
je les > jes, ges	*ne te > net*	*si me > sim*
je me > jem	*ne se > nes*	*si se > sis*
jo le > jol	*qui le > quil*	*si en > sin*
jo les > jos	*qui les > quis*	*se le > sel, seu*
tu le > tul	*qui me > quim*	*se les > ses*
tu me > tum	*qui se > quis*	
lui en > luin	*qui en > quin*	

Other enclitic forms are sometimes found, especially in early texts, e.g. *si est > sist, ço est > çost.*

APPENDIX C. VERBS: WEAK AND STRONG PERFECTS

Later twelfth-century forms are given below, but early infinitives with stems in *ḍ, ei > oi* or *l > u* are included. Common alternative infinitives are added.

The first person singular of strong perfects is given in brackets, followed by the second person singular in the case of vocalic alternation. The perfect stem of weak perfects can be derived from PI.4. Compounds use the same perfect as the simple verb.

For the meaning of verbs which are not the same in ModFr, see Chapters 5, 6 or the glossary.

* Asterisked verbs use additional perfects (see Appendix E).

1. **Weak/a Perfect** (well over 1000 Class 1a verbs in *-er*)

   amer, apeler, ariver, chanter, clamer, comander, durer, entrer, gaber, laver, lever, livrer, mander, mener, monter, parer, peser, plorer, porter, soner, torner, trembler, trover, etc. (P.1 *amai*, PP *amé*, etc.).

2. **Weak/a² Perfect** (well over 500 Class 1b verbs in *-ier*)

   aidier, apoiier†, araisnier, chevalchier > chevauchier, comencier, conseillier, cuidier, deignier, espleitier > esploitier, jugier, laissier, noncier,

otreiier > otroiier†, preisier > proisier, repairier, etc. (P.1 *aidai*, PP *aidié*, etc.).

† *ii* soon > *i* (§15).

3. **Weak/i Perfect** (over 100 Class II and Class III verbs in -*ir*)

Class II verbs:

cherir, choisir, fenir, florir, garantir, garir, obeïr, perir, etc. (P.1 *cheri*, PP *cheri*, etc.).

Class III verbs:

coillir, dormir, faillir, ferir (PP *feru*), *mentir, oḍir > oïr, sentir, sortir*, etc. (P.1 *coilli*, PP *coilli*, etc.).

4. **Weak/i² Perfect** (about 20 Class III verbs in consonant +-*re*)

*atendre, batre, cosdre, defendre, descendre, entendre, espandre, fendre, fondre, pendre, perdre, rendre, *respondre, rompre, *sivre, tendre, vendre*, etc. (P.1 *atendi*, PP *atendu*, etc.). Also originally: *iraistre* (P.1 *irasqui*, PP *irascu*), *naistre* (P.1 *nasqui*, PP *nascu*), *veintre* (P.1 *venqui*, PP *vencu*), *vivre* (P.1 *vesqui*, PP *vescu*).

5. **Weak/u Perfect** (about 10 Class III verbs)

chaloir, corre, doloir, moldre > moudre (P.1 *molui*), *morir* (PP *mort*), *paroir, secorre, soloir, *valoir*, etc. (P.1 *corui*, PP *coru*, etc.).

6. **Strong/i Perfect** (4 Class III verbs)

tenir (*tin/tenis*, PP *tenu*), *venir* (*vin/venis*, PP *venu*), *veḍeir > veoir* (*vi/veïs*, PP *veü*), *voloir* (P.1 *vol*, PP *volu*).

7. **Strong/s Perfect** (about 50 Class III verbs in -*re* and a few others)

(a) **Vocalic perfect stem**: Vocalic alternation usual. Intervocalic *s*, when marked *ş*, is increasingly omitted (§69.2). Past participle in -*s*, if not given.

cloḍre > clore (*clos/cloşis*), *conclure* (*conclus/conclusis*), *despire* (*despis/despeşis*, PP -*t*), *dire* (*dis/desis*, PP -*t*), *faire* (*fis/feşis*, PP *fait*), *frire* (*fris/fresis*, PP -*t*), *manoir, maindre* (*mes/masis, mesis*), *metre* (*mis/meşis*), *ociḍre > ocire* (*ocis/oceşis*), *prendre* (*pris/preşis*), *querre* (*quis/queşis*), *reḍre > rere* (*res/rasis*), *remanoir, remaindre* (*remes*), *riḍre > rire* (*ris/reşis*), *seḍeir > seoir* (*sis/seşis*), etc.

(b) **Consonant perfect stem**: No vocalic alternation. Intervocalic *s* often appears as *ss* (§69.2). Past participle in -*t*, if not given.

Note: The perfect stems of *escorre, escrivre* and *pondre*, like perfect stems in vowel +*i*, formerly ended in a consonant.

aërdre (*aërs*, PP -*s*), *ardre* (*ars*, PP -*s*), *ataindre* (*atains*), *braire* (*brais*), *ceindre* (*cⱷins*), *conduire* (*conduis*), *construire* (*construis*), *criembre, criendre*, etc. (*criens*) *cuire* (*cuis*), *destruire* (*destruis*), *duire* (*duis*), *escorre* (*escos*, PP -*s*), *escrivre, escrire* (*escris*), *espardre* (*espars*, PP -*s*), *esteindre* (*esteins*), *estraindre* (*estrains*), *feindre* (*feins*), *fraindre* (*frains*), *joindre* (*joins*), *luisir, luire* (*luis*), *mordre* (*mors*, PP -*s*), *oindre* (*oins*),

peindre (*peins*), *plaindre* (*plains*), *poindre* (*poins*), *pondre* (*pos*, PP *post*), *redembre* > *raembre* (*raens*), *semondre* (*semons*, PP *-s*), *soldre* > *soudre* (*sols* > *sous*, PP *-s*, *-t*), *sordre* (*sors*, PP *-s*), *terdre* (*ters*, PP *-s*), *tordre* (*tors*, PP *-t*, *-s*), *traire* (*trais*), etc.

8. Strong/u Perfect

(a) P.1 in -oi (6 verbs)

avoir (*oi*), *paistre* (*poi*), *plaisir*, *plaire* (*ploi*), *podeir* > *pooir* (*poi*), *savoir* (*soi*), *taisir*, *taire* (*toi*). (PP *eü*, *peü*, etc.)

(b) P.1 in -ui (about 20 verbs)

beivre > *boivre* (*bui*), *conceivre*† (*conçui*), *conoistre* (*conui*), **creidre* > *croire* (*crui*), *creistre* > *croistre* (*crui*), *deceivre*† (*deçui*), *devoir* (*dui*), **ester* (*estui*), *estovoir* (P.3 *estut*), *gesir* (*jui/geüs*, etc.), *leisir* > *loisir* (P.3 *lut*), **lire* (*lui*), *movoir* (*mui*), **nuisir*, *nuire* (*nui*), *perceivre*† (*perçui*), *plovoir* (P.3 *plut*), *receivre*† (*reçui*), etc. (PP *beü*, *conceü*, etc.). † In these stems *ei* > *oi*, and *-c* is now written *-ç* before *o* and *u*, e.g. *receivre* > *reçoivre* (*reçui/receüs*). These verbs also have an infinitive in *-oir*, e.g. *recevoir*.

APPENDIX D. VERBS: VOCALIC ALTERNATION

Well over a hundred Class I and Class III verbs have vocalic alternation in their present tenses (see §76 and Table 10). The main types are given below, with eighty fairly common verbs affected. Infinitives usually use the unstressed stem.

A few of these verbs have palatalised forms in PI.1 and the present subjunctive, which may not show vocalic alternation (see §78 and Appendix E).

The first column lists standard spelling changes in stressed and unstressed stems respectively; their pronunciation is added in brackets.

For the meaning of verbs which are not the same in ModFr see Chapters 5, 6 or the glossary.

VA type Verbs showing this vocalic alternation

a/e   *acheter*, PI.3 *achate*. VA [a/ə].

ai/a (+nas.)
   amer, *clamer* ; *manoir*, etc. PI.3 *aime*, etc. VA [ẽi/ã].

e/a   *comparer*, *laver*, *parer* ; *haïr* ; *paroir*, *savoir*, etc. PI.3 *compere*, etc. VA [é:/a].

ei > oi/e   *adeser*, *celer*, *conreer*, *errer*, *esperer*, *peser*, *sevrer* ; (a) *perçoivre**, *boivre**, *conçoivre**, *croire**, *deçoivre**, *reçoivre** ; *devoir*, *veoir*, etc. PI.3 *adeise* > *adoise*, etc. VA [ei > oi/ə].
   * These infinitives use the stressed stem *ei* > *oi*, but all except *boivre* and *croire* also have an e-stem infinitive in *-evoir*, e.g. *recevoir*.

ei/e (+nas.)
   mener, *pener*, etc. PI.3 *meine*, etc. VA [ẽi/ə].

i̲/ei > oi *empoirier (empirier), loiier* (lier), noiier* (nier), otroiier* (otrier), ploiier* (plier), proiier* (prier), proisier (prisier); oissir (issir)*, etc. PI.3 *empire*, etc. VA [i/ei > oi]. These verbs first use the *ei > oi* stem in the infinitive, and later also the stressed stem. A few, like *oissir*, soon adopt the stressed stem throughout.
 * In these verbs *-ii-* is soon spelt *-i-* (§15).

ie̲/e   *achever, crever, geler, grever, lever; assegier, depecier; ferir; querre; cheoir, seoir*, etc. PI.3 *achieve*, etc. VA [ié/ə] > [yé/ə] 13th c.
ie̲/e (+nas.)
    tenir, venir; criembre, etc. PI.3 *tient*, etc. VA [iẽ/ə] > [yẽ/ə] 13th c.
o̲(>eu)/ o > ou
    aorer, avoer, demorer, esposer, (h)onorer, laborer, plorer, savorer; cosdre, etc. PI.3 *aoure, aeure*, etc. VA [ó:/ó] > [ö/u] or [u/u] 13th c.
    Stressed *o* at times becomes [ö], spelt *eu*, in the thirteenth century, but more often [u], spelt *ou*, ≠ the unstressed stem, in which case alternation ends.
ue̲/o > ou
    prover, rover, trover; coillir, covrir, (en)foïr, morir, ovrir, sofrir; moudre; doloir, estovoir, movoir, plovoir, pooir, soloir, voloir, etc. PI.3 *prueve*, etc. VA [ö/ó] > [ö/u] 13th c.
ui̲/oi   *apoiier*, aproismier, enoiier**, etc. PI.3 *apuie*, etc. VA [üi/oi] > [ẅi/oi] 13th c.
 * In these verbs *-ii-* is soon spelt *-i-* (§15).

In a few verbs vocalic alternation does not affect the spelling, e.g. *apeler*, VA [è/ə], *aprochier*, VA [ò/ó].

In the twelfth century already the use of the stressed or unstressed stem was at times extended (e.g. Ren: 1502/6: F.4 *reprïerons*, F.5 *proieriez*), and this levelling process became more frequent in the thirteenth century.

Note: Vocalic alternation, a characteristic of OFr, is also found in about half the strong perfects (§65, Table 9.2 and App.C), in a few Class III nouns (§16.2) and in a fair number of related words (§§16.3, 18).

APPENDIX E. IRREGULAR VERBS

The verb forms listed are those of standard OFr of the later twelfth century, but earlier infinitives with stems in *d̨* or in *ei > oi* are included. Glide or intrusive consonants (§75) are bracketed in infinitives, and vocalic alternation is given if it affects the spelling.

PI.4 forms with palatalised stems are asterisked to explain second person plural forms in *-iez* and PS.4 in *-iens* (§§66.1, 67) and PI.2 in *-z* after [l'] or [n']. Palatalised forms of PI.1 are also asterisked, as well as the corresponding PS.1 (§78), as a key to stem changes and PS.4,5 in *-iens, -iez*. Early forms with *-l* are added to account for later vocalised stems, while a few other early forms are given for the sake of conformity; the rare PI.1 *plaz** (v. *plaire*) thus explains PS.1 *place** (§78).

The present indicative is given in full, together with relevant forms of the present subjunctive, while the PS.1 of the subjunctive in *-ge* (§68.6) is shown for

verbs which use some of these forms in Francien. Usually only the singular of the imperative is listed, in which case I've 4 and 5 are the same as PI.4 and 5. The present participle and Impf.1 are given if they cannot be derived from PI.4 (§66.1,2).

Only the first person singular is shown for other tenses, except that P.2 is given in the case of vocalic alternation. The imperfect subjunctive, although usually regular, is added as a check on P.2 (§66.6), hence on the perfect type. Some of the forms shown, e.g. certain PS.4 or 5 forms, could not be checked in texts, but all are probable, and given for the sake of uniformity.

It must be stressed that over half the verbs listed below are regular, if account is taken of verb classes, perfect types, vocalic alternation and standard modifications as explained in Chapter 6. Verbs whose only irregularities are consonant modifications (§§72–4) are omitted if affected forms are easily understood, e.g. PI.3 *rent* (v. *rendre*), or rarely used, like PS.2 *loz* (v. *loḍer* > *loer*).

For other standard variations, not included below, see §§67–9; thus many Class III verbs in *-ir* also use Class II forms. Verbs showing vocalic alternation are listed in Appendix D.

Note that where forms seemed irregular, e.g. due to palatalisation or to vocalic alternation, they were often gradually supplemented and eventually usually replaced by analogical forms. Where two forms are given, e.g. PI.1 *tieng**, *tien* (v. *tenir*) or PI.4 *faimes*, *faisons* (v. *faire*), the second is usually a later creation. In the thirteenth century many more analogical forms were added, and other changes took place (§§7.3, 11.8,9 and 21.14); thus $z > s$ in the singular, *-o* often became *-ou*, and *-ue* was at times written *-eu*.

Throughout the OFr period further deviations were possible due to the influence of dialects or the whim of scribes, but once the basic patterns are grasped these variations are easily recognised and should prove a source of delight.

1. Irregular verb tables

Almost all these verbs, as can be seen from the infinitive, belong to Class III. For the meaning of verbs which are not the same in ModFr see Chapters 5, 6 or the glossary.

Note: Forms for the 1st, 2nd and 3rd persons singular and plural are separated by dashes. Variant forms for the same person are separated by commas.

Aidier (see §77)

Pres.Ind. *aiu, aï–aiues, aïes–aiue, aïe–aidons*–aidiez–aiuent, aïent*
Pres.Subj.
        aiu, aï–aiuz, aïz–aiut, aït, aïst, aie–aidons–aidiez–aiuent, aïent

Perf.	*aidai* Wk/a^2		I've *aiue, aïe*

Impf.Subj.
        aidasse   Fut. *aiderai*

PP   *aidié*

  ai- = 1 syll.; *aï, aï-* = 2 sylls.

  Early 12th c. forms: PI.1 *aiuṭ, aïṭ ;* PI.3 *aiuḍeṭ, aïḍeṭ,* etc.

Aler

Pres.Ind. *vois**, *vai–vais, vas–vait, va–alons–alez–vont*
Pres.Subj.

	1. *voise** 3. *voise, voist* 4. *voisiens (-ons)* 5. *voisiez*
or	1. *aille** 3. *aille, alt > aut* 4. *alons, ailliens (-ons)* 5. *alez, ailliez*
	(also *alge > auge*)

Perf.   *alai* Wk/a   I've *vas, va*
Impf.Subj.

       alasse   Fut. *irai*
PP   *alé*

Benedis(t)re > Beneïs(t)re, Beneïr

Pres.Ind. *beneï**, *beneïs–beneïs–beneïst, beneïst–beneïssons*–beneïssiez–beneïssent*
Pres.Subj.

| | 1. *beneïe**   4. *beneïiens (-ons)*   5. *beneïiez* |
| or | 1. *beneïsse*   4. *beneïssons*   5. *beneïssiez* |

Perf.   *beneï, benesqui* Wk/i²   I've *beneï, beneïs*
Impf.Subj.

       beneïsse, benesquisse   Fut. *beneïrai,*
PP   *beneeit > beneoit, beneï*   *beneïstrai*
eï (< eḍi) = 2 sylls.; ii soon > i (§15)
This verb adopts many Cl.II forms.

Bolir, Boillir

Pres.Ind. *boil*–bols > bous–bolt > bout–bolons, boillons*–bolez, boilliez–bolent,*
      boillent
Pres.Subj.

       1. *boille**   4. *boilliens (-ons)*   5. *boilliez*
Perf.   *boli, boilli* Wk/i, also P.3 *bolu*
      Wk/u   I've *bol, boil*
Impf.Subj.

       bolisse, boillisse   Fut. *boldrai/boildrai*
PP   *boli, boilli, bolu*   *> boudrai*

Cein(d)re

Pres.Ind. *ceing–ceinz–ceint–ceignons*–ceigniez–ceignent*
Pres.Subj.

       1. *ceigne*   4. *ceigniens (-ons)*   5. *ceigniez*
Perf.   *ceins* St/s   I've *ceing*
Impf.Subj.

       ceinsisse   Fut. *ceindrai*
PP   *ceint*

Chaloir (Impersonal) VA ie/a

Pres.Ind. 3. *chielt, chalt > chaut*   Impf.Ind. 3. *chaloit*
Pres.Subj.   Pres.Part.

    3. *chaille*   *chalant*

Perf.   3. *chalu* Wk/u, *chalst* > *chaust*
        St/s   Fut. 3. *chaldra* > *chaudra*
Impf.Subj.
        3. *chalust, chalsist* > *chausist*
PP   *chalu*

Chedeir > Cheoir, Chadeir > Chaoir, Chedir, Chadir VA <u>ie</u>/e, a

Pres.Ind. *chié–chiez–chiet–cheons, chaons–cheez, chaez–chiéent*
Pres.Subj.
        1. *chiée*   4. *cheons, chaons*   5. *cheez, chaez*   6. *chiéent*
Perf.   *chei, chaï* Wk/i   I've *chié*
        chui–cheüs St/u   Fut. *cherrai, charrai*
Impf.Subj.
        cheïsse, chaïsse, cheüsse
PP   *chei, cheü, cheoit* (or *chaï*, etc.)

Coillir, Cueillir, Cueil(d)re / Cuel(d)re > Cueu(d)re VA <u>ue</u>/o

Pres.Ind. *cueil*–cueilz* > *cueuz–cueilt* > *cueut–coillons*–coilliez–cueillent*
Pres.Subj.
        1. *cueille** 4. *coilliens (-ons), cueilliens (-ons)*   5. *coilliez, cueilliez*
        6. *cueillent*   (also *colge*)
Perf.   *coilli* Wk/i   I've *cueil*
Impf.Subj.
        coillisse   Fut. *coildrai* > *cueudrai*
PP   *coilli*
    The stem *cueill-* is generalised in the 13th c., e.g. PI.1 *cueille*, PI.4 *cueillons*,
P.1 *cueilli*.

Conois(t)re

Pres.Ind. *conois–conois–conoist–conoissons*–conoissiez–conoissent*
Pres.Subj.
        1. *conoisse*   4. *conoissiens(-ons)*   5. *conoissiez*
Perf.   *conui–coneüs* St/u   I've *conois*
Impf.Subj.
        coneüsse   Fut. *conoistrai*
PP   *coneü*

Cos(d)re, Coudre VA <u>o</u> > eu/o > ou

Pres.Ind. *keus–keus–keust–cousons–cousez–keusent*
Pres.Subj.
        1. *keuse*   4. *cousons*   5. *cousez*   6. *keusent*
Perf.   *cosi* Wk/i[2]   I've *keus*
Impf.Subj.
        cosisse   Fut. *cosdra*
PP   *cosu*
    The 13th c. forms of *cosdre* are given, since the earlier vocalic alternation
[ó:]/[ó] does not affect the spelling. *K* or *qu* replaces *c* before *eu*.

Covrir VA ue/o > ou

Pres.Ind. *cuevre–cuevres–cuevre–covrons–covrez–cuevrent*
Pres.Subj.
       1. *cuevre* 4. *covrons* 5. *covrez* 6. *cuevrent*
Perf.   *covri* Wk/i   I've *cuevre*
Impf.Subj.
    covrisse   Fut. *covrerai*
PP   *covert, covri*

Creiḍre > Croire VA ei > oi/e

Pres.Ind. *croi–croiz–croit–creons–creez–croient*
Pres.Subj.
       1. *croie* 4. *creons* 5. *creez* 6. *croient*
Perf.   *crui–creüs* St/u, *creï* Wk/i   I've *croi*
Impf.Subj.
    creüsse, creïsse   Fut. *crerai*
PP   *creü*

Creis(t)re > Crois(t)re

Pres.Ind. *crois–crois–croit–croissons*–croissiez–croissent*
Pres.Subj.
       1. *croisse* 4. *croissiens (-ons)* 5. *croissiez*
Perf.   *crui–creüs* St/u   I've *crois*
Impf.Subj.
    creüsse   Fut. *croistrai*
PP   *creü*

Criem(b)re, Crien(d)re, Crem(b)re, Cremir, etc. **VA** ie/e

Pres.Ind. *criem–criens–crient–cremons–cremez–criement*
Pres.Subj.
       1. *crieme* 4. *cremons* 5. *cremez* 6. *criement* (also *crienge*)
Perf.   *criens, crens* St/s   I've *criem*
             cremi Wk/i, *cremui* Wk/u   Fut. *criendrai*
Impf.Subj.
    criensisse, crensisse, cremisse, cremusse
PP   *crient, crent, cremu*
    The stem *craign-* (≠ *plaindre*, etc.) appears in the 13th c., e.g. PI.4 *craignons*.

Cuire

Like *luire*, or occasionally *duire*, e.g. PI.6 *cuisent* or *cuient*. St/s perfect *cuis*. Also spelt *quire*, stem *quis-*.

Devoir VA ei > oi/e

Pres.Ind. *doi*–dois–doit–devons–devez–doivent*
Pres.Subj.
       1. *doie*, *doive* 4. *doiiens (-ons), devons* 5. *doiiez, devez* 6. *doient, doivent*

Perf.   *dui–deüs* St/u   I've —
Impf.Subj.
        deüsse   Fut. *devrai*
PP   *deü*
  ii soon > *i* (§15).

Dire

Pres.Ind. *di–dis–dit–dimes, dions*, disons*–dites–dient*
Pres.Subj.
        1. *die* 4. *diiens (-ons), disiens (-ons)* 5. *diiez, disiez* 6. *dient*
Perf.   *dis–desis* St/s   I've *di*
Impf.Subj.   Impf.Ind.
        desisse   *disoie*
PP   *dit*   Pres.Part.
                            disant
                            Fut. *dirai*

Doloir VA uc/o > ou

Pres.Ind. *doil*, dueil*, duel–duels > dueus–duelt > dueut > dolons–dolez–*
        duelent
Pres.Subj.
        1. *dueille** 4. *doilliens (-ons), dueilliens (-ons)* 5. *doilliez, dueilliez*
        6. *dueillent*
Perf.   *dolui* Wk/u   I've *duel*
Impf.Subj.   Pres.Part.
        dolusse   *dolant,*
PP   *dolu*   *doillant, dueillant*
                            Fut. *doldrai > doudrai*
  -ueu- (PI.2,3) can become *-ieu-*.

Doner

Pres.Ind. *doing*, doins*–dones–done–donons–donez–donent*
Pres.Subj.
        1. *doigne** 3. *doigne, doint, dont* 4. *donons, doigniens (-ons)*
        5. *donez, doigniez* 6. *doignent*
  or   1. *doinse** 3. *doinse, doinst* 4. *doinsiens (-ons)*
        5. *doinsiez* (also *donge*)
Perf.   *donai* Wk/a   I've *done*
Impf.Subj.
        donasse   Fut. *donrai, dorrai, darai*
PP   *doné*

Duire

Pres.Ind. *dui–duis–duit–duions*–duiiez–duient*
Pres.Subj.
        1. *duie* 4. *duiiens (-ons)* 5. *duiiez*
Perf.   *duis* St/s   I've *dui*

Impf.Subj.	Impf.Ind.
duisisse	*duisoie*
PP *duit*	Pres.Part. *duisant*
	Fut. *duirai*

ii soon > *i* (§15). The use of the stem *duis-** is soon extended, e.g. PI.5, PS.5 *duisiez*.

Alternative P.2,4,5 and IS in *ss*, e.g. P.2 *duissis* (§69.2.iii).

Eissir, Issir VA i̲/ei(>oi)

Pres.Ind. *is–is–ist–eissons**, *issons**–eissiez, issiez–issent*
Pres.Subj.

	1. *isse* 4. *eissiens (-ons), issiens (-ons)* 5. *eissiez, issiez* 6. *issent*
Perf. *eissi, issi* Wk/i	I've *is*
Impf.Subj.	
eississe, ississe	Fut. *eistrai, istrai*
PP *eissu, issu*	

Weak stems in *-ei* are usually replaced by analogical stems in *-i* before *ei* > *oi*.

Escrivre, Escrire

Pres.Ind. *escrif–escris–escrit–escrivons–escrivez–escrivent*
Pres.Subj.

	1. *escrive* 4. *escrivons*
Perf. *escris* St/s	I've *escrif*
Impf.Subj.	
escrisisse	Fut. *escrivrai, escrirai*
PP *escrit*	

Perfect also with VA i̲/e, e.g. P.2 *escresis* and IS *escresisse*, etc.
Alternative P.2,4,5 and IS in *ss*, e.g. P.2 *escrissis, escressis*.

Ester

Pres.Ind. *estois**–estas, estais–esta, estait–estons–estez–estont*
Pres.Subj.

	1. *estoise**, estace** 3. *estoise, estoist, estace* 4. *estons* 5. *estez*
	6. *estoisent, estacent*
Perf. *estui–esteüs* St/u, *estai* Wk/a	I've *esta*
Impf.Subj.	
esteüsse, estasse	Fut. *esterai*
PP *esté, esteü*	

Distinguish between the verbs *ester* and *estre* (Table 8).

Estovoir (Impersonal) VA ue̲/o > ou

Pres.Ind. 3. *estuet*
Pres.Subj.

	3. *estuisse, estuist, estuece*	
Perf. 3. *estut* St/u	Impf.Ind. 3. *estovoit*
Impf.Subj.	
3. *esteüst*	Fut. 3. *estovra*
PP *esteü*	

Like *plovoir*, except for palatal stems in the present subjunctive.

Faire

Pres.Ind. *faz*, fai–fais–fait–faimes, faisons*–faites–font*
Pres.Subj.

      1. *face**   4. *faciens, façons*   5. *faciez*

Perf.	*fis–feşis* St/s	I've *fai*
Impf.Subj.		Impf.Ind.
	feşisse	*faisoie*
PP	*fait*	Pres.Part.
		faisant
		Fut. *ferai*

  ai (+ cons.) soon also spelt *ei* or *e* (§12), e.g. Impf. 3 *feisoit*, Pl.3 *fet*.

Falir, Faillir

Pres.Ind. *fail*–fals > faus–falt > faut–falons, faillons*–falez, failliez–falent, faillent*
Pres.Subj.

      1. *faille**   4. *failliens (-ons)*   5. *failliez*

Perf.	*fali, failli* Wk/i	I've *fail*
Impf. Subj.		
	faillisse	Fut. *faldrai > faudrai*
PP	*fali, failli*	

Ferir VA ie/e

Pres.Ind. *fier–fiers–fiert–ferons–ferez–fierent*
Pres.Subj.

      1. *fiere*   4. *feriens (-ons)*   5. *feriez*   5. *fierent*   (also *fierge*)

Perf.	*feri* Wk/i	I've *fier*
Impf.Subj.		
	ferisse	Fut. *ferrai*
PP	*feru*	

Foïr, Fuïr (to flee)

Pres.Ind. *fui–fuis–fuit–fuions*–fuiiez–fuient*
Pres.Subj.

      1. *fuie*   4. *fuiiens (-ons)*   5. *fuiiez*

Perf.	*foï, fuï* Wk/i	I've *fui*
Impf.Subj.		
	foïsse, fuïsse	Fut. *fuirai*
PP	*foï, fuï*	

  fui, fui- = 1 syll.; *fuï, fuï-* = 2 sylls.; *ii* soon > *i* (§15).

Garir

Class II. Extra future: *garrai*. Extra perfect: *garis–garesis* St/s.

Gesir, Gisir

Pres.Ind. *gis–gis–gist–gisons*–gisiez–gisent*
Pres.Subj.

      1. *gise*   4. *gisiens (-ons)*   5. *gisiez*

Perf.   *jui–geüs* St/u   I've *gis*
Impf.Subj.
         geüsse   Fut. *gerrai, girrai*
PP   *geü*
  j replaces *g* before *-u* in P.1,3,6.

Guerpir

Class II or III, e.g. Pr.Ind. *guerp–guers–guert–guȩrpons* etc., or *guerpis–guerpis–guerpist–guerpissons*, etc.

Haḍir > Haïr VA ȩ/a

Pres.Ind. *haz*, hé–hez–het–haons–haez–héent*
Pres.Subj.
         1. *hace** 4. *haciens, haçons* 5. *haciez*
or   1. *hée* 4. *haons* 5. *haez* 6. *héent*
Perf.   *haï* Wk/i   I've *hé*
Impf.Subj.
         haïsse   Fut. *harrai, harai*
PP   *haï*
  Occasional Cl.II forms are found, e.g. PI.6 *haïssent*.

Joḍir > Joïr

Pres.Ind. *joi*–joz–jot–joons–joez–joent*
Pres.Subj.
         1. *joie** 4. *joiiens (-ons)* 5. *joiiez*
Perf.   *joï* Wk/i   I've *joi*
Impf.Subj.
         joïsse   Fut. *jorai, joïrai*
PP   *joï*
  joi, joi- = 1 syll.; *joï, joï-*(*<joḍi*) = 2 sylls.; *ii* soon > *i* (§15).
  After 1150 additional forms are built on the stem *joi-*, e.g. PI.3 *joit*, Pres.Pt. *joiant*.
  Occasional Cl.II PI and PS forms are found, e.g. PI.1 *joïs*, PI.4 *joïssons*, PS.1 *joïsse*.

Join(d)re

Pres.Ind. *joing–joinz–joint–joignons*–joigniez–joignent*
Pres.Subj.
         1. *joigne* 4. *joigniens (-ons)* 5. *joigniez*
Perf.   *joins* St/s   I've *joing*
Impf.Subj.
         joinsisse   Fut. *joindrai*
PP   *joint*

Laiier > Laier, Laire

Pres.Ind. *lai–laies, lais–laie, lait–laions*–laiiez–laient*
Pres.Subj.
         lai–lais–lait, laie–laions–laiiez–laient

Perf.   *laiai* Wk/a   I've *lai, laie*
Impf.Subj.

      laiasse   Fut. *lairai, lerrai*
PP   *laié*
   ii soon > *i* (§15); *ai* (+cons.) occasionally spelt *ei* or *e* (§12), e.g. F.1 *leirai*,
PI.3 *let*.
   Laier is used as an alternative to *laissier* (see below), especially in the future
and conditional. The rare PI.3 *laist* may combine *lait* and *laisse*.

Laissier
Pres.Ind. *lais–laisses–laisse–laissons*–laissiez–laissent*
Pres.Subj.

      lais–lais–laist–laissons–laissiez–laissent
   Regular (but see §§72, 73) except for an extra I've 2: *lais*.
   ai (+cons.) soon also spelt *ei* or *e* (§12), e.g. Inf. *leissier*, PS.3 *lest*.
   See note on *laier* (above).

Leisir > Loisir (Impersonal)
Pres.Ind. 3. *loist*   Impf. Sub. 3. *leüst*
Pres.Subj.

      3. *loise*   PP   *leü*
Perf.   3. *lut* St/u

Lire
Pres.Ind. *li–lis–lit–lisons*–lisiez–lisent*
Pres.Subj.

      1. *lise*   4. *lisiens (-ons)*   5. *lisiez*
Perf.   *lui–leüs* St/u, *lis–leșis* St/s
Impf.Subj.

      leüsse, lesisse   I've *lis*
PP   *leü, lit*   Fut. *lirai*

Luisir, Luire
Pres.Ind. *luis–luis–luist, luit–luisons*–luisiez–luisent*
Pres.Subj.

      1. *luise*   4. *luisiens (-ons)*   5. *luisiez*
Perf.   *luisi* Wk/i, *luis* St/s   I've *luis*
Impf.Subj.

      luisisse   Fut. *luirai*
PP   *luit*
   Alternative P.2,4,5 and IS in *ss*, e.g. P.2 *luissis* (§69.2.iii).

Manoir, Main(d)re VA ai/a
Pres.Ind. *maing*, main–mains–maint–manons–manez–mainent*
Pres.Subj.

      1. *maigne**   4. *maigniens (-ons)*   5. *maigniez*
Perf.   *mes–masis, mesis* St/s, *mains* St/s

Impf.Subj.

    masisse, mainsisse   I've *main*

PP   *manu, masu, mes*   Fut. *mandrai, maindrai*

Mol(d)re > Mou(d)re VA ue/o > ou

Pres.Ind. *muel, mueil*–muels > mueus–muelt > mueut–molons–molez–muelent*
Pres.Subj.

       1. *muele*   4. *molons*   5. *molez*   6. *muelent*

   or   1. *mueille**   4. *mueilliens (-ons)*   5. *mueilliez*

Perf.   *molui* Wk/u   I've *muel*
Impf. Subj.

    molusse   Fut. *moldrai > moudrai*

PP   *molu*

   -ueu- (PI.2,3) can become *-ieu-*. Rare St/s perfect *mols*, PP *mols*.

Morir VA ue/o > ou

Pres.Ind. *muir*–muers–muert–morons–morez–muerent*
Pres.Subj.

       1. *muire**   4. *morons, muiriens (-ons)*   5. *morez, muiriez*   6. *muirent*

       Later: 1. *muere*, etc. (also *muerge*)

Perf.   *morui* Wk/u, *mori* Wk/i   I've *muir*
Impf.Subj.

    morusse, morisse   Fut. *morrai*

PP   *mort*

Movoir VA ue/o > ou

Pres.Ind. *muef–mues–muet–movons–movez–muevent*
Pres.Subj.

       1. *mueve*   4. *movons*   5. *movez*   6. *muevent*

Perf.   *mui–meüs* St/u   I've *muef*
Impf.Subj.

    meüsse   Fut. *movrai*

PP   *meü*

Nais(t)re

Pres.Ind. *nais–nais–naist–naissons*–naissiez–naissent*
Pres.Subj.

       1. *naisse*   4. *naissiens (-ons)*   5. *naissiez*

Perf.   *nasqui* Wk/i[2]   I've *nais*
Impf.Subj.

    nasquisse   Fut. *naistrai*

PP   *nascu, né*

   ai (+cons.) soon also spelt *ei* or *e* (§12), e.g. PI.6 *neissent*, PI.3 *nest*.

Norrir, Norir

Class II or III, Wk/i. Extra perfect: *noris–noresis* St/s.

Nuisir, Nuire

Pres.Ind. *nuis–nuis–nuist, nuit–nuisons*–nuisiez–nuisent*
Pres.Subj.
     1. *nuise*   4. *nuisiens (-ons)*   5. *nuisiez*
Perf.   *nui–neüs* St/u, *nuis* St/s   I've *nuis*
Impf.Subj.
     neüsse, nuisisse   Fut. *nuirai*
PP   *neüt, nuit*

Ociḍre > Ocire

Pres.Ind. *oci–ociz–ocit*, etc. St/s perfect: *ocis–oceșis*, etc.
  Extra future: *ocirrai*.

Oḍir > Oïr

Pres.Ind. *oi*–oz–ot–oons–oez–oent*
Pres.Subj.
     1. *oie**   4. *oiiens (-ons)*   5. *oiiez*
Perf.   *oï–oïs–oï* Wk/i   I've *o, oz, oi*
Impf.Subj.
     oïsse   Fut. *orrai, orai*
PP   *oï*
  oi, oi- = 1 syll.; *oï, oï-* (*<oḍi*) = 2 sylls.
  ii soon > *i* (§15).
  After 1150 additional forms are built on the stem *oi*, e.g. PI.6 *oient*, I've 5 *oiez*.

Ofrir, Offrir

Like *covrir*. Occasional Pr.Ind. *ofre–ofres–ofre–ofrons*, etc.

Pais(t)re

Like *naistre*, except for St/u perfect: *poi–peüs*, Impf.Sub. *peüsse* and PP *peü*.

Pareis(t)re > Parois(t)re

Like *creistre*, but uses the Wk/u perfect and, at times, the Impf.Subj. and PP of
paroir (see below), similar in meaning, e.g. P.1 *parui*.

Paroir VA e/a

Pres.Ind. *pair*, per–pers–pert–parons–parez–perent*
Pres.Subj.
     1. *paire*, pere*   4. *parons*   5. *parez*   6. *pairent, perent*   (also *perge*)
Perf.   *parui* Wk/u   I've *per*
Impf.Subj.
     parusse   Fut. *parrai*
PP   *paru*
  ai (+cons.) soon also spelt *ei* (§12), e.g. PS.1 *peire*.
  Used as an alternative to *pareistre*, especially in the perfect.

Plain(d)re

Pres.Ind. *plaing–plainz–plaint–plaignons*–plaigniez–plaignent*
Pres.Subj.
      1. *plaigne* 4. *plaigniens (-ons)* 5. *plaigniez* (also *plange*)
Perf.   *plains* St/s   I've *plaing*
Impf.Subj.
    plainsisse   Fut. *plaindrai*
PP   *plaint*

Plaisir, Plaire

Pres.Ind. *plaz**, *plais–plais–plaist–plaisons*–plaisiez–plaisent*
Pres.Subj.
      1. *place** 4. *placiens, plaçons* 5. *placiez*
or   1. *plaise* 4. *plaisiens (-ons)* 5. *plaisiez*
Perf.   *ploi–pleüs* St/u   I've *plais*
Impf.Subj.
    pleüsse   Fut. *plairai*
PP   *pleü*
    ai (+cons.) soon also spelt *ei* or *e* (§12), e.g. PS.3 *pleise*, PI.3 *plest*.

Plovoir (Impersonal) VA ue/o > ou

Pres.Ind. 3. *pluet* 6. *pluevent*

Pres.Subj.	Impf.Ind.
3. *plueve*	3. *plovoit*
Perf. 3. *plut* St/u	Pres.Part.
Impf.Subj.	*plovant*
3. *pleüst*	Fut. 3. *plovra*
PP *pleü*	

Poḍeir > Pooir VA ue/o > ou

Pres.Ind. *puis*–puez–puet–poons–poez–pueent*
Pres.Subj.
      1. *puisse** 3. *puisse, puist* 4. *puissiens (-ons)* 5. *puissiez*
Perf.   *poi–peüs* St/u   I've —
Impf.Subj.   Pres.Part.
    peüsse   *poänt, puissant*
PP   *peü*   Fut. *porrai*

Prendre

Pres.Ind. *preing**, *pren–prenz–prent–prenons–preṇez–prenent*
Pres.Subj.
      1. *preigne** 4. *prenons, preigniens (-ons)* 5. *prenez, preigniez*
      6. *preignent* (also *prenge*)
Perf.   *pris–preṣis* St/s   I've *pren*
Impf.Subj.
    preṣisse   Fut. *prendrai*
PP   *pris*
    PI stems in *-d* appear in dialects, e.g. PI.4 *prendons*.
    Later also *prandre*, present stems *pran-*, *praigne-**.

Querre VA <u>ie</u>/e

Pres.Ind. *quier–quiers–quiert–querons–querez–quierent*
Pres.Subj.
      1. *quiere*   4. *querons*   5. *querez*   6. *quierent* (also *quierge*)
Perf.   *quis–quesis* St/s   I've *quier*
Impf.Subj.
      quesisse   Fut. *querrai*
PP   *quis*

Receivre > Reçoivre, Recevoir VA <u>ei > oi</u>/e

Pres.Ind. *reçoif, reçoi–reçois–reçoit–recevons–recevez–reçoivent*
Pres.Subj.
      1. *reçoive*   4. *recevons*   5. *recevez*   6. *reçoivent*
Perf.   *reçui–receüs* St/u   I've *reçoif*
Impf. Subj.
      receusse   Fut. *recevrai*
PP   *receü*

Reḍem(b)re > Raem(b)re, Raiem(b)re, Raein(d)re, etc. VA <u>ie</u>/e

Pres.Ind. *raiem–raiens–raient–raemons–raemez–raiement*
Pres.Subj.
      1. *raieme*   4. *raemons*   5. *raemez*   6. *raiement*
Perf.   *raens, raiens* St/s   I've *raiem*
Impf.Subj.
      raensisse, raiensisse   Fut. *raembrai, raiembrai*
PP   *reent, raent, raient*, etc.
  Many variations possible, e.g. PI.5 *raembez*.

Remanoir, Remain(d)re

Like *manoir*, but perfect: *remes–remesis* St/s, *remains* St/s.
Extra PP *remasu, remanoit*.

Respondre

Pres.Ind. *respoing*, respon–responz–respont–respondons–respondez–respondent*
Pres.Subj.
      1. *respoigne**   4. *respoigniens (-ons)*   5. *respoigniez*
  or   1. *responde*   4. *respondons*
Perf.   *respondi* Wk/i², also P.3 *respost*   I've *respont*
Impf. Subj.
      respondisse   Fut. *respondrai*
PP   *respondu, respons*
  Forms also found without *-d* ≠ *repon(d)re*, e.g. PI.6 *responent*.

Savoir VA <u>e</u>/a

Pres.Ind. *sai*–ses–set–savons–savez–sevent*
Pres.Subj.
      1. *sache**   4. *sachiens (-ons)*   5. *sachiez*

Perf.   *soi–seüs* St/u

Impf.Subj.

    seüsse

PP   *seü*

I've 1. *sachez*

    4. *sachiens*   5. *sachiez*

Pres.Part.

    savant, sachant

Fut. *savrai, sarai*

Seḍeir > Seoir VA ie/e (Pres.Subj. also i/ei)

Pres.Ind. *sié–siez–siet–seons–seez–siéent*

Pres.Subj.

    1. *siée* 4. *seons* 5. *seez* 6. *siéent*

  or   1. *sië* 4. *seiiens (-ons)* 5. *seiiez* 6. *siënt*

Perf.   *sis–seṣis* St/s

Impf.Subj.

    seṣisse

PP   *sis*

I've *sié*

Fut. *serrai*

  ii soon > *i* (§15).

Semon(d)re, Somon(d)re

Pres.Ind. *semoing*, semon–semons–semont–semonons–semonez–semonent*

Pres.Subj.

    1. *semoigne** 4. *semonons, semoigniens (-ons)* 5. *semonez, semoigniez*

    6. *semoignent* (also *semonge*)

Perf.   *semons* St/s

Impf.Subj.

    semonsisse

PP   *semons*

I've *semon*

Fut. *semondrai*

  Alternative stem: *somon-*.

Sivre, Siure, Sivir, etc.

Pres.Ind. *siu–sius–siut–sevons, sivons–sevez, sivez–sivent, siuent*

Pres.Subj.

    1. *sive* 4. *sevons* 5. *sevez* 6. *sivent*

  or   1. *siue* 4. *sivons* 5. *sivez* 6. *siuent*

Perf.   *sivi* Wk/i[2], *sui–seüs* St/u

Impf.Subj.

    sivisse, seüsse

PP   *sivi, seü*

I've *siu*

Fut. *sevrai, sivrai, siurai*

  The triple stem changes iu,iv/ev (PI.1,6,4 *siu, sivent, sevons*) led to an extended use of the stressed stems (with variations like *ui-, uiv-*). Some examples are given above.

Sofrir, Soffrir

Like *covrir*. Occasional Pr.Ind. *sofre–sofres–sofre–sofrons*, etc.

Sol(d)re > Sou(d)re

Pres.Ind. *soil*, sols–sols > sous–solt > sout–solons–solez–solent*

Pres.Subj.

    1. *soille** 4. *soilliens (-ons)* 5. *soilliez*

Perf.   *sols > sous* St/s   I've *sol*
Impf.Subj.
       solsisse > sousisse   Fut. *soldrai > soudrai*
PP   *solt > sout, sols > sous, solu*

Sordre

Pres.Ind. *sort–sorz–sort–sordons–sordez–sordent*
Pres.Subj.
      1. *sorde* 4. *sordons* (also *sorge*)
Perf.   *sors* St/s   I've *sort*
Impf.Subj.
      sorsisse   Fut. *sordrai*
PP   *sors*
  Occasional stems: *sorg-, sorj-*, e.g. PI.6 *sorgent*, Pres. Part. *sorjant*.

Tenir VA ie/e

Pres.Ind. *tieng*, tien–tiens–tient–tenons–tenez–tienent*
Pres.Subj.
      1. *tiegne** 4. *tiegniens (-ons)* 5. *tiegniez* (also *tienge, tenge*)
Perf.   *tin–tenis–tint–tenimes–tenistes–tindrent, tinrent* St/i
Impf.Subj.
      tenisse   I've *tien*
PP   *tenu*   Fut. *tendrai*
  The palatalised stem *tie-gn-* can also be spelt *tie-ign* or *tie-ngn*.
  The stems *teign*, taign-** are analogical (cf. v. *prendre*).

Tol(d)re > Tou(d)re, Tolir

Pres.Ind. *toil*, tol–tols > tous–tolt > tout–tolons–tolez–tolent*
Pres.Subj.
      1. *toille** 4. *toilliens (-ons)* 5. *toilliez*
  or   1. *tole* 4. *tolons* (also *tolge > touge*)
Perf.   *toli* Wk/i, *tols > tous* St/s, *tolui* Wk/u
Impf.Subj.
      tolisse, tolsisse > tousisse, tolusse   I've *tol*
                             Fut. *toldrai > toudrai*
PP   *tolu, toleit > toloit, tolt > tout*

Tordre

Like *sordre*, but no stems in *g,j*. Occasional stressed stems in *-ue*, e.g. PI.3 *tuert*, or in *-t*, from the earlier infinitive *tortre*, e.g. PI.6 *tortent*. Extra PP *tort*.

Torner

PS.2 *torz*, PS.3 *tort* (§73). Extra future: *torrai* (§66.7a).

Traire

Pres.Ind. *trai–trais–trait–traions*–traiiez, traites–traient*
Pres.Subj.
      1. *traie* 4. *traiiens (-ons)* 5. *traiiez*

Perf.   *trais* St/s   I've *trai*
Impf.Subj.
         traisisse   Fut. *trairai*
PP   *trait*
   ii soon > *i* (§15); *ai* (+cons.) soon also spelt *ei* or *e* (§12), e.g. Inf. *treire*, PP.
tret.
   Alternative P.2,4,5 and IS in *ss*, e.g. P.2 *traissis* (§69.2.iii).

Trover VA ue/o > ou

Pres.Ind. *truis*–trueves–trueve–trovons–trovez–truevent*
Pres.Subj.
         1. *truisse** 3. *truisse, truist* 4. *trovons, truissiens (-ons)* 5. *trovez,*
         truissiez 6. *truissent* (Later: 1. *trueve*, etc.)
Perf.   *trovai* Wk/a   I've *truisse*
Impf.Subj.
         trovasse   Fut. *troverai*
PP   *trové*

Valoir

Pres.Ind. *vail*, val–vals > vaus–valt > vaut–valons, vaillons*–valez, vailliez–*
         valent, vaillent
Pres.Subj.
         1. *vaille** 4. *vailliens (-ons)* 5. *vailliez*
Perf.   *valui* Wk/u, *vals > vaus* St/s   I've —
Impf.Subj.
         valusse, valsisse > vausisse   Fut. *valdrai > vaudrai*
PP   *valu*

Veḍeir > Veoir VA ei > oi/e

Pres.Ind. *voi*–voiz–voit–veons–veez–voient*
Pres.Subj.
         1. *voie** 4. *veons, voiiens (-ons)* 5. *veez, voiiez* 6. *voient*
I've   1 *voi* 4. *veons* 5. *veez, vez*
Perf.   *vi–veïs–vit–veïmes–veïstes–virent* St/i
Impf.Subj.   Pres.Part.
         veïsse   *veant, voiant*
PP   *veü, vis*   Fut. *verrai*
   -eï- (< *eḍi*) = 2 sylls.; *ii* soon > *i* (§15).

Vein(t)re (13th c. *Veincre*)

Pres.Ind. *venc, veinc–veinz–veint–venquons, veinquons–venquez, veinquez–*
         venquent, veinquent
Pres.Subj.
         1. *venque* 4. *venquons*
   or   1. *veinque* 4. *venquons* 5. *venquez* 6. *veinquent*
Perf.   *venqui* Wk/i²   I've *veinc*
Impf.Subj.
         venquisse   Fut. *veintrai*
PP   *vencu, veincu*   (13th c. *veincrai*)

qu- replaces *c-* before *e*, *i*, and often ≠ before *a* or *o*, thus PI.4 *vencons* or *venquons*.

-ai can replace *-ei*, e.g. Inf. *vain(t)re*, PI.3 *vaint*.

Vestir

Class III, PI.2 *vez*, PI.3 *vest* (§73) Wk/i perfect. Additional PP *vestu*.

Vivre

Pres.Ind. *vif–vis–vit–vivons–vivez–vivent*
Pres.Subj.

	1. *vive* 4. *vivons*		
Perf.	*vesqui* Wk/i[2]	I've	*vif*
Impf.Subj.			
	vesquisse	Fut.	*vivrai*
PP	*vescu*		

Voloir VA <u>ue</u>/o > ou

Pres.Ind. *voil*, vueil*, vuel–vuels > vueus, vues–vuelt > vueut, vuet–volons–*
          volez–vuelent, volent
Pres.Subj.
          1. *vueille**   4. *voilliens (-ons), vueilliens (-ons)* 5. *voilliez, vueilliez*
          6. *vueillent*
I've   1. *vueilles* 4. *vueilliens (-ons)* 5. *vueillez*
Perf.   *voil, vol–volis–volt > vout–volimes–volistes–voldrent > voudrent* St/i,
        vols > vous St/s, *voli, volsi > vousi* Wk/i
Impf.Subj.

	volisse, volsisse > vousisse	Pres.Part.	*volant, voillant,*
PP	*volu*		*vueillant*
		Fut.	*voldrai > voudrai*

-ueu- (PI.2,3) can become *-ieu-*.
Alternative Pres.Subj. and I've stems: *voill-, vuell-*.
Alternative St/s P.2,4,5 and IS in *ss*, e.g. P.2 *voussis* (§69.2.iii).

2. Other irregular verbs

amer : see Table 10.
aperceivre > aperçoivre, apercevoir: like *receivre*, etc.
araisnier: see Table 11.
atain(d)re* : like *plaindre*.
avoir : see Table 7.
beivre > boivre : see Table 6.
conceivre > conçoivre, concevoir: like *receivre*, etc.
constuire : like *duire*.
deceivre > deçoivre, decevoir: like *receivre*, etc.
deraisnier, desraisnier : see Table 11.
destrain(d)re* : like *plaindre*.
destruire : like *duire*.

disner : see Table 11.
estein(d)re : like *ceindre*.
es(t)re : see Table 8.
estrain(d)re* : like *plaindre*.
fein(d)re : like *ceindre*.
frain(d)re :* like *plaindre*. Extra PP: *frait*.
garder : Class 1, abbreviated I've 2: *gar*.
irais(t)re : like *naistre*.
issir : see *eissir*.
jalir, jaillir : like *falir, faillir*.
mangier : see Table 11.
oin(d)re : like *joindre*.
ovrir : like *covrir*.
parler : see Table 11.
pein(d)re : like *ceindre*.
perceivre > perçoivre, percevoir : like *receivre*.
poin(d)re : like *joindre*.
prover : like *trover*.
rover : like *trover*.
salir, saillir : like *falir, faillir*.
soloir : like *doloir*.
taisir, taire : like *plaisir, plaire*.
terdre : like *sordre*.
venir : like *tenir*.
veoir : see *vedeir > veoir*.
    * or like *ceindre*, with stem in *-ein-*.

3. Irregular compounds

The following prefixes are frequently used to modify the meaning of verbs:

> *a, as, com con, contre, de, des, en, entre, es, for, mal > mau, mes, par, por, pro, re, sor.*

These prefixes have a wide variety of meanings (for *re-* see §193); a dictionary study of verbs listed with these prefixes will give some idea of their use.

The compounds given below are conjugated like their stem verb.

cheoir, chaoir, etc.: *escheoir, mescheoir,* etc.
coillir : *acoillir, recoillir.*
conoistre : *mesconoistre, reconoistre.*
croire : *mescroire, recroire.*
croistre : *acroistre, decroistre, escroistre.*
dire : *contredire, desdire, entredire, mesdire.* Also *maudire* (with some forms in *-iss*).
duire : *aduire, conduire, deduire, reduire.*
ester : *arester, rester* (P.3 in *-ut*, etc., but many forms remodelled on Cl.1).
faire : *contrefaire, desfaire, forfaire, malfaire, mesfaire, parfaire.*
ferir : *aferir, s'entreferir.*
joir : *esjoir.*
lire : *eslire.*

manoir, maindre : parmanoir, remanoir, etc.
moldre > moudre : esmoldre, etc.
movoir : esmovoir, removoir.
plaindre : complaindre.
prendre : emprendre, entreprendre, esprendre, mesprendre, porprendre, sorprendre.
querre : aquerre, conquerre, enquerre, porquerre, requerre.
saillir : assaillir, tressaillir.
seoir : asseoir.
sivre, etc.: *aconsivre, consivre, ensivre, parsivre, porsivre,* etc.
soldre > soudre : assoldre, dissoldre, resoldre, etc.
tenir : contretenir, maintenir, retenir, etc.
toldre > toudre : destoldre, etc.
traire : atraire, detraire, portraire, retraire, sostraire.
valoir : contrevaloir.
venir : avenir, co(n)venir, mesavenir, parvenir, revenir, etc.
veoir : porveoir, reveoir.
vestir : fervestir, revestir.

Key to exercises

Note on translations: Phrases for translation in Chapters 7–10 are taken from literary texts. The suggested translation fits the context in each case, but is not necessarily the only version possible.

Chapter 1

(a)

NS	*li rois*	*li frere*	*uns traître*	*une novele*
OS	*le roi*	*le frere*	*un traïtor*	*une novele*
NP	*li roi*	*li frere*	*un traïtor*	*unes noveles*
OP	*les rois*	*les freres*	*uns traïtors*	*unes noveles*
NS	*la clamor(s)*	*Eve*		
OS	*la clamor*	*Evain*		
NP	*les clamors*			
OP	*les clamors*			

(b) *li maistre, les paroles, les serors, li lion, li baron, li païs, les flors.*

(c) *la mere, uns pelerins, Charles, li pere, une loi(s), Berte, uns trovere.*

(d) *les maisons, uns livres, les seignors, les nonains, unes letres, les paiens.*

(e) 1. *Li provoire oient les voiz.* 2. *Li frere fierent les traïtors.* 3. *Or voient les serors les maistres.* 4. *'Pelerin! ferez les lions!'* 5. *Or oient li conte les troveors.* 6. *'Seignor! veez les barons!'*

(f) 1. 'Knights! see the queen!' 2. Now the infidels strike. 3. The daughter of the count hears the clamour. 4. Now they hear knights. 5. The nuns see Charles the king. 6. 'Carry the news to the lord!' 7. Now the pilgrim sees the house of the priest.

Chapter 2

(a) *amis, amirauz, anz, chasteaus, chevaus, chiés, cieus, cous, conseuz, corz, cous, dras, dus, dueus, escuz, fiz, ganz, genouz, jorz, monz, nons, oz, periz, piez, poinz, sainz, sans, sers, travauz, vaslez, vassaus, Bernarz, Raous.*

(b) 1. *Li chastel sont sor les monz.* 2. *'Veez les escuz as vaslez!'* 3. *Es nés oient li fil les corz des oz.* 4. *Li cheval sont as amirauz.* 5. *Or oient li troveor les nons des sers.* 6. *Si trenchent as paiens les piez, les poinz, les chiés.*

(c) 1. 'See the saints in the cities!' 2. The duke hears the opinions of the armies. 3. Now the friend strikes the knights. 4. He sees the body at the feet of the count. 5. Bernard has a pair of gloves in the (=his) hand. 6. 'Raoul, see the ships of the emirs!'

Chapter 3

(a) *beaus, blans, bons, chaitis, chaus, chenuz, douz, durs, enfers, fers, frans, freis, froiz, grés, iriez, lars, las, lons, malades, nus, prez, sainz, seus, tarz, tierz, toz, vermeuz, vieuz, vis.*
autre, povre, tendre.
briés, coranz, fous, forz, gentis, granz, loiaus, mortieus, noveaus, puissanz, roiaus, tels (also *tieus, teus*)*, vaillanz, vis.*
graindre, mieudre, pire.
chantez, coverz, escriz, eüz, gariz, ocis, trovez, venuz, chantanz, trenchanz.

(b) *bele, blanche, bone, chaitive, chauve, chenue* (*< chenuḍe*)*, douce, dure, enferme, ferme, franche, fresche, froide, greque, iriee* (*< irieḍe*)*, large, lasse, longe, malade, nule, preste, sainte, seule, tarde, tierce, tote, vermeille, vieille, vive.*
chantee (*< chanteḍe*)*, coverte, escrite, eüe* (*< eüḍe*)*, garie* (*< gariḍe*)*, ocise, trovee* (*< troveḍe*)*, venue* (*< venuḍe*)*, chantant, trenchant.*

(c) *brief, autre, fort, graindre, povre, pire.*

(d) 1. *Une bone suer.* 2. *Nus pire periz.* 3. *Granz est li oz / l'oz.* 4. *Uns sers loiaus e forz.* 5. *Li vieuz dus povre et enfers.* 6. *Li ber est morz et ocis.*

(e) 1. *'Fier, frans chevaliers!'* 2. *Or ot li prestre le brief conseil de la nonain.* 3. *Molt par est puissanz li sire.* 4. *Li pelerins chaitis voit le paien irié.*

Chapter 4

(a) 1. *Cil saintismes hom.* 2. *La soe suer Eve.* 3. *Lor niés chaitis et fous.* 4. *Cist beaus travauz.* 5. *S'amor(s), ceste graindre folie.* 6. *Nostre povre fiz, tes compaing.*

(b) 1. NP. 2. NP. 3. NS. 4. NP. 5. NS / OS. 6. NP. 7. OS / NP. 8. NS / OS.
OP phrases: 1. *Les vostres nons.* 2. *Iceus lons jorz.* 3. *Tes granz merciz.* 4. *Les tuens forz poinz.* 5. *Celes batailles mortieus.* 6. *Mes enfanz trovez.* 7. *Noz vieuz dus loiaus.* 8. *Les toes amies ocises.*

(c) 1. Here you have / Here is his brother, that valiant and noble king! 2. He has found his old father. 3. See these ill and weary lords. 4. His nephew is dead.
1. *Es vos sa seror, cele reïne vaillant e franche!* 2. *Cele a trové la soe vieille mere.* 3. *Veez cez dames enfermes et lasses.* 4. *Morte est sa niece.*

(d) 1. His friends and mine. 2. Ah! noble count, valiant man! 3. The city is mine! ('This city', see §30, would fit the context better.) 4. Bernard my brother, the hoary and the white-haired. 5. The flowers are scarlet from the blood of our barons.

Chapter 5

(a) 1. PI: *dur, dures, dure, durons, durez, durent.*
   PI: *floris, floris, florist, florissons, florissez, florissent.*
   PI: *trai, trais, trait, traions, traiiez, traient.*
   PS: *dur, durs, durt, durons, durez, durent.*
   PS: *florisse, florisses, florisse, florissons, florissez, florissent.*
   PS: *traie, traies, traie, traiiens (traions), traiiez, traient.*
   I've: *dure, durons, durez.*
   I've: *floris, florissons, florissez.*
   I've: *trai, traions, traiiez.*
 2. PI.3 *durẹt,* PS.3 *florissẹt,* PS.3 *traiẹt.*
 3. *laissiez* or *otroiiez* in each case.

(b) 1. *plorant, choississant.*
 2. Early 12th c. imperfect:
   garisseie, garisseies, garisseit, garissiiens, garissiiez, garisseient.
   veḍeie, veḍeies, veḍeit, veḍiiens, veḍiiez, veḍeient.
   Later 12th c. imperfect:
   garissoie, garissoies, garissoit, garissiiens, garissiiez, garissoient.
   veoie, veoies, veoit, veiiens, veiiez, veoient.
 3. *venge, venges, venge, vengiens (venjons), vengiez (-ez), vengent.*

(c) 1. *amai, amas, ama, amames, amastes, amerent.* Wk/a. PP: *amé.*
   aidai, aidas, aida, aidames, aidastes, aidierent. Wk/a². PP: *aidié.*
   oï, oïs, oï, oïmes, oïstes, oïrent. Wk/i. PP: *oï.*
   perdi, perdis, perdié, perdimes, perdistes, perdierent. Wk/i². PP: *perdu.*
   dolui, dolus, dolu, dolumes, dolustes, dolurent. Wk/u. PP: *dolu.*
   vin, venis, vint, venimes, venistes, vindrent. St/i. PP: *venu.*
   mis, mesis, mist, mesimes, mesistes, mistrent (or: *mis, meis,* etc. §69.2). St/s
   (vocalic perf. stem). PP: *mis.*
   crens, crensis, crenst, crensimes, crensistes, crenstrent. St/s (consonant perf.
   stem). PP: *crient.*
   soi, seüs, sot, seümes, seüstes, sorent. St/u (P.1 in -*oi*). PP: *seü.*
   dui, deüs, dut, deümes, deüstes, durent. St/u (P.1 in -*ui*). PP: *deü.*
 2. *dis, deïs, dist, deïmes, deïstes, distrent.*
 3. *aidasse, aidasses, aidast, aidissons (-iens), aidissoiz (-ez, -iez), aidassent.*
   *choisisse, choisisses, choisist, choisissons (-iens), choisissoiz (-ez, -iez),
   choisissent.*
   dolusse, dolusses, dolust, dolussons (-iens), dolussoiz (-ez, -iez), dolussent.
   mesisse, mesisses, mesist, mesissons (-iens), mesissoiz (-ez, -iez), mesissent (or:
   meïsse, etc. §69.2).
   deüsse, deüsses, deüst, deüssons (-iens), deüssoiz (-ez, -iez), deüssent.

(d) 1. *noncerai, nonceras, noncera, noncerons, nonceroiz (-ez), nonceront.*
   dirai, diras, dira, dirons, diroiz (-ez), diront.
 2. *direie, direies, direit, diriiens, diriiez, direient.*
   diroie, diroies, diroit, diriiens, diriiez, diroient.

(e) 1. F.1: *ier, er, serai, estrai.* Impf.2: *ieres, eres, estoies.*
F.5: *avroiz, aroiz*; or *avrez, arez.*
2. *soie, soies, soit, soiiens (soions), soiiez, soient.*
3. Impf.3 or F.3: *(i)ert.* Impf.6 or F.6: *(i)erent.*

Chapter 6

(a) 1. *boivre*: unstressed stem *bev-* (§66.1); VA oi/e; consonant modifications in PI.1 (final $v > f$), PI.2 (Rule 1) and PI.3 (R.2).
2. *soudre*: stem *sol-* (§66.1), with final *-l* palatalised in PI.1 and vocalised in PI.2,3 before consonants.
3. *conoistre*: stem *conoiss-*; consonant modifications in PI.1 (final $ss > s$), PI.2 (final $ss + s > s$) and PI.3 ($ss + t > st$). PI.5 in *-iez* (§67).
4. *pooir*: VA ue/o; stem formerly ended in *-ḍ*; consonant and vowel modifications in PI.1 (palatalised stem), PI.2 ($ḍ + s > z$) and PI.3 ($ḍ + t > t$).
5. *coillir*: VA ue/o; stem ends in *l'* (*-il* when final in PI.1, *-ill* between vowels in PI.4–6); *l'* is vocalised before consonants in PI.2 and 3, with $l' + s > uz$ in PI.2. PI.5 in *-iez* (§67).

(b) 1. *boivre*: unusual use of stressed stem for infinitive. PS.1 *boive*, PS.5 *bevez.*
2. *soudre*: stem *sol-*; $l + r > ldr > udr.$ PS.1 *soille*, PS.5 *soilliez.*
3. *conoistre*: stem *conoiss-*; $ss + r > str$; [s] spelt *ss* between vowels, *s* before a consonant. PS.1 *conoisse*, PS.5 *conoissiez.*
4. *pooir*: early 12th c. *ḍ* has disappeared and *ei* has become *oi*. Normal use of unstressed stem for the infinitive. PS.1 *puisse*, PS.5 *puissiez.*
5. *coillir*: normal use of the unstressed stem in *-o*; intervocalic *l'* spelt *-ill.* PS.1 *cueille*, PS.5 *coilliez* or *cueilliez.*

(c) *pert, perz, pert ; perdez.*
duel, dueus, dueut ; dolez.
joing, joinz, joint ; joigniez.

(d) PS: *lief, lies, liet, levons, levez, lievent.*
PS: *comenz, comenz, comenzt, començons, comenciez, comencent.*
I've: *cuevre, covrons, covrez.*
I've: *reçoif, recevons, recevez.*
I've: *manjue, manjons, mangiez.*

Chapter 7 (see 'Note on translations', p. 168)

(a) 1. The infidels arm themselves to defend themselves.
2. When my lord Gawain sees her
He does not delay to go toward her
And he greets her and she him.
3. As it seems to me.
4. Tristan leans on the rock.
He laments bitterly to himself all alone.
5. And he replies: 'Gawain, be quiet about it.'
6. And he said: 'Knight, you have struck me.'
– 'Truly, he says, I have struck you.'

7. As they did to me.
8. 'Give them up to us, I ask it of you.'
9. Yvain sees to them (=their) tears fall,
   He comes towards them and greets them.
10. 'Mercy! Do not kill me!'
11. Come and rest! (§82)
12. And the duke immediately asks of her
    That she tell (it) to him at once.
13. 'Is he armed?' – 'Indeed, that he is (=yes).'
    – 'I will go (and) speak to him.'
14. He shatters him the (=his) helmet.
15. 'Do you want to make me have it (=the ring)
    By force?' – 'Not that (=no) truly, sweetheart.'

Chapter 8 (see 'Note on translations', p. 168)

1. 'Who killed them?' asks Galahad.
2. I am looking for that, which I cannot find.
3. He (Charlemagne) no longer knows to whom he should give it (the city of Narbonne).
4. Troy, of which Laomedon was king.
5. I do not find anyone who might tell me what love is.
6. I ask you about a city which I see there,
   To whom it belongs (whose it is) and what name it has.
7. Cassandra . . . of whom we have spoken.
8. I am William, the beard of whom (whose beard) you have pulled.
9. They will hear something about which they will be distressed.
10. I hate the hour in which (§101) I am alive.
11. There is not one, who has not a castle or a city.
12. God! What shall I do? Why do I live so long?
    Why is death delaying? What is it waiting for?

Chapter 9 (see 'Note on translations', p. 168)

1. All the birds were singing.
2. Poverty makes many a man foolish.
3. To each, whoever he may be.
4. He who serves a scoundrel wastes his time.
5. You will tell the queen something similar.
6. She did not ever wake anyone there / She never woke anyone there. (Or, more likely, with *nului* NS: No one ever woke there.)
7. All that they see pleases them greatly.
8. I have no need to love another.
9. One cannot find (no one can find, §138) food here.
10. I do not know what else to say about it.
11. No one asked for a supply of anything, whatever it might be.
12. Alexander, who showed his wrath to so many princes.
13. Some killed and the majority drowned.

14. Whatsoever way I may follow / Wherever I may go.
15. The news was not pleasing to some / did not please some.
16. You should have seen him hurl one (down) dead on the other!

Chapter 10 (see 'Note on translations', p. 168)

1. Roland now laughs about it. (See §187.)
2. He went quickly back again.
3. Again they will have Orange, my city.
4. Now the wretch is probably drunk.
5. He makes the knights draw back.
6. He loves more basely (=a woman of lower rank).
7. St Peter left with a rapid step / quickly.
8. William, do sit down. – I will not do (it), (my) lord.
9. There will never again be a day when (§101) Charles will not lament.
10. His sweetheart, who will be sold very dearly to him.
11. Tristan did not ever love so cordially / Tristan never loved so sincerely.
12. There is an armed knight outside.
13. With drawn sword he came to the convent.
14. Have I come too early now?
15. She lay down completely naked.
16. William hears it, he is almost out of his mind.

Old French texts

1. **CHRÉTIEN DE TROYES: YVAIN** *c.* 1175

Lunete helps Yvain to marry her mistress Laudine, but soon after the wedding
Yvain leaves for King Arthur's court, failing to return on the agreed date, and
Laudine refuses to see him again. Here Yvain succumbs to remorse and grief
near Laudine's castle, unaware that Lunete, accused of treachery for having
encouraged the marriage, is imprisoned in a small chapel near by.

   This blend of adventure and analysis is typical of Chrétien's Arthurian
romances, which show a skilful handling of dialogue and verse.

> Que que il ainsi se demente,
> Une chaitive, une dolente
> Estoit en la chapele enclose,
> Qui vit et oï ceste chose
> Par le mur, qui estoit crevez.   5
> Maintenant qu'il fu relevez
> De pasmoisons, si l'apela.
> 'Des!' fait ele, 'cui oi je la?
> Qui est, qui se demente si?'
> Et cil li respont: 'Et vos, qui?'   10
> 'Je sui', fait ele, 'une chaitive,
> La plus dolente riens, qui vive.'
> Et il respont: 'Tais, fole riens!
> Tes dueus est joie, tes maus biens
> Envers le mien, dont je languis.   15
> Tant com li om a plus apris
> A delit et a joie vivre,
> Plus le desvoie et plus l'enivre
> Dueus, quant il l'a, que un autre ome.
> Uns faibles om porte la some   20
> Par us et par acostumance,
> Qu'uns autre de graignor puissance
> Ne porteroit por nule rien.'
> 'Par foi!', fait ele, 'je sai bien,
> Que c'est parole tote voire;   25
> Mais por ce ne fait mie a croire,

Que vos aiiez plus mal de moi;
Et por ce mie ne le croi,
Qu'il m'est avis, que vos poez
Aler, quel part que vos volez,   30
Et je sui ci emprisonee,
Si m'est teus faeisons donee,
Que demain serai çaenz prise
Et livree a mortel juïse.'
'Ha, Des!' fait il, 'por quel forfait?'   35
'Sire chevaliers! ja Des n'ait
De l'ame de mon cors merci,
Se je l'ai mie desservi!
Et neporquant je vos dirai
Le voir, que ja n'en mentirai,   40
Por quoi je sui ci en prison:
L'on m'apele de traïson,
Ne je ne truis, qui m'en defende,
Que l'on demain ne m'arde ou pende.'
'Or primes', fait il, 'puis je dire   45
Que li miens dueus et la moie ire
A la vostre dolor passee;
Qu'estre porriiez delivree,
Par cui que soit, de cest peril.
Don ne porroit ce estre?' – 'Oïl;   50
Mais je ne sai encor, par cui.
Il ne sont el monde que dui,
Qui osassent, por moi defendre,
Vers trois homes bataille emprendre.'
'Comment? por Dé! sont il donc troi?' 55
'Oïl, sire! a la moie foi.
Troi sont, qui traître me claiment.'
'Et qui sont cil, qui tant vos aiment,
Dont li uns si hardiz seroit,
Qu'a trois combatre s'oseroit,   60
Por vos sauver et garantir?'
'Je le vos dirai sans mentir:
Li uns est mes sire Gauvains,
Et li autre mes sire Yvains,
Por cui demain serai a tort   65
Livree a martire de mort.'

2.   VILLEHARDOUIN: LA CONQUESTE DE
CONSTANTINOPLE *c.* 1210

Geoffrey de Villehardouin, Marshal of Champagne, gives a vivid eye-witness
account in this work of the events before and during the fourth crusade (1202–4)
which ended with the capture of Constantinople. This excerpt describes the
departure from Venice and the siege of Zara.

Adonc furent departies les nés et li huissier por
les barons. Ha, Diex! tant bon destrier i ot mis! Et
quant les nés furent chargiées d'armes et de vïandes
et de chevaliers et de serjanz, et li escu furent pendu
et portendu environ des borz et des chastiax des nés,   5
si drecierent les banieres dont il avoient tant de
beles. Et sachiez que il porterent es nés de perrieres
et de mangoniax plus de CCC et toz les engins qui ont
mestier a vile prendre a grant plenté, ne onques plus
bele estoire ne parti de nul port; et ce fu as huitieves   10
de la saint Remi, en l'an de l'incarnacïon Jhesu Christ
M et CC et II anz. Ainsi partirent del port de Venise,
com vos avez oï.
    La veille de la saint Martin vindrent devant Gadres
en Esclavonie, si virent la cité fermee de hauz murs   15
et de hautes torz, et por nient demandissiez plus bele
ne plus fort ne plus riche. Et quant li pelerin la
virent, il se merveillierent mult et distrent li uns
a l'autre: 'Comment porroit estre prise tel vile par
force, se Diex meïsmes nel fait?' Les premieres nés   20
vindrent devant la vile et aancrerent et atendirent
les autres et al matin fist molt bel jor et molt cler,
et vindrent les galies totes et li huissier et les
autres nés qui estoient arrieres, et pristrent le port
par force et rompirent la chaaine qui molt ere forz et   25
bien atornee, et descendirent a terre, si que li porz
fu entre eus et la vile. Lor veïssiez maint chevalier
et maint serjant issir des nés et maint bon destrier
traire des huissiers, et maint riche tref et maint bel
paveillon.   30
    Ainsi se loja l'oz et fu Gadres assegiée le jor de
la saint Martin . . . L'endemain de la saint Martin
issirent de ceus de Gadres et vindrent parler le duc
de Venise qui ere en son paveillon, et li distrent que
il li rendroient la cité et totes les lor choses saus   35
lor cors en sa merci. Et li dus dist qu'il n'en
prendroit mie cestui plait ne autre, se par le conseil
non as contes et as barons, et qu'il en iroit a eus
parler.

3.   LE CHÂTELAIN DE COUCI: CHANSON DE
CROISADE 1189?

Renowned as a lyric poet and great lover, the Châtelain de Couci took part in both the third and fourth crusades. This song, a sincere expression of the courtly love of the later twelfth century, may already have been written before the third crusade in 1189. During the fourth crusade, according to Villehardouin, soon after the fleet left Andros in 1203 'they suffered a great misfortune, for a nobleman of high standing in the army, Guy, Châtelain de Couci, died and was buried at sea.'

     A vos, amant, plus qu'a nule autre gent
     Est bien raison que ma dolor complaigne,
     Car il m'estuet partir outreement
     Et dessevrer de ma loial compaigne;
     Et quant la pert, n'est rien qui me remaigne.   5
     Et sachiez bien, amors, seürement,
     S'ainc nus moru por avoir cuer dolent,
     Ja mais par moi n'ert meüz vers ne lais . . .

     Par Dieu, amors, grief m'est a consirer
     Del grant solaz et de la compaignie   10
     Et des deduiz que me soloit mostrer
     Cele qui m'ert dame, compaigne, amie;
     Et quant recort sa simple cortoisie,
     Et les douz moz dont sot a moi parler,
     Comment me puet li cuers el cors durer?   15
     Quant ne s'en part, certes, trop est mauvais . . .

     Je m'en vois, dame; a Dieu le creator
     Comant vo cors, en quel lieu que je soie;
     Ne sai se ja verroiz mais mon retor:
     Aventure est que ja mais vos revoie.   20
     Por Dieu vos pri, ou que tiegne ma voie,
     Que voz covenz tenez, viegne ou demor;
     Et je pri Dieu qu'ainsi me doint honor
     Com je vos ai esté amis verais.

Authors and works quoted

Reference numbers, unless indicated otherwise, apply to lines, e.g. Ad.731.

v = a listed variant of the phrase quoted, e.g. Tr.687.v.
C.F.M.A. = *Classiques Français de Moyen Age.*
S.A.T.F. = *Société des Anciens Textes Français.*

Ad. *Le Mystère d'Adam*, ed. by P. Studer (Manchester, 1918).

Al. *Aliscans*, ed. by F. Guessard and A. de Montaiglon (Paris, 1870).

Alex. *La Vie de saint Alexis*, ed. by G. Paris, *C.F.M.A.* (Paris, 1903).

Auc. *Aucassin et Nicolette*, ed. by M. Roques, *C.F.M.A.* (Paris, 1929). (Numbers refer to section.)

Ay. *Aymeri de Narbonne*, ed. by L. Demaison, *S.A.T.F.* (Paris, 1887).

Ch.N. *Le Charroi de Nîmes*, ed. by J.-L. Perrier, *C.F.M.A.* (Paris, 1931).

Cl. *Chrestomathie du Moyen-Age*, ed. by L. Clédat, 12th ed. (Paris, 1932). (Numbers refer to page.)

Cou. *Chansons attribuées au Chastelain de Couci*, critical edition by A. Lerond (Paris, 1964). (Numbers refer to lyric.)

En. *Eneas*, ed. by J.-J. Salverda de Grave, *C.F.M.A.* (2 vols., Paris, 1925, 1929).

Er. Chrétien de Troyes, *Erec et Enide*, ed. by M. Roques, *C.F.M.A.* (Paris, 1952).

F. *Twelve Fabliaux*, ed. by T. B. W. Reid (Manchester, 1958). (Numbers refer to fabliau and line.)

Fb. *Fabliaux*, ed. by R. C. Johnston and D. D. R. Owen (Oxford, 1957). (Numbers refer to fabliau and line.)

Gr. *La Queste del Saint Graal*, ed. by A. Pauphilet, *C.F.M.A.* (Paris, 1923). (Numbers refer to page.)

Omb. Jehan Renart, *Le Lai de l'Ombre*, ed. by J. Orr (Edinburgh, 1948).

Or. *La Prise d'Orange*, ed. by C. Régnier (Paris, 1967).

Per. Chrétien de Troyes, *Le Roman de Perceval*, ed. by W. Roach (Geneva, 1956).

Ren. *Le Roman de Renart*, ed. by M. Roques, *C.F.M.A.* (6 vols., Paris, 1948–63).

Rol. *La Chanson de Roland.* See any edition of the Digby MS (Bodleian Library, Oxford), e.g. as ed. by F. Whitehead, 2nd ed. (Oxford, 1946).

R.Tr. *Le Roman de Troie en prose*, ed. by L. Constans and E. Faral, *C.F.M.A.* (Paris, 1922). (Numbers refer to section.)

SB. Schwan-Behrens, *Grammatik des Altfranzösischen*, French translation by O. Bloch, *Grammaire de l'ancien français*, 3rd ed. (Leipzig, 1923).

(Numbers refer to the 89 charters in Part III: *Matériaux pour servir à l'étude des dialectes de l'ancien français*.)

Th. *Le Miracle de Théophile*, in Rutebeuf, *Oeuvres Complètes*, critical edition by E. Faral and J. Bastin (2 vols., Paris, 1960).

Tr. Béroul, *Tristran*, ed. by A. Ewert (Oxford, 1939).

Tx. OFr Text included in this work. (Numbers refer to extract and line.)

Ver. *La Chastelaine de Vergi*, ed. by L. Whitehead, 2nd ed. (Manchester, 1951).

VP. Huon Le Roi, *Le Vair Palefroi*, ed. by A. Långfors, *C.F.M.A.* (Paris, 1921).

Yv. Chrestien de Troyes, *Yvain*, ed. by W. Foerster (Halle, 1912). See also the photographic reproduction of W. Foerster's critical text with introduction, notes and glossary by T. B. W. Reid (Manchester, 1942).

Source of Old French Texts

1. Chrestien de Troyes, *Yvain*, ed. by W. Foerster (Halle, 1912), lines 3563–628. This excerpt has been normalised.

2. The passage from Villehardouin is based on the 14th c. MS 4972 (Bibl. Nat., Paris), with minor additions from MS 15100. Both versions are given in K. Bartsch, *Chrestomathie de l'ancien français*, 5th ed. (Leipzig, 1884). A few changes have been made to normalise this extract.

3. There are over a dozen versions of this six-verse song in 13th and 14th c. MSS (see A. Lerond, *op. cit.* under Cou. above). The normalised rendering of verses 1, 3 and 6 given here is based on a 13th c. text, but incorporates variants from other MSS.

Select bibliography

The following works are suggested for further study:

1. Old French phonology, morphology and syntax

*M. K. Pope, *From Latin to Modern French* (Manchester, 1934), reprinted with corrections and supplementary bibliography, 1952.

*A. Ewert, *The French Language*, 2nd ed. (London, 1943), reprinted with corrections and bibliographical additions, 1964.

*G. Price, *The French language, present and past* (London, 1971).

J. Fox and R. Wood, *A Concise History of the French Language* (Oxford, 1968).

L. Kukenheim, *Grammaire historique de la langue française*, (2 vols., Leiden, 1967–8).

J. Anglade, *Grammaire élémentaire de l'ancien français*, 14th ed. (Paris, 1963).

L. Foulet, *Petite syntaxe de l'ancien français*, C.F.M.A., 3rd revised ed. (Paris, 1928), reprinted 1968.

P. Ménard, *Manuel d'ancien français : 3, Syntaxe* (Bordeaux, 1968).

P. Fouché, *Le verbe français : étude morphologique* (Strasbourg, 1931), new edn. (Paris, 1967).

   * For supplementary reading consult the detailed bibliographies in these works.

2. Anthologies of Old French literature

P. Studer and E. G. R. Waters, *Historical French Reader, Medieval Period* (Oxford, 1924).

P. Groult and V. Emond, *Anthologie de la littérature française du moyen age*, 3rd ed. revised by G. Muraille (2 vols., Gembloux, 1967).

Penguin Book of French Verse, with plain prose translations of each poem (4 vols.). *Vol. I : To the Fifteenth Century*, ed. by B. Woledge (Harmondsworth, 1961).

3. Dictionaries

A. J. Greimas, *Dictionnaire de l'ancien français* (Paris, 1969).

K. Urwin, *A Short Old French Dictionary for Students* (Oxford, 1946).

Glossary

The OFr words and meanings given here are mainly those needed for an understanding of texts and quotations in this work. For further information consult an OFr dictionary. Words with the same meaning today are usually not listed if they can be found in a small French/English dictionary, but forms which would present difficulties to those with no knowledge of ModFr are included.

Words in *ʈ* are added to explain listed inflected forms in *-z*. These early forms and regular 13th c. forms with *ou* or *eu* for *o* (§ 11.8,9) are recorded as variants; for an explanation of other variants see § 21.

For noun, adjective and verb classes, where not given, see §§ 24, 25, 41–4 and 62. Verbs shown as irregular will be found in Appendix E, while those marked VA are included in Appendix D. Since the use of verbs is flexible (§ 187) they have not been classified as transitive, intransitive or reflexive; for the same reason (§ 194.1) combinations with *se*, *en* or *s'en* are not all recorded.

Text references, e.g. 3.16, and a few other references are given for convenience. For abbreviations such as var., 'variant (of), and i.f., 'inflected form', see p. xi.

a, aḍ (1), prep., to, at, of, from, by, with, in, against; §§ 164, 191.
a, aḍ (2), PI.3 v.*avoir*; (*i*) *a* : see *avoir*.
aancrer, v., anchor.
acostumance, nf., custom.
adeser, v.VA, approach, touch, injure.
adober, v., arm, equip.
adonc, adv., then, at that time.
aërdre, v., seize, cling.
ai, PI.1 v. *avoir*.
aidier, irr.v.SA, help.
aïe, PI/PS.3 v. *aidier*.
aiiez, PS/Iv.5 v. *avoir*.
aille, PS.1,3 v. *aler*.
aime, PI.3, Iv.2 v. *amer*.
aiment, PI.6 v. *amer*.
ainc, adv., ever; (+ *ne*) never.
ainsi, adv., so, thus; 3.23–4: *ainsi* . . . *com*, in the same measure as.

ainz, adv.conj.prep., rather, but, before; *ainz que* (+ subj.), before.
ait, PS.3 v. *avoir*.
al = *a* + *le*.
alé, PP v. *aler*.
Alemant, nm., Aleman, German.
aler, irr.v., go, leave; *s'en aler*, go off (+ Pres.Pt: § 185.1).
alge, PS.1,3 in *-ge* of *aler*.
Alixandre, Alexander.
aloit, Impf.3 v. *aler*.
alquant, see *auquant*.
alsi, adv., so, also.
alsiment, adv., also, likewise.
altre, see *autre*.
amant, nm., lover.
ame, nf., soul.
amener, v.VA, bring.
amer, v.VA, love.

amie, nf., friend, sweetheart.
amistié, nf., friendship.
amor, nm/f., love, Love
  (personified).
an, nm., year.
anz, i.f. of *an*.
aorer, v.VA, worship.
aoust, nm., August.
apeler, v.VA, call, address, accuse.
aperçoivre, irr.v.VA, perceive.
apoier (s'), *apoiier (s')*, v.VA, lean.
aprester (s'), v., prepare.
apris, PP v. *aprendre*.
aprochier, v.VA, approach.
aproismier, v.VA, approach.
apuie, PI.3, Iv.2 v. *apoier*.
ardre, v., burn.
arester, irr.v., stop.
ariver, v., land, arrive.
armé, PP v. *armer*; nm., armed
  knight.
armer, v., arm.
arrier(e), *arriere(s)*, adv., back, behind.
as (1), *a + les*.
as (2), PI.2 v. *avoir*.
assaut, nm., assault.
assegier, v.VA, besiege.
asseoir, irr.v.VA, place, seat, besiege;
  (+ *se*), sit down.
assez, adv., very, enough.
assis, PP v. *asseoir*.
ataindre, irr.v., reach, touch, wound.
atant, var. PI.3 v. *atendre*.
atendre, v., await, wait for.
atorner, v., fashion, equip; 2.26: *bien
  atornee*, well-wrought.
au = *a + le*.
auquant, pr.adj., NP form, some,
  several, a certain number; § 121.
autel, pr.adj., the like, like, similar;
  § 119.
autre, pr.adj., other, another, second;
  § 107.
autrui, stressed OS of *autre*; § 137.
avenir, irr.v.VA, arrive, happen, suit.
aventure, nf., adventure, event,
  chance; 3.20: *aventure est*, it is
  possible.

avez, PI.5 v. *avoir*.
avis, nm., opinion; *il m'est avis*, it
  seems to me.
avoer, v.VA, admit, recognise.
avoir, irr.v., have, §§ 186.2, 189; *(il)
  a*, *(il) i a*, there is, there are;
  §§ 83, 188.5; nm., possessions.
avront, F.6 v. *avoir*.
avuec, *avueque(s)*, with, together with.

bacheler, nm., young man.
bacon, nm., bacon, ham.
baillie, nf., power, possession.
baillier, v., give, grant, rule.
baniere, nf., banner.
barbe, nf., beard.
baron, nm. Cl.III, NS *ber*, baron,
  lord, husband.
bas, adj., low, base.
batre, v., beat.
beaus, i.f. of *bel*.
bel, adj., beautiful, fine, fair; *estre
  bel a*, be pleasing to; 2.7: *tant de
  beles*, so many fine ones.
beneïstre, irr.v., bless.
besoing, nm., need.
bien, adv., well, very, much, right;
  nm., good, goodness; 1.14: good
  fortune, blessing.
boçu, nm., hunchback.
bolir, irr.v., boil.
bort, nm., side (of ship), bulwark.
braire, v., roar.
brief, nm., letter; adj. Cl.III, short.
briément, adv., briefly.
bués, i.f. of *buef*, nm., ox.

çaenz, dem.adv., herein, here; § 60.3.
car, conj., for, because, since; often
  stresses orders or wishes: (+ Iv.)
  please, do; (+ Subj.) would that,
  if only; § 150.2.
Carles, var. *Charles*, Charles.
Cassandre, Cassandra.
ce, dem.pr., this, that, it; §§ 59, 83,
  188; *por ce* (. . . *que*), see *por*.
cel, dem.pr./adj., that one, that;
  §§ 57, 58.

celeement, adv., secretly.
celer, v.VA, hide.
celui, stressed OS of *cel*; §58.5; *n'i a celui* (+*ne*+subj.), there is not one who . . ., §99.
certes, adv., indeed; §152.
cest, dem.pr./adj., this one, this; §§57, 58.
ceus, (M) OP of *cel*.
cez, M/F OP of *cest*.
chaaine, nf., chain.
chaitif, adj., captive, unfortunate; nm., prisoner, poor wretch.
chaloir, irr.v.VA, matter, concern; §188.
chanter, v., sing.
chapele, nf., chapel.
char(*n*), nf., flesh, meat.
chargier, v., load.
chascun, pr.adj., each; §108.
chastel, nm., castle.
chastiax, var. i.f. of *chastel*; 2.5: castles (of ship = wooden structures erected fore and aft).
chauces, nf.pl., hose.
cheoir, irr.v.VA, fall.
chesne, nm., oak.
chevalier, nm., knight.
chevauchier, v., ride.
chevaus, i.f. of *cheval*, nm., horse.
chevel, nm., hair.
chier, adj., dear.
choisir, v. Cl.II, notice, distinguish, choose.
chose, nf., something, thing, matter; §114; 2.35: *totes les lor choses*, all their possessions.
ci, adv., here; §60.1.
cil, NS of *cel*; that one, that, he.
cité, nf., city.
claiment, PI.6 v. *clamer*.
clamer, v.VA, call, declare.
cler, adj., bright, clear.
clerc, nm., scholar, clerk, cleric.
coi, var. *quoi*.
col, nm., neck.
com, adv.conj., as, how, like, when; §§50, 102.5, 154.3.

comander, v., order, entrust, commend.
comant, PI/PS.1 v. *comander*.
combatre, v., fight.
comencier, v., begin.
coment, var. *comment*.
comment, adv.conj., how; 1.55: what! §§102.5, 103.4, 133.
compaigne, nf., companion, friend.
compaignie, nf., company.
complaigne, PS.1 v. *complaindre*.
complaindre, irr.v., complain, lament.
conçoivre, irr.v.VA, conceive.
conquerre, irr.v.VA, conquer.
conquist, P.3 v. *conquerre*.
conreer, v.VA, arrange, care for.
conseil, nm., opinion, advice, decision.
consirer (+*de*), v., part with, do without.
contre, prep., against, towards.
co(*n*)*venir*, irr.v.VA, assemble, be necessary.
convertir, v. Cl.III, convert.
coral, adj. Cl.III, cordial.
corre, v., run.
cors, nm., body; 3.18: *vo cors*, you; §90.7.
cort (1), nf., court.
cort (2), adj., short.
cort (3), PI.3 v. *corre*.
cortoisie, nf., courtesy, graciousness.
costume, nf., custom.
couchier (*se*), v., lie down.
covent, nm., agreement, promise.
covenz, i.f. of *covent*.
covient, PI.3 v. *co*(*n*)*venir*.
creator, nm., creator.
creras, F.2 v. *croire*.
crever, v.VA, crack.
criembre, criendre, irr.v.VA, fear.
croire, irr.v.VA, believe.
croistre, irr.v., grow.
cuer, nm., heart.
cui, rel./int.pr., stressed OS form, whom, to whom, whose, etc. §§93, 96, 98.3, 128; 1.49: *cui que*, OS of *qui que*; §130.
cuidier, v., think, believe.

d', elided form of *de*.

dame, nf., lady.

de, prep., of, from, with, about, to, by; §§165, 191; (partitive use) some, some of, etc.: §32; (in comparisons) than; §50.

Dé, var. *Dieu*; 1.55: *por Dé!* for God's sake! good heavens!

deçoivre, irr.v.VA, deceive.

dedenz, adv. prep., in, into.

deduit, nm., amusement, pleasure; 3.11 (pl.): love's favours.

defendre, v., defend, protect.

defors, adv.prep., outside.

del = de÷le.

delez, adv.prep., alongside, next to.

delit, nm., delight.

demander (*+a*), v., ask (of), demand (of).

demant, PI.1, Iv.2 v. *demander*.

dementer (*se*), v., lament (bitterly).

demorer, v.VA., remain, delay, stay.

departir, v. Cl.III, share out, distribute.

depecier, v.VA, break to pieces.

derier(e), adv.prep., behind.

des = de + les.

Des, i.f. of *Dé*.

descendre, v., descend, dismount; *descendre a terre*, land.

desoz, adv.prep., below.

despire, v., despise.

desservir, v. Cl.III, deserve.

dessevrer, v., separate, part.

destraindre, irr.v., restrain, oppress.

destrier, nm., war-horse, horse.

destruire, irr.v., destroy.

destruit, PP v. *destruire*.

desus, adv.prep., above, upon.

desvoier, v., mislead, distract.

Deu, var. *Dieu*.

deus, nm/f., adj., (M) NP *dui*, two; §174.

devant, adv.prep., before, in front, in front of.

devoir, irr.v.VA, should, must, owe.

Dex, var. i.f. of *Deu*.

die, PS.1,3 v. *dire*.

Dieu, nm., God; *par Dieu*, by God; *por Dieu*, for God's sake.

Diex, var. i.f. of *Dieu*.

diras, F.2 v. *dire*.

dire, irr.v., say, speak, tell.

dist, P.3 v. *dire*.

distrent, P.6 v. *dire*.

doie, PS.1,3 v. *devoir*.

doint, PS.3 v. *doner*.

dolant, Pres.Pt. v. *doloir*; used as adj., unhappy, distressed.

dolent, adj. Cl.I (< Cl.III), unhappy, distressed; 3.7: grieving; *dolente*, nf., unhappy woman.

dolor, nf., grief, sorrow, pain.

don, var. *donc*, *dont* (esp. before a consonant).

donc, *donque(s)*, adv.conj., then; *donc ne*: §102.7.

doner, irr.v., give, grant.

dont (1), pron.adv., whose, of whom, of which, of what, with which, whence; §102.2.

dont (2), var. *donc*.

dormir (*se*), v. Cl.III, sleep.

doter, v., fear, doubt.

douz, adj., sweet.

drecier, v., raise.

drue, nf., sweetheart.

duc, nm., duke.

duel, nm., grief, pain.

dueus, i.f. of *duel*.

dui, see *deus*.

duire, irr.v., lead, please.

dulz, var. *douz*.

dus, i.f. of *duc*.

e, *et*, conj., and; §157.2.

el (1), pr., something else, anything else; §116.

el (2), var. *ele*.

el (3) = *en + le*.

ele, pers.pr., she, it.

elme, var. *heaume*.

empirier, v.VA, injure, grow worse.

emplir, v. Cl.III, fill.

emprendre, irr.v., undertake.

emprisoner, v., imprison.

en (1), pron., of (from, by, about)+ him (her, it, them), etc.; §84.

en (2), adv., from thence, away (from); frequently used with verbs of motion; often expletive; §194.1.

en (3), prep., in, into, on, onto; §168.

en (4), var. *on*, see *ome*.

enclos, PP v. *enclore*, enclose, shut in; 1.3: imprison.

encontrer, v., meet.

encor(e), adv., still, yet, again.

endemain, nm., morrow, next day; 2.32: *l'endemain de*, on the day after.

endormir (*s'*), v. Cl.III, fall asleep.

enfoïr, irr.v.VA, bury.

engin, nm., machine, military engine.

englotir, v. Cl.III, swallow up.

enivrer, v., intoxicate, bewilder.

enoier, enoiier, v.VA, annoy.

enserrer, v., enclose, imprison.

envers, prep., towards, in comparison with.

environ (*de*), adv.prep., about, around.

enz, adv.prep., in, inside.

ere, Impf.1,3 v. *estre*.

errant, adv., immediately.

ert, Impf/F.3 v. *estre*.

es = *en*+*les*.

esba(h)ir (*s'*), v., be astonished.

eschaper, v., escape.

Esclavonie, Sclavonia.

escorcier, v., flay.

escorre, v., shake.

escouter, v., listen.

escrier (*s'*), v., call, cry out.

escrin, nm., chest, box.

escrire, escrivre, irr.v., write.

escut, nm., shield.

esforcier, v., strengthen; (+*se*), make an effort.

esgarder, v., see, notice.

espandre, v., spread out, spill.

espardre, v., scatter.

espee, nf., sword.

espiét, nm., lance, spear.

esploitier, v., accomplish, hasten.

espoir, nm., hope; adv., perhaps, probably; §150.3.

esposer, v.VA, marry.

est, PI.3 v. *estre*.

esté, PP v. *estre*.

esteindre, irr.v., extinguish.

ester, irr.v., stand, stop, remain.

estes, PI.5 v. *estre*.

estoie, Impf.1 v. *estre*.

estoient, Impf.6 v. *estre*.

estoire, nm/f., fleet; nf., history, story.

estoit, Impf.3 v. *estre*.

estovoir, irr.v.VA, be necessary; *estuet*, it is necessary; (*il*) *m'estuet*, I must.

estraindre, irr.v., clasp, press.

estre, irr.v., be; §§185.1, 186.1, 188.4,5, 189; *estre a*, belong to.

estrier, nm., stirrup.

estuet, PI.3 v. *estovoir*.

esveillier, v., wake.

et, see *e*.

eure, nf., hour.

eus, stressed pers.pr. (M), them, themselves.

face, PS.1,3 v. *faire*.

faeison, nf., fate.

faible, adj., weak.

faire, irr.v., do, make, say, ask, commit, carry out, etc.; §192; *faire bon, bel*, be good, fine; §188.1; *faire a* (+inf.), should be, deserves to be (+PP); §192.

fait, PI.3, PP v. *faire*.

felon, adj. Cl.IV, NS *fel*, treacherous, cruel, terrible, wicked; nm., scoundrel, traitor.

fenestre, nf., window.

fenir, v. Cl.II, finish.

ferai, F.1 v. *faire*.

ferir, irr.v.VA, strike, attack.

feroie, C.1 v. *faire*.

fermer, v., enclose, fortify, fasten.

feru, PP v. *ferir*.

fet, var. PI.3, PP v. *faire*.

fier, adj., fierce, haughty.

fil, nm., son.
filz, var. i.f. of *fil*.
firent, P.6 v. *faire*.
fist, P.3 v. *faire*.
fiz, i.f. of *fil*.
foi, nf., faith, loyalty, honour; 1.24,
   56: *par foi, a la moie foi*, upon my
   word, indeed.
foïr (1), v.VA, Cl.III, dig.
foïr (2), var. *fuïr*.
fol, nm., fool; adj. Cl.III, foolish.
forches, nf.pl., gallows.
forfait, nm., misdeed, transgression.
forment, adv., strongly, greatly.
fors, adv. prep., out, outside, except.
forsener, v., be mad/be out of one's
   mind (with rage).
fort, adj. Cl.III, strong.
forz, i.f. of *fort*.
fraindre, irr.v., shatter.
fraint, PI.3 v. *fraindre*.
frais, adj., fresh.
fu, P.3 v. *estre*.
fuïr (s'en), irr.v., flee.
furent, P.6 v. *estre*.
fust, IS.3 v. *estre*.

g', elided form of *ge*, var. *je*.
Gadres, Zara.
gaire(s), adv., much, long; (+*ne*), not
   very, etc.
Galaad, Galahad.
galie, nf., galley.
garantir, v. Cl.II, protect, defend.
garder, v., keep, protect, look, watch.
garir, irr.v., protect, defend, save,
   heal.
gars, var. *garz*, NS of *garçon*, nm.
   Cl.III, boy, servant.
gas, i.f. of *gap*, nm., joke, boast.
Gauvain, Gavain, Gawain.
ge, var. *je*.
gent, nf. sing. (+sing. or pl. verb),
   usually nm. in the plural: people,
   race, army, household.
gesir, irr.v., lie, lie down.
geter, v., throw.
gié, stressed var. of *je*.

gloton, nm. Cl.III, NS *glot*, glutton,
   scoundrel, wretch.
graignor, adj. Cl.IV, NS *graindre*,
   greater.
granment, adv., greatly, much.
grant, adj. Cl.III, tall, large, great.
grevos, adj., hard, distressing.
grief, adj. Cl.III, heavy, hard,
   distressing.
guere(s), var. *gaire(s)*.
guerpir, irr.v., abandon.
Guillelme, William.
guster, v., taste.

ha!, ah!
haïr, irr.v.VA, hate, detest.
hardit, adj., brave, bold.
haster, v., hasten.
haut, adj. Cl.III, high.
hé, PI.1 v. *haïr*.
heaume, nm., helmet.
home, var. *ome*.
huissier (< *huis*, nm., door), nm.,
   transport vessel (ship with side
   door used for transporting horses).
huitieves, nf.pl., octave; 2.10: *as
   huitieves*, during the octave.
hurter, v., knock, strike.

i, adv., there, here; to (in)+him (it,
   them) etc.; §84; (*il*) *i a*, see *avoir*.
il, pers.pr., he, it, they; neuter NS;
   §§83, 188.
iluec, adv., there; §60.2.
incarnacïon, nf., incarnation.
irai, F.1 v. *aler*.
iraistre, irr.v., make / become angry.
ire, nf., wrath, grief, distress.
ireement, irieement, adv., angrily, in
   grief, in distress.
irer, irier, v., annoy.
irez, F.3 v. *aler*.
ir(i)é, PP v. *ir(i)er*.
iroit, C.3 v. *aler*.
isnel, adj., quick.
isnelement, adv., quickly.
issir, irr.v.VA, go out, come out.
ivre, adj., drunk.

ja, adv., formerly, already, now, soon, ever; (+*ne*), never. At times expletive. §149.

jaiant, nm., giant.

jamais = *ja*+*mais*, adv., ever before, ever again, ever; (+*ne*), never, etc. §149.

je, pers.pr., I.

jel = *je*+*le*.

Jhesu, Jesus.

jo, var. *je*.

joïr, irr.v., enjoy, rejoice.

jor(n), nm., day.

juïse, nm., judgement; 1.34: *livrer a mortel juïse*, bring to trial for one's life, sentence to death.

jus, adv., below, down.

jusque, conj.prep., until, to, up to, down to, as far as.

ki, var. *qui*.

l', elided form of *le, la, li*.

la (1), def.art. (F) sing.; pl. *les*, the.

la (2), pers.pr., her, it.

la (3), dem.adv., there; §60.1.

laborer, v.VA, labour.

lai, nm., lay, song.

laier, laiier, laire, irr.v., leave, abandon, allow; *ne laier* (+*ne*+ subj.), not fail to, etc.; §194.2.

laissier, irr.v. (meaning and use as for *laier*).

lait, adj., ugly, base.

languir, v. Cl.ii, languish.

Laomedon, Laomedon.

le (1), def.art. (M) OS; NS/P *li*, OP *les*, the.

le (2), pers.pr., him, it.

lerme, nf., tear.

les (1), see *le* (1), *la* (1).

les (2), pers.pr., them.

lever, v.VA, lift, raise; (+*se*), rise; *bien soiez vos levez*, may you have risen well, good morning.

li (1), see *le* (1).

li (2), pers.pr.; stressed (F) form: her, herself, etc.; unstressed M/F form: him, to him, etc., her, to her, etc.

lïer, v.VA, tie, fasten.

lieu, nm., place; 3.18: *en quel lieu que*, wherever.

liez, i.f. of *liét*, adj., happy.

lire, irr.v., read.

lisiez, PI/PS/Iv.5 v. *lire*.

livraison, nf., supply.

livrer, v., hand over, deliver.

loer, v., advise, approve.

loge, nf., shelter, tent, hut.

logier (se), v., lodge, dwell, encamp.

loial, adj. Cl.iii, loyal.

loiaument, adv., loyally, honorably.

loing, adv., far.

loisir, irr.v., be allowed.

loja, P.3 v. *logier*.

Lonbart, nm., Lombard.

lor, pers.pr., poss.pr./adj., them, to them, etc., themselves, theirs, their.

lor(e), lore(s), adv., then.

lui, pers.pr., stressed (M) form: him, himself, etc.

m', elided form of *ma, me*.

ma, poss.adj. (F), my.

Mahomez, i.f. of *Mahomet*, Mohammed.

maint, pr.adj., much, many, many a; §124.

maintenant, adv., at once, immediately; *maintenant que*, as soon as.

mais, adv., more, any more, before, again, ever; (+*ne*), never; §149; conj., but.

mal, nm., evil, harm, misfortune, illness; adj., bad, wicked; 1.27: *avoir mal*, be badly off.

mander, v., order, summon, send, announce.

mangier, irr.v.SA, eat.

mangoniax, var. i.f. of *mangonel*, nm., mangonel (military machine for hurling missiles).

mar(e), adv., in an evil hour, unfortunately.

Martin: la (*feste*) saint *Martin*, the feast of St Martin, St Martin's day.

matin, nm., morning; adv., early; *al matin*, in the morning.

maus, i.f. of *mal*.

mauvais, adj., bad, wicked, base, vile; 3.16: unworthy.

me, pers.pr., me, to me, etc., myself.

meisme, adj.adv., same, self, even, also; §§46.2, 90.5.

meison, var. *maison*, nf., house, home.

menacier, v., threaten.

mener, v.VA, lead, conduct.

menjoient, var. Impf.6 v. *mangier*.

mentir, v. Cl.III, lie.

merci, nf., pity, mercy, grace; 2.36: *rendre en la merci de*, place at the discretion of.

mercier, v., reward, thank.

merveillier (*se*), v., marvel.

merveillos, adj., marvellous, terrible.

mesprendre, irr.v., do wrong, transgress, behave badly.

mespris, PP v. *mesprendre*.

messagier, nm. (usually *mes* or *message*, nm.), messenger.

messire, NS of *monseignor*, my lord.

mestier, nm., service, profession, business, job, need; 2.9: *avoir mestier a*, be needed for.

metre, v., put, place.

meüz, i.f. PP v. *movoir*.

mi, nm., adj., centre, middle; *en mi*, in the middle of, in; *par mi*, in, in half, right through.

mie, nf., crumb, bit; adv., in the least; (+*ne*), not at all, not anything, not; §148.1.

mien, poss.pr./adj. (M), mine, my.

mieuz, neut.adj., adv., better, rather, best, most.

mis, PP v. *metre*.

moi, stressed pers.pr., me, to me, myself.

moie, poss.pr./adj. (F), mine, my.

moins, neut.adj., adv., less.

molt, *mout*, pr.adj.adv., many, numerous, very, greatly.

monstrer, v., show.

morir, irr.v.VA, die; *avoir mort*, have killed; §187.

mort, nf., death; adj., dead; PP v. *morir*.

moru, P.3 v. *morir*.

morz, i.f. of *mort*.

mostier, nm., monastery, convent, church.

mostrer, v., show.

mot, nm., word.

movoir, irr.v.VA, move, stir up, cause, depart; 3.8: compose.

moz, i.f. of *mot*.

murir, var. *morir*.

n', elided form of *ne* (1), (2).

navrer, v., wound.

ne (1), conj., and, or, nor; §158.

ne (2), adv., negative particle, not; §§138, 146, 148; at times expletive; §148.6; *ne ... que*, only.

nef, nf., ship.

neiét, var. PP of *noier*.

nel = *ne*+*le*.

nenil (<*nen*+*il*), not he, not that, not they, no; §§90.8, 148.4.

neporquant, adv.conj., however, nevertheless.

nés, i.f. of *nef*.

nient, nm., nothing; *por nïent*, in vain.

nier, *noier*, *noiier*, v.VA, deny.

noier, *noiier*, *nier*, v.VA, drown.

nom, *non*, nm., name; *avoir nom*, be called.

nomer, v., name.

non, stressed adv., no, not; §§146-7.

norrir, irr.v., nourish, rear.

nos, pers.pr., us, to us, etc., ourselves.

novele, nf., news.

nu, adj., naked.

nuisir, irr.v., harm.

nul, pr.adj., someone, some, anyone, any; §112; (+*ne*), no one, none, no; §138.

nului, stressed OS of *nul*; §137.
nus, i.f. of *nul*.

o, ou (1), dem.pr., this, that.
o, ou (2), adv., where, in which, in
    whom, when; §102.1; *ou que*,
    wherever; §132.
o, ou (3), prep., with.
o, ou (4), conj., or; *o . . . o*, either . . .
    or.
ocire, v., kill.
ocis, PP v. *ocire*.
ocist, P.3 v. *ocire*.
oï, P.1,3, PP v. *oïr*.
oil (< *o* + *il*), that he is, that it is,
    that they are, yes; §90.8.
oïr, irr.v., hear.
oisel, nm., bird.
om, NS of *ome*.
ome, nm. Cl.III, NS *om, on, uem*,
    man; unstressed NS form *on*, pr.,
    one, someone: §117; 1.42: *l'on
    m'apele de*, I am accused of.
on, see *ome*.
onc, var. *onque*.
onque(s), adv., ever; (+ *ne*), never;
    §149.
ont, PI.6 v. *avoir*.
or(e), adv., now, just now, then.
ore, nf., hour.
Orenge, Orange.
orront, F.6 v. *oïr*.
oser (*s'*), v., dare.
ost, nm/f., army.
ot (1), P.3 v. *avoir*.
ot (2), PI.3 v. *oïr*.
otroier, otroiier, v.VA, grant, allow.
ou, see *o*.
outreement, adv., utterly, completely.
ouvri, var. P.1,3 v. *ovrir*.
ovrir, irr.v.VA, open.
oz, i.f. of *ost*.

paien, nm., infidel.
paienor, indecl.adj., of the infidels,
    infidel.
païs, nm., country, land.
paistre, irr.v., feed, graze.

par (1), prep., by, through, across,
    past, because of, out of, in the
    name of, on behalf of; §166.
par (2), intensive particle; §52.
parler, irr.v.SA, talk, speak; 2.33:
    parler le duc, see §29.4.
paroir, irr.v.VA, appear.
paroistre, irr.v., appear.
part, nf., side, part; *quel part que*,
    wherever.
parti, P.3, PP v. *partir*.
partir, v. Cl.III, divide, leave, depart.
pas, nm., step; *ne . . . pas*, not at all,
    not; §148.1.
pasmoison, nf. (also pl.), swoon,
    fainting fit.
passer, v., pass, surpass.
paveillon, nm., tent, pavilion.
pelerin, nm., pilgrim.
pendre, v., hang.
pendu, PP v. *pendre*.
pener, v.VA, torment, harass.
peor, var. *paor*, nf., fear.
per, nm., peer, equal.
perçoivre, irr.v.VA, perceive.
perdre, v., lose.
perriere, nf., petrary, catapult (for
    hurling stones, etc.).
perron, nm., rock, stone block.
pert, PI.1, Iv.2 v. *perdre*.
Pierre, Peter.
piét, nm., foot.
pis, neut.adj., adv., worse.
plaignet, var. PS.3 v. *plaindre*.
plaindre (*se*), irr.v., complain, lament.
plaisir, nm., pleasure; irr.v., please.
plait, nm., trial, speech, agreement;
    2.37: *prendre cestui plait*, enter into
    this agreement.
plenté, nf., plenty; 2.9: *a grant
    plenté*, in abundance.
plorer, v.VA, weep, lament.
plovoir, irr.v.VA, rain.
plus, nm., adv., more; *plus de / que*,
    more than; §50.
plusor, pr.adj., NP form, several,
    many; *li plusor*, the majority;
    §122.

poi, nm., adj.adv., few, little; *a poi*
  (+*ne*), almost; §151.
pooir, irr.v.VA, be able; nm., power,
  ability.
por, prep., for, because of, in order
  to, for the sake of, in exchange for,
  etc.; §§167, 194.3; *por ce*, therefore; *por ce que* (+ind.), because,
  (+subj.), so that; 1.65: *por cui*, on
  whose account; 3.7: *por avoir*,
  through having.
porpenser, v., think, plan.
porriiez, C.5 v. *pooir*.
portendu, PP v. *portendre*, display.
porter, v., carry, bear.
porteroit, C.3 v. *porter*.
povretez, i.f. of *povretét*, nf., poverty.
prendre, irr.v., take, hold, catch,
  accept.
prenent, PI.6 v. *prendre*.
prent, PI.1,3, Iv.2 v. *prendre*.
pres, adv.prep., near by, near.
pri, PI/PS.1 v. *prier*.
prier, *proier*, *proiier*, v.VA, beg,
  implore, pray (to).
primes, adv., firstly; 1.45: *or primes*,
  now indeed.
prince, nm., prince.
pris, nm., price, worth.
pristrent, P.6 v. *prendre*.
proisier, v.VA, value, esteem.
prover, irr.v.VA, prove.
prudenment, adv., prudently.
pucele, nf., maiden, young girl.
puet, PI.3 v. *pooir*.
puis, PI.1 v. *pooir*.
puisse, PS.1,3 v. *pooir*.

qu', elided form of *que* or *qui*; §98.1.
quanque, pr., all that, as much as,
  however much; §134.
quant, conj., when, since, if; §159.1.
quar, var. *car*.
que (1), rel./int.pr., whom, what,
  which; §§93, 95, 98.2, 99.2; why;
  §103.2.
que (2), rel.adv., when, where, etc.;
  §101.

que (3), conj., that, so that, for,
  because, since; §§154.2, 155, 156;
  (after a comparative), than; §50.
que que (1), see *qui que*.
que que (2), conj., while.
quel, pr.adj. Cl.III, which, what;
  §§39.9, 102.3; *le quel*, etc., who,
  whom, which; §102.4; *quel . . . que*,
  whichever, whatever; *quel part
  (lieu) que*, wherever; §131.
querre, irr.v.VA, seek, wish, ask.
qui, rel./int.pr. NS/P, who, what,
  which; §§93, 94, 95.1, 98.1, 99;
  he who, whoever, if one; §§128,
  182.4d; at times in error for *cui*.
qui que, *que que*, etc., pr., whoever,
  whatever; §130; *qui que (ce) soit*,
  whoever it may be; §130.
quoi, rel./int.pr., which, what; §§93,
  97; *por quoi*, why; §103.2.

r- (+verb), elided form of *re-*.
raembre, irr.v.VA, redeem.
raison, nf., speech, reason; 3.2: *estre
  raison*, be fitting.
re-, verbal prefix, again, back, also,
  etc.; §193. Sometimes expletive.
recorder, v., remember, recall.
regne, nm., kingdom.
reine, nf., queen.
relever (se), v.VA, rise, get up.
remaigne, PS.1,3 v. *remanoir*.
remanoir, irr.v.VA, stay, remain.
Remi: la (feste) saint Remi, St
  Remigius' day.
rendre, v., give, give up, return.
repairier, v., return.
reposer (se), v., rest.
rere, v., cut down, shave.
resplendir, v. Cl.III, shine.
respondre, irr.v., reply.
respont, PI.1,3, Iv.2 v. *respondre*.
retor, nm., return.
retorner, v., return.
reveoir, irr.v.VA, see again.
revoie, PS.1,3 v. *reveoir*.
riche, adj., powerful, magnificent,
  rich.

rien, nf., person, creature, thing, someone, something, anyone, anything; §113; (+ *ne*), no one, nothing; §138.
rire (se), v., laugh.
roi, nm., king.
Rollant, Roland.
rompre, v., break.
rover, irr.v.VA, ask, desire.

s', elided form of *sa, se, si*.
sa, poss.adj. (F), his, hers, its; §§53, 54.
sachiez, PS/Iv.5 v. *savoir*.
sai, PI.1 v. *savoir*.
saillir, irr.v., leap up, rush out.
saint, nm., saint.
sainz, i.f. of *saint*.
sale, nf., hall.
saluer, v., greet.
sans, prep., without.
sanz, var. *sans*.
sarcueu, nm., coffin.
sauf, adj., safe.
saus, i.f. of *sauf*; 2.35: *saus lor cors*, their lives being spared, provided their lives were spared.
savoir, irr.v.VA, know, be able.
savorer, v.VA, be fragrant.
se (1), unstressed refl.pr., himself, herself, itself, themselves, to himself, etc.; each other; at times expletive; §§82, 187.
se (2), conj., if; §182; *se . . . non*, except; §159.2.
secorre, v., help.
seez, PI/PS/Iv.5 v. *seoir*.
seignor, nm. Cl.III, NS *sire*, lord, master.
sembler, v., seem, appear.
semondre, irr.v., urge.
sent, PI.3 v. *sentir*, feel.
seoir, irr.v.VA, sit, seat, be seated.
sera, F.3 v. *estre*.
serai, F.1 v. *estre*.
serjant, nm., sergeant (tenant owing military service to his lord), servant.

seroit, C.3 v. *estre*.
seront, F.6 v. *estre*.
sert, PI.3 v. *servir*.
servir, v. Cl.III, serve.
servise, nm., service.
sesi, var. P.3 v. *saisir*, seize.
set (1), nm/f., adj., seven.
set (2), PI.3, v. *savoir*.
seul, var. *sol*.
seürement, adv., surely.
sevrer, v.VA, separate.
si (1), adv., thus, so, as; §150.1.
si (2), conj., and, so, since, yet, but; *si com*, just as, as; *si que*, so that; *si* can introduce a main clause after a subordinate clause, as in 1.7, 2.6; often expletive; §157.1.
simple, adj., simple, natural.
sire, NS of *seignor*.
sivre, irr.v., follow.
soef, adj., sweet, gentle.
sofrir, irr.v.VA, suffer, allow.
soi, stressed refl.pr., himself, herself, itself, themselves, to himself, etc.; each other; at times expletive; §82.
soie, PS.1 v. *estre*.
soiez, PS.5 v. *estre*.
soir, nm., evening.
soit, PS.3 v. *estre*.
sol, adj.adv., alone, only.
solaz, nm., delight, comfort.
soleilz, var. i.f. of *soleil*, sun.
soloir, irr.v.VA, be used to, be wont to.
soloit, Impf.3 v. *soloir*.
some, nf., sum, total, burden.
somes, PI.4 v. *estre*.
son, poss.adj. (M), his, her, its; §§53, 54.
sont, PI.6 v. *estre*.
soper, nm., supper.
sor(e), adv. prep., above, over, on, onto.
sordre, irr.v., spring (up).
sorent, P.6 v. *savoir*.
sot, P.3 v. *savoir*.
sotil, adj. Cl.III, ingenious.

sotiment, adv., ingeniously.
soudre, irr.v., pay, absolve.
sovent, adv., often.
su, var. *sus*.
sui, PI.1 v. *estre*.
sun, var. *son*.
sus, adv.prep., above, up, on, upon.

t', elided form of *te*.
tais, PI.1,2, Iv.2 v. *taisir*.
taisir (se), irr.v., be silent.
tandis, adv., meanwhile.
tant, adj.adv., so, so great, so many, so much, so long, so far, etc.; many a; §125; *tant que*, until; *tant com*, as long as; 1.16–18: *tant com ... plus ... plus*, the more ... the more.
tarder (se), v., delay.
te, pers.pr., you, to you, etc., yourself.
tel, pr.adj. Cl.III, adv., such a one, such, some; *tel i a*, someone; §§118, 175.6.
tendre, adj., tender.
tenir, irr.v.VA, keep, hold.
tens, nm., time, times, weather.
terdre, irr.v., wipe.
tere, var. *terre*, nf., land.
tes, i.f. of poss. adjs, *ton*, *ta*, your.
teus, i.f. of *tel*.
tex, var. i.f. of *tel*.
tiegne, PS.1,3 v. *tenir*.
tint, P.3 v. *tenir*.
tirer, v., pull.
toi, stressed pers.pr., you, to you, yourself.
tor(n), nf., tower.
torner, v., turn, turn back, return, go; *s'en torner*, leave, depart.
tort, nm., wrong; *a tort*, wrongly.
torz, i.f. of *tor(n)* or *tort*.
tot, pron.adj.adv., NP *tuit*, everyone, everything, every, all, quite, completely; §126, §140.
toudre, irr.v., take away.
toz, i.f. of *tot*.

trahison, var. *traïson*.
traire, irr.v., pull, draw, bring, suffer, tear out; *se traire*, move, withdraw.
traïson, nf., treason, treachery; *en traïson*, by treachery.
trait, PP v. *traire*.
traître, NS of *traïtor*, nm. Cl.III, traitor.
tref, nm., tent.
trenchier, v., cut, hew.
tres (1), adv., very.
tres (2), var. P.1 v. *traire*.
tresŏr, nm., treasure.
trestot, pr.adj.adv., everyone, everything, all, completely; §127.
Tristan, *Tristran*, Tristan.
trop, adv., very, too, too much, too long, etc.
trover, irr.v.VA, find, invent.
Troye, Troy.
truis, PI.1 v. *trover*.
Turc, nm., Turk.

un, indef.art., a, an; §§23, 31; pr.adj., someone, one; §106.
us, nm., habit.

vassal, nm., vassal, knight.
vassaument, adv., valiantly.
veille, nf., vigil, day before.
veïssiez, IS.5 v. *veoir*.
veist, IS.3 v. *veoir*.
veistes, P.5 v. *veoir*.
vendu, PP v. *vendre*, sell.
venir, irr.v.VA, come, arrive.
Venise, Venice.
venoison, nf., venison.
venoit, Impf.3 v. *venir*.
venu, PP v. *venir*.
veoir, irr.v.VA, see.
verai, adj., true, faithful.
verroiz, F.5 v. *veoir*.
vers (1), nm., verse, song.
vers (2), prep., towards, against, about.
vespre, nm/f., evening.
viande, nf., food; pl., provisions.

viegne, PS.1,3 v. *venir.*
viegnes, PS.2 v. *venir.*
vien, Iv.2 v. *venir.*
vient, PI.3 v. *venir.*
vif (1), adj., alive.
vif (2), PI.1 v. *vivre.*
vilain, nm., peasant, wretch.
vile, nf., town.
vindrent, P.6 v. *venir.*
vint, P.3 v. *venir.*
virent, P.6 v. *veoir.*
vit, P.3 v. *veoir.*
vive (1), (F) of *vif* (1).
vive (2), PS.1,3 v. *vivre.*
vivre, irr.v., live.
vo, var. of poss.adj. *vostre,* your; cf.
   §213.5.

voi, PI.1 v. *veoir.*
voie, nf., way, road; *sa voie tenir,* go
   one's way; 3.21: *ou que tiegne ma
   voie,* wherever I may go.
voient, PI.6, v. *veoir.*
voir, nm., truth, adj.adv., true, truly.
voire, nf., truth, adv., truly.
vois, PI.1 v. *aler.*
voit, PI.3 v. *veoir.*
volenté, nf., will, desire.
voloir, irr.v.VA, wish, want, desire.
vorroie, var. C.1 v. *voloir.*
vos, pers.pr., you, to you, etc.,
   yourself, yourselves.
voz, i.f. of poss. adj. *vostre,* your.

Yvain, Yvain.